THE VOICE OF
JESUS

*Discernment, Prayer and
the Witness of the Spirit*

GORDON T. SMITH

InterVarsity Press
Downers Grove, Illinois

InterVarsity Press
P.O. Box 1400, Downers Grove, IL 60515-1426
World Wide Web: www.ivpress.com
E-mail: mail@ivpress.com

InterVarsity Press® is the book-publishing division of InterVarsity Christian Fellowship/USA®, a student movement active on campus at hundreds of universities, colleges and schools of nursing in the United States of America, and a member movement of the International Fellowship of Evangelical Students. For information about local and regional activities, write Public Relations Dept., InterVarsity Christian Fellowship/USA, 6400 Schroeder Rd., P.O. Box 7895, Madison, WI 53707-7895, or visit the IVCF website at <www.ivcf.org>.

Cover design: Cindy Kiple

Cover and interior image: Lowe Art Museum/SuperStock

ISBN 0-8308-2390-5

Printed in the United States of America ∞

Library of Congress Cataloging-in-Publication Data

Smith, Gordon T., 1953-
The voice of Jesus: discernment, prayer, and the witness of the
Spirit/Gordon T. Smith.
p. cm.
Includes bibliographical references and index.
ISBN 0-8308-2390-5 (pbk.: alk. paper)
1. Discernment (Christian theology) I. Title.
BV5083S655 2003
248.4—dc21   2003006827

P   19   18   17   16   15   14   13   12   11   10   9   8   7   6   5   4

Y   18   17   16   15   14   13   12   11   10   09   08

To five who have been pastors and spiritual mentors to me, with appreciation, esteem and affection (1 Thess 5:13):

The Rev. Dr. Miguel Lecaro

The Rev. Robert Willoughby

The Rev. Dr. Alex Aronis

Fr. Thomas H. Green, S.J.

The Rev. Darrell W. Johnson

CONTENTS

INTRODUCTION

❧

Every Christian should be able to answer two questions. First, what do you think Jesus is saying to you at this point in your life, in the context of the challenges and opportunities you are facing? Second (and just as critical), what indicators give you some measure of confidence that it is indeed Jesus speaking to you rather than someone or something else? This book addresses these questions through an examination of the inner witness of the Spirit, with the conviction that the Spirit is present to each person and that each of us has the capacity to respond intentionally to this witness.

The inner witness has definition. It is not so imprecise that it is reduced to ill-defined impulses about which we can only make vague references. Rather, the Christian tradition on this subject gives us something definite about which we can speak and to which we can hold one another accountable. We do not need to be silent when others say that Jesus told them something. We can discuss their experience in a manner that is both wise and discerning. By time-proven standards of authentication, we can test whether their experience is truly of the Spirit of Christ.

This is a book, then, about discernment. We need to take as a given the possibility of a false witness that may be confused with the voice of Jesus. Thus we must be discerning.

The word _discernment_ implies (at least in English) three different concepts simultaneously. First, it includes the idea of *insight*, which speaks of the capacity to see something clearly—the acumen to recognize that which is. Second, discernment includes the idea of *discretion*, the capacity to distinguish between good and evil as well as between the good and the better. A wine taster, for example, has the particular capacity to distinguish between good wine and even better wine. And third, discernment includes the idea of *judgment*. To be a discerning person is to be a wise woman or man capable of making a good assessment, a judgment that is informed by knowledge and understanding. Through the regular practice of discernment, a person grows in wisdom—a wisdom evident in the quality of one's choices.

The ability to discern the voice of Jesus is a critical spiritual skill, basic to our capacity to make vocational and moral choices. What we long for are the insight, discretion and judgment that would enable us to respond with integrity in the face of emotional turmoil and perplexing alternatives. As we yearn to know the voice of Jesus at the critical moments of our lives, we have a wonderful Christian heritage that can inform and guide this longing and help us make sense of the voices in our heads. We can learn how to discern, how to listen for the voice of Jesus and how to speak of this voice within the community of faith.

God speaks to his people in various ways; this book addresses one aspect of this speaking: the inner witness. The inner witness is known only when we recognize each way in which God speaks to us, whether it be through Scripture, through a prophetic word that comes within the community of faith or through the structures of the living church. But my concern in this volume is to consider how we recognize the voice of Jesus through the inner witness of his Spirit to our hearts.

1) insight
2) discretion, goal, will · Goal: [wisdom]
3) judgment

1

in knowledge by
knowledge; JESUS AND THE SPIRIT
understanding

A Christian is a person who has deliberately and eagerly decided to live
by the Word of God. Holy Scripture makes the extraordinary assumption
that God the Creator has chosen to speak to us. In the Old Testament era
this speaking was through the prophets. At that time, if one was to listen to
God, one had to attend to the prophets; they were the mouthpieces of God.
With the advent of the New Covenant, however, there came an astonishing
transition, described cogently in the opening words of the letter to the Hebrews: "Long ago God spoke to our ancestors in many and various ways by
the prophets, but in these last days he has spoken to us by a Son" (Heb 1:1-2).

The life of God is found in knowing the voice of the Son—the voice of
Jesus. God has spoken to us through Jesus.

THE WORDS OF JESUS

Jesus is the incarnate second person of the Trinity, but the Scriptures remind us that he is also a Teacher who speaks on behalf of God, and his
words are the words of life. As Jesus said to his disciples, "The words that I
have spoken to you are spirit and life" (Jn 6:63). And so Jesus himself announced that if we attend to the voice of the Son of God, we will live (Jn
5:25). For what Jesus speaks, he speaks on behalf of the Father (Jn 12:50).

The words of Jesus are the bread by which we live (Jn 6), the living water
for which we thirst (Jn 7:37-38) and the light of the world (Jn 8:12). He is
water, bread and light to those who listen to his voice. Jesus is the good
shepherd, and so of course his sheep hear his voice (Jn 10:4).

This voice is powerful. Jesus commanded Lazarus to come out of the tomb and back from the dead (Jn 11:43). This same voice tenderly called Mary Magdalene by name in the garden following the resurrection (Jn 20:16). And on some level this is what we all long for—to hear Jesus call *our* names. We yearn to hear the redemptive voice that, in the words of the hymn writer, "calms our fears and bids our sorrow cease." But more, we long to hear the voice of Jesus in the midst of the competing demands and expectations that we all face in the world and in the church. This is the voice that will give clarity, meaning and direction to our lives, enabling us to know who we are and who we are called to be. We somehow know that the voice of Jesus will enable us to live with courage and grace in a broken world.

In our early adult years we yearn to know Jesus' voice because we are making critical life choices. In midlife the issues are no less demanding as we seek to know that we are not alone, that Jesus is there for us. In our senior years the longing to know the voice of Jesus is, if anything, even more pronounced, for then we need to hear the voice of comfort, the voice of courage, the voice assuring us that indeed we know God and God knows us. Thus one of the deepest desires we have as Christians is to know the voice of Jesus.

As often as not, this longing arises when we face an important decision and yearn for God to speak to us and give us wisdom, direction and assurance in the midst of perplexing circumstances. The choices we make affect our lives and the lives of those we love; we long for the guidance of God. Further, in times of suffering and disappointment, we ardently seek to hear Jesus that we may know grace, comfort and hope in the midst of our pain.

This longing seems accentuated for those who live in busy and noisy cities. The city confronts us with a bewildering and confusing array of choices. We will live with sanity only if we are able to nurture the capacity to discern—to know the voice of Jesus in the midst of the choices we must make and in the midst of the myriad of competing voices we hear.

To discern is to make a distinction between the voice of Jesus and those competing voices that invariably speak in our hearts and minds. Sometimes these voices are nothing more than our own inner emotional turmoil; sometimes the voices we hear are the spoken and unspoken expectations of others; and there is no doubt that sometimes we come face to face with the subtleties of the evil one.

In the last book of the Bible, the Revelation of St. John, the apostle wrote of a series of visions that included seven messages for the seven churches of Asia (Rev 2—3). The Christian community over the centuries has always been taken by one in particular, the remarkable words spoken to the church in Laodicea. It is a sobering assessment of this church. The Lord said they were neither cold nor hot, and they were seemingly content in their lukewarmness. The angel of the Lord called them to repentance with words that echo deeply in our hearts.

I can vividly remember one of my experiences of these words. I was attending a concert put on by the Vancouver Chamber Choir and the Pacific Baroque Orchestra on December 3, 1999. The concert included the oratorio by Johann Sebastian Bach called *Nun komm, der Heiden Heiland* ("Now Come, Savior of the Nations"), which contains a wonderful recitative that is sung by the baritone. Derrick Christian was the baritone that evening, and I sat there and heard him sing the words to the Laodicean church, as found in Revelation 3:20: "Listen! I am standing at the door, knocking; if you hear my voice and open the door, I will come in to you and eat with you, and you with me." As he sang, I realized that I longed for nothing so deeply as that I would hear and know the voice of Jesus. These words called to the deepest part of my being.

I am not alone in this; the church over the centuries has found great comfort in Christ's promise. But there is an irony in this because these are words of warning and judgment on the church in Laodicea. Christians of all generations and cultures see their own failure reflected here. We are often deeply conscious of how we have failed (and are still failing) to live in a manner consistent with our confession and with the call of Jesus. Thus the words of judgment to the Laodicean church are for us words of mercy and reassurance; the Lord is inviting this pathetic congregation (and us!) to hear his voice with the promise that if we listen, he will enter and we will be with him and he will be with us.

But what is this voice? If Jesus is the good shepherd and his sheep hear his voice, how do we hear it? How is it recognized and known?

THE WITNESS OF THE SPIRIT

For one thing, the voice of Jesus is found in the words of the apostles, as inscripturated in the New Testament. Indeed the whole of holy Scripture is the word of Christ (Col 3:16). Furthermore, many Christians would affirm the role of the church and of those within the church who are called to speak for Christ in the life and witness of the Christian community. But Christians of all traditions are appreciating more and more that the voice of Jesus is also present to the Christian community through the inner witness of the Holy Spirit. As I hope to show, this inner witness is always grounded in the written witness of the Spirit—holy Scripture—and it is recognized by those who live in mutual submission within the community of faith. With these two anchors in place, Christians can know and live by the remarkable reality that God speaks to us through his Son, Jesus Christ, and that Jesus is present to us by his Spirit. We hear the voice of Jesus as we attend to the inner witness of the Spirit.

Earlier I referred to the words quoted in Revelation 3:20: "Listen! I am standing at the door, knocking; if you hear my voice and open the door, I will come in." As mentioned, these words were spoken to the Laodicean church, one of seven "messages" that were given to seven different churches. It is noteworthy that each of these seven messages concludes with a standard phrase with little variation: "Let anyone who has an ear listen to / what the Spirit is saying to the churches" (Rev 3:22). The link with the voice of Jesus is very apparent—we attend to the voice of Jesus by listening to what the Spirit is saying. We find this same link in the letter to the Romans, where we are reminded that we are children of God when we are led by the Spirit (Rom 8:14) and that the kingdom of God is "righteousness and peace and joy in the Holy Spirit" (Rom 14:17).

The connection between hearing the voice of Jesus and listening to the Spirit should come as no surprise to those familiar with the Gospel of John. An underlying thread of this Gospel is that the disciples learned to live by the voice of Jesus. Then in chapter 14 Jesus announced that he would be returning to the Father and that this meant he would be physically absent from them and from the world. They would no longer be able to see and touch him or hear his audible voice—the voice that had come to mean so much to them. Yet he also urged them not to be anxious about this. He would not leave them orphaned (Jn 14:18); rather, he would send them "another." This other was an Advocate, the Spirit of Truth, who would testify on behalf of Jesus (Jn 15:26).

John 14 opens with wonderful words of reassurance from Jesus: "Do not let your hearts be troubled." The chapter concludes with these same words (Jn 14:27), spoken immediately after Jesus had assured the disciples that the Holy Spirit would come. The entire ministry of Jesus was one that was empowered by and guided by the Spirit (Lk 4:18). And at the conclusion of his ministry, as a final gesture of love and empowerment for his disciples, he would breathe his Spirit on them (Jn 20:22). That being the case, we read that "by this we know that [Christ] abides in us, by the Spirit that he has given us" (1 Jn 3:24).[1]

This is the heart of the matter. John 15 is a call to live in union with Christ, as branches that are grafted into the vine and that bear fruit because we abide in Jesus. This union is known through the ministry of the Spirit. We abide in Christ when we are a people who receive his Spirit and live by his Spirit. As is highlighted earlier in the Gospel of John, Jesus is the one who speaks the words of God, "for he gives the Spirit without measure" (Jn 3:34).

It comes as no surprise, then, that the early church was a community that lived in intentional response to the Spirit, as is evident throughout the book of Acts. In Acts 13, for example, we read that "the Holy Spirit said, 'Set apart

---

[1]Hans Urs von Balthasar put this well when he wrote, "The Son is the prototype of those 'who are led by the Spirit of God' (Rom 8:14)" (Hans Urs von Balthasar, *Prayer*, trans. Graham Harrison [San Francisco: Ignatius Press, 1986], p. 188).

for me Barnabas and Saul for the work to which I have called them' " (Acts 13:2). And the church in Antioch obeyed because they knew that in so doing they were following Jesus, the Lord of the church.

The Spirit has come in place of the bodily presence of Jesus, and so the church follows Christ only insofar as it intentionally responds to the Spirit. Therefore, when we long to hear the voice of Jesus, what we seek is not an audible voice that we hear with our senses. Rather, we listen to Jesus and live by his "voice" when we attend to the Spirit—when we are, in the words of Romans 8:14, led by the Spirit. Jesus is known, and thus the voice of Jesus is known, through the ministry of the Spirit.

This theological principle brings to mind two subtle errors that we must avoid. First, we cannot conclude from this development (Jesus' return to the Father) that the presence of the Spirit is a minimally acceptable alternative to Christ. Not so! Rather, through the gift of the Spirit, we have the capacity to experience the entire Trinity and to live in dynamic union with Father, Son *and* Spirit. Second, we cannot suggest that the gift of the Spirit supplements what we have in Christ—that, having received Christ, we now need in addition to have an encounter with the Spirit. Indeed it is by the Spirit that we know the crucified and risen Christ in personal experience.

ATTENDING TO THE SPIRIT

As we have seen, it is by the Spirit that we are enabled to know the voice of Jesus. This leads to the following conclusion: The genius of the Christian life is the resolve, willingness and capacity to respond personally and intentionally to the prompting of the Spirit. To be a Christian is to walk in the Spirit, to be led by the Spirit, to respond to the Spirit, who transforms us into the image of Christ. What made the day of Pentecost so significant was that this event established our claim that every believer can know the immediate presence of the Spirit in our lives.

It is helpful to speak of this presence as *the inner witness of the Spirit.* By this we mean a direct impression on our inner consciousness, usually but not necessarily occasioned by some event or circumstance in our lives. God can, of course, bring a deep inner peace or awareness of his presence through no apparent catalyst. But whatever the means, the Spirit of God can and will make a direct, unmediated impression on the heart and mind of the Christian believer. It is possible to experience this witness and know with confidence that this is the inner work of the Holy Spirit—to know it is the voice of Jesus.

This witness is available to each individual Christian. But we can also affirm that God speaks to us as a community. As individuals, we develop the capacity to hear the voice of Jesus. But then as communities of faith, we can also seek and urgently need to develop our capacity to listen together to the witness of the Spirit. We need to know, corporately, as part of our patterns of governance and decision making, how to attend to the Spirit and know what the Spirit is saying to the community as a whole.

For us as individuals, the danger is that we might never develop an inner life. It is easy to live by duty, the expectations of others, the routines of our work and the inertia of culture and religious traditions. Surely what we long for, though, is an authentic interior life in which we know to the core of our beings that the Spirit of God is present to us and speaking life to us—a life that is personally and dynamically our own. With a well-developed interior life, we live our lives in response to the Spirit. We choose to live that which we are called to live—our life, not someone else's life.

The same could be said for churches and religious organizations. We do not genuinely fulfill what God is calling us to be and do as a community unless we develop the capacity to hear together the voice of Jesus in our midst—his voice of assurance and comfort, but also his voice of call and guidance. It is easy for churches or religious organizations to look elsewhere for models or trends to follow. Some church leaders are easily attracted to attending a conference or reading the most recent how-to book to learn how to help their church or organization develop in the same way as some remarkable church on the other side of the continent or the ocean. Others, in contrast, are nostalgic about a tradition, about the way things have always been done in this particular community, and speak of it as "our way."

Yes, we need to learn from others. And surely we are right to stress the value of the heritage we have within our church communities and organizations. But both our search for new models and the love for our own way of doing things can undermine our capacity to hear the new word that Jesus has for us as a community. We urgently need to develop a corporate capacity to respond to the voice of Jesus and have the courage both to hear this voice and to respond eagerly to the particular way God is calling us at this time and in this place.

This is life: an intentional response to the voice of Jesus, a voice that comes through the presence of the Spirit. Discernment is the discipline of attending to this presence and responding to this leading.

DYNAMIC TENSIONS IN CHRISTIAN DISCERNMENT

To attend to the Spirit is to discern the witness of the Spirit to our hearts and minds. This discernment is possible only if we are alert to several dynamic tensions that shape and guide the task of attending to the Spirit. The tension between heart and mind will be the focus of chapter three, but at least four other such tensions will guide our thinking and our response to the Spirit.[2]

1. *Divine initiative and human response.* Christian theology affirms the priority of God, and when it comes to discernment, this means that God is always the initiator. Before we can seek God, God has already sought us. Christian spirituality is *always* a spirituality of response. It is God who reaches out to us, speaks to us and enables us to hear his word. The genius of discernment is learning how to respond to this initiative. As God is always prior, discernment is the task of engaging this priority, seeking to know how God is speaking to us in this place and in this time.

However, while we can and must affirm the priority of God, we should

---

[2]In using the language of "tension," we acknowledge what is often the case in Christian theology—that frequently truth is found in sustaining two polarities and that error arises when we affirm, intentionally or inadvertently, one side of the equation over the other. So when it comes to the theology and practice of Christian discernment, it is helpful to think in terms of the dynamic tensions we must preserve if we are to discern well.

never do so in such a way as to discount the significance of what we ourselves do. The fact that God has priority and that all spirituality presumes God's initiative does not for a moment imply that we cannot accept responsibility for how we respond. Rather, the initiative of God calls forth our response. Christian discernment rests in this tension between the priority of God on the one hand and the call for genuine human action and responsibility on the other.

The response to the initiative of God requires both receptivity and skill. Receptivity is the fundamental disposition of openness to the priority of God, a desire to know the Word of God and an eagerness to respond in truth with our whole beings to this Word. The prayer that best captures this posture of receptivity is wonderfully expressed in the words of young Samuel when he said, "Speak, LORD, for your servant is listening" (1 Sam 3:10). However, discernment is also a learned art. Good will and good intentions are not enough. Many have been eager and willing to hear God but live deluded lives, doing harm when they presume to be doing good, living by their own ambitions when they say and believe they are doing the will of God. In other words, we need to learn discernment because it is quite possible, even if we are eager and sincere, to be led by our own misguided desires, motives and inclinations.

We must learn to distinguish, for not all "spiritual" experience finds its source in God. Scripture urges us, "Beloved, do not believe every spirit, but test the spirits to see whether they are from God" (1 Jn 4:1). We see the same dual concern in 1 Thessalonians 5 when Paul urged his readers to a radical openness ("do not quench the Spirit," 1 Thess 5:19) but also urged them to be discerning ("test everything; hold fast to what is good; abstain from every form of evil," 1 Thess 5:21-22).

Yet how do we know that what we are experiencing is truly from God? How do we know that God is present to us and that our experience is the fruit of God's grace? How do we know it is God and not just self-delusion? We need to somehow determine that we are not merely hearing what we want to hear but instead are encountering the triune God who is revealed in holy Scripture.

Further, the demands and expectations of others, while not necessarily evil, can easily sway us if we are generous people. Self-knowledge demands that we recognize our capacity for self-deception. A feeling of joy and contentment may be nothing more than our own enjoyment of recognition or a subtle desire to escape responsibility. In other words, a sincere heart must be complemented with a discerning mind. The capacity to discern, then, is a critical sign of spiritual maturity. The author of the letter to the Hebrews chided the readers for failing to be more mature in their faith and identified discernment as the sign of this maturity (Heb 5:12-14). It is as discerning people that we are able to grow in righteousness (Phil 1:9-11).

In this study on discernment, therefore, I will address the matter of our inner disposition. We can learn not only how to respond but also how to foster a genuine openness to the Spirit of Christ. I recognize, though, that no amount of study or critical analysis is a substitute for the disposition of humility—a poverty of spirit that is reflected in a childlike simplicity of heart (Mt 11:25-26; Lk 10:21). Humility is the first requirement for effective discernment. Yet Jesus taught his disciples how to lift up their hearts toward God, how to become receptive and vulnerable to the gracious initiative of God. Surely we have the capacity to learn with them.

While we foster this posture of receptivity, we must stress that discernment is also about our skillful response. We can learn much about this aspect of discernment from the wealth of our spiritual heritage, specifically how to test the movements of the heart, how to be alert to evil that masquerades as an angel of light and how we can be men and women who have both eager hearts and alert minds. Our resolution is to listen with heart and mind, and we listen well when we attend to both the priority of God's speaking and the necessity of an eager but discerning response.

2. *The context of our lives and the particularity of the voice of Jesus.* In discernment we need to attend to the tension that we experience between the specific context of our own lives and the capacity of the Spirit to speak uniquely into that context.

All religious experience is contextual and socially conditioned. All experience, including the experience of God, is located in the particularities of our lives and the factors that have shaped them. Many assume that if God is at work, this somehow overrides the specifics of our lives and makes them irrelevant. But God always speaks into the particular. If we hear the voice of Jesus, it is in part because we have learned to be attentive to the details of our lives. This includes the formative elements of our experience—the environment in which we grew up and the religious tradition that has shaped and informed our experience of God (particularly our language for God)—as well as the current aspects of our life circumstances.

We have a greater capacity to listen to Jesus if we are frank with ourselves about who we are, where we have come from, what we have experienced and what we hope for. Only then can we develop the ability to attend to the inner witness of the Spirit. We turn from sentimentality and pretense; we affirm things as they actually are, not as we wish they were. We strive to see and accept the actual circumstances of our lives rather than live and act as though they were otherwise. This includes honesty about our history, what we have been and what we have done. But further, it includes accepting what has been wrong about our lives, whether we are to blame or not, whether or not we have been all that we had hoped to be. It also means that we turn from the propensity to indulge in a wistful memory of some better time in the past.[3]

Some affirm all of this and go too far. They insist that all religious experience can be explained by social and cultural analysis. This perspective essentially denies the possibility of God's gracious intervention in human affairs.

Religious experience cannot be reduced to social and cultural analysis, or to a critical understanding of our environment, however important this is. The voice of Jesus can never be explained solely by our circumstances. While God speaks into the particularities of our lives, understanding and accepting

---

[3]This was aptly put by William Barry when he wrote, "The wisdom necessary for discernment requires an acceptance of the present environment as the one and only theatre for my action" (William A. Barry, "A Theology of Discernment," *The Way Supplement: The Place of Discernment*, spring 1989, p. 138).

these particularities never constitutes the whole of discernment. God may well surprise us! And God is clearly capable of saying one thing to one person and another thing to another, both of whom may have remarkably similar circumstances. While we must affirm that God speaks to us within our context, the voice of Jesus is never determined by or reduced to those circumstances. I am impressed, for example, by the contrast we see between two men whose encounters with Jesus are described in Luke 18—19.

In Luke 18 we read that a rich young ruler came to Jesus with a question: "Good Teacher, what must I do to inherit eternal life?" (Lk 18:18).[4] Jesus responded with some standard rabbinic questions and observations. But this man persisted in his search for an answer, so Jesus gave it to him: "Sell all that you own and distribute the money to the poor, . . . then come, follow me" (Lk 18:22). The man was very rich, and these words from Jesus saddened him. We read in the parallel account in Matthew's Gospel that he went away.

However, we should not discount him. He was probably a sincere seeker. I often imagine that though he was dispirited by Jesus' response, he nevertheless continued to follow, but at a distance, trying to reconcile his longing for Jesus with his wealth. And if he did continue down the road with Jesus, he would have been surprised at what happened. For we read in the next chapter, Luke 19, that Jesus had another encounter with a wealthy man, but this time with a very different outcome.

Luke portrayed the rich young ruler of Luke 18 as a good man. He had acquired his wealth by honorable means. The disciples were bewildered that his wealth could be an obstacle to the kingdom of God. But the wealthy man of Luke 19, Zacchaeus, is portrayed as just the opposite—he was the chief tax collector of that region. He had aligned himself with the oppressor, and his wealth had likely come by less than honorable means.

The rich man of Luke 18 sought Jesus out and asked his question. In contrast, the rich man of Luke 19 climbed a tree so that from a distance he

---

[4]Luke describes him merely as a "ruler." It is from Matthew 19:22 that we know he was young.

What is that to you?
John 21:22

could see Jesus over the heads of the people in the crowd who lined the path into Jericho. And Zacchaeus must have been amazed, if not shocked, that Jesus approached him and announced that he would join Zacchaeus in his home! Jesus declared by this deed what he also announced in word, that salvation had come to the home of this tax collector. With an eager response, Zacchaeus proclaimed that he would give half of his money to the poor and pay back those whom he had defrauded.

Now imagine if the rich young ruler of Luke 18 overheard this interchange between Jesus and Zacchaeus. It seems to me that he might have approached Jesus a second time with a legitimate question: "You call me to sell everything and give it to the poor, but to this man—this tax collector—you say nothing about his money and he announces that he will give one-half of his wealth to the poor! Why this discrepancy?"

The answer could easily have been something along the following lines: "My word to you is different than my call to Zacchaeus." In other words, though they were both wealthy men, there was not some standard way by which they were both to live.

A common temptation in discernment is that of assuming that God's word in one set of circumstances is the same for someone else in a similar situation. We are continually tempted to compare ourselves to others or assume that we know God's word for others. But God may well lead one person, whose circumstances resemble ours, in ways very different from his call to us.

John 21 describes an experience of St. Peter that is instructive in this regard. After the powerful encounter with Jesus when he was called to "feed my sheep," Peter looked over at the one who is called the beloved disciple (presumably John himself) and asked Jesus, "What about him?" (Jn 21:21). Jesus' response was intentionally vague as he spoke of his call to the other disciple. Then he said, "What is that to you?" (Jn 21:22). Peter's responsibility was to hear the call of Jesus on *his* life. This implies that we should avoid being curious about what God is saying to others, comparing ourselves with others or, even worse, presuming to know what God is saying to others.

Discernment, then, calls us to consider our circumstances, certainly, but this is only the first act of discernment. The contrast between the rich young ruler and Zacchaeus is a constant reminder of the fundamental principle of discernment: we cannot discern for one another. No matter how well I understand your circumstances, I am never able to tell you what God is saying to you. No one can presume to discern for another. Even if I am your pastor and know you well, I can never say that I know what God is saying to you. I may suggest possibilities; and I may even go so far as to suggest what I suspect the Lord is saying. But in the end, only *you* can discern what God is saying to you.[5]

This is why discernment is such a vital skill in the Christian life. We can discern only for ourselves. Further, we mature in the Christian faith only when we learn to discern for ourselves and thus develop the capacity, and hopefully the courage, to listen and to act in a manner congruent with the voice of Jesus.

It is important to make an additional point here. Discernment is indeed a matter of recognizing what God is saying to us now, at this time and place. But sometimes this means that we hear that voice through the spiritual discipline of retrospection. Sometimes, perhaps often, we do not hear the voice of Jesus in the moment, but later we look back and consider the signs of the Spirit's presence in our lives. At these times we might chide ourselves and wonder why we missed the voice of Jesus earlier, when in retrospect we can clearly see that he was speaking to us. Indeed sometimes it may seem that we should have been able to recognize his voice and failed to do so because we were not receptive or attentive. On the other hand, it is often the case that we cannot discern *except* in retrospect. God wants us to hear something now that we can appreciate only as we consider how God has been present to us and has led us in the past. Our past begins to make sense through retrospec-

---

[5]I need to stress, of course, that the general will of God—God's word for all people of all time—is clearly laid out in the Scriptures. What I am speaking to here is the particular call, that is, how one person is called to live out the specifics of God's will in the world. We certainly are to call one another to obedience, but it is another matter when a person is wrestling with a choice that is morally neutral.

tion, and how we are being called to act in the present makes sense as we see the gracious hand of God present in our past circumstances.

Yet all of this is intended to enable us to hear God speak to us today, in the present context of our lives. The tension is that we cannot hear God except in the actual context of our lives but that the context is never the whole of what God is saying to us. God speaks into the particularities of our lives, and God is always able to surprise us in those particularities.

3. *The voice of Jesus in prayer and in the world.* There is a third critical tension in discernment that we need to take into account: the dynamic interplay between what happens in prayer and what happens in the rest of our lives. One side of this tension calls us to affirm that God is present everywhere. When it comes to discernment, one of the most common errors is to assume that God speaks only in particular kinds of contexts or only in specific modes. This error minimizes God's voice, usually with an assumption that God only speaks in religious settings. The complementary error is the assumption that if we are in a religious setting, then surely what we hear is God speaking and never the expression of evil. Neither is true; God is present in the world and evil is present within the church.

The danger is that we might miss the voice of Jesus because we are unwilling to hear him through the mode by which he is speaking. We reject what we are hearing and presume that this could not possibly be the voice of Jesus because of the source or the venue. However, a discerning person learns to be alert and attentive to the voice of Jesus in every context of life and, potentially, through unexpected channels of communication. Augustine's conversion came in response to the words of a child playing outside his window. His experience is a reminder that God may well surprise us and speak to us through those whom we might initially discount because of their youth or other factors. But discerning people know that God often chooses to confound the wisdom of the "wise" by challenging the teacher through her students, the father through the words of his teenage daughter, the grandparent through the questions raised by a grandson. A wise person knows that those with less education, or even those of another faith tradition, are often a source of crucial insight. Is it possible for God to speak to me through a Buddhist or through my agnostic neighbor? As I ride the bus to work, can God speak to me through the person sitting next to me? Or do I always assume that if they are not Christians, or if they do not have as much theological education or experience as I have, they cannot be a means by which I hear the voice of Jesus?

Effective discernment requires that we be open to surprises, to the strange and wonderful ways in which God may want to encounter our hearts and minds, inform our conscience and call us to be his followers. However, while we must affirm that God can speak to us anywhere and through whatever means, to become discerning people it is necessary that we learn to listen in prayer. While we must avoid the error of thinking that God is only present to us in religious settings such as worship and prayer, we also need to appreciate that if we are able to recognize God's presence in the whole of life, it is because we are people of prayer.

To put it differently, while God speaks to us in the whole of our lives and potentially within just about any circumstance and through any person who comes our way, we will not recognize the voice of Jesus unless we establish the pattern of listening to the Spirit in our prayers. We learn to listen in prayer. Then, in time, the whole of our lives will be marked by our capacity to listen. Thus mature pray-ers are those who are not just attentive to Jesus in prayer; they have over time become women and men who are able to discern the inner witness of the Spirit in the midst of life and work. Whether on the bus or in a committee meeting, whether in a worship service or a sporting event, they are individuals of discernment alert to the ways in which God is present and speaking. But they learn to be discerning people by first developing the capacity to attend to the inner witness of the Spirit in the context of their prayers. Discerning people are pray-ers.

But as we are reminded in Romans 8:26, we do not know how to pray. "The Spirit helps us in our weakness; for we do not know how to pray as we ought, but that very Spirit intercedes with sighs too deep for words." Our inability to pray is a recognition that we are deeply dependent on the *defined; Prayer*

Spirit to guide us in our praying. Indeed it is precisely at this point that we seek to follow and respond to the Spirit. Without a conscious dependence on the Spirit in our prayers, we are always in danger of talking to ourselves rather than to God. The Spirit guides our prayers such that our praying is in obedience to this inner witness. Obedience here is not so much compliance as it is an eager and hearty response—an unqualified yes to the initiative of the Spirit. Too often our inclination in prayer is to propose an agenda for God, but true prayer is first and foremost an act of response to God's initiative. In prayer we certainly learn to speak, but our speaking arises out of our listening.[6]

Prayer is an intentional response to the Spirit. We acknowledge that we do not know how to pray but also appreciate that the Spirit will guide us in our praying. Surely this is at least in part what the apostle Paul meant when he called his readers to "pray in the Spirit at all times" (Eph 6:18; compare Jude 20) and at another time spoke of Christians as those who are "led by the Spirit" (Gal 5:18). In prayer, as in all of life, we seek to respond to the initiative of the Spirit.

For some, then, this book will be a guide to prayer—to what it means to both listen and discern in their praying. The hope is that, in learning to listen well in prayer, we might learn to listen well wherever we are. If we are genuinely attentive to Christ in prayer, we will more likely be attentive to the witness of Christ's Spirit in every dimension of our lives.

4. *The individual and the community.* Here is another dynamic tension in discernment. The community is both a threat and an indispensable aid to discernment. As individuals, we can and must develop the capacity to listen to the voice of Jesus for ourselves, quite apart from the potentially weighty influence of the community. But we are never alone in our listening; we are always hearing Jesus from within community with its network of relationships.

---

[6]"Prayer is a conversation with God in which God's word has the initiative and we, for the moment, can be nothing more than listeners" (Balthasar, *Prayer*, p. 15). Some might suggest that this sounds like a form of quietism that undermines the legitimate place of human agency. However, though the spiritual life is one of response, it is an *active* response—an eager, willful engagement with the initiative of the Spirit.

On the one hand, this means that as communities we must take the individual seriously. As I hope to show in the chapters on communal discernment (chapters eleven and twelve), the community will not be able to listen to the voice of Jesus until we appreciate that God speaks through individuals within the community. Conversely, as individuals, we face the challenge of learning what it means to listen to God for ourselves, in light of our personal experience and call. For us to mature, our faith and our experience of Christ cannot be derivative of others' faith. It must be our own, forged through our own experience. A personal faith is developed as we trust God, experience his grace and recognize that the God of creation calls us by name. We learn to hope in God—as individuals—and learn to live in radical dependence on the gracious work of God in our lives and in our world.

We cannot look to our surrounding culture or society to provide us with support. On the contrary, in a post-Christian era the intellectual, moral, artistic, judicial and educational streams of our societies will either take no account of our religious convictions or actually be adversarial to them. Fundamentalism seeks to stay the cultural tide (that is, it puts its energy into fighting the decline toward secularism) or else denies that any significant cultural change has occurred. Perhaps the better alternative would be to recover the dynamic of authentic spiritual experience.

What if we accept that we now live in a religious, moral and spiritual desert—a social and cultural landscape that is not hospitable? Then the only alternative is to draw strength from our own experience of divine grace. An inhospitable culture is part of the context for the experience of God. This is not something that is new per se. It was the contextual reality for the psalmists (see Psalm 12, for example) and for the Christians of the first and second centuries.

This does not mean that we abandon culture and society or remain passive. It means, rather, that our posture can be one in which we do not expect the culture and society to sustain us. Our point of reference is *our* experience of divine grace. The great mystics did not go the way of pure negation. They sought God in the world, believing that God is found in all things (to use a wonderful line from Ignatius Loyola). They demonstrated that the true contemplative is a contemplative in action—engaged in generous service in response to the pain of the world.

Some contend that this emphasis on personal experience is too subjective. However, our experience is always of an external, tangible reality that is encountered by the believer. Furthermore, while our experience is personal and unique, it is always mediated by and sustained by the community of faith. The community does not lose its role when there is an emphasis on a highly personal, experiential religious faith. Rather, as Louis Dupré contended, the community is that entity which enables the individual to experience the ancient reality on which faith is based. Dupré noted, "By providing the believer with sacraments, Scriptures, and a whole system of representations, the religious community enables the individual to integrate his or her private spiritual life within a living communion."[7]

But herein lies a tension that is central to our pursuit of discernment. Though the community is an essential bastion of support in the face of a post-Christian or non-Christian social environment, we also need to acknowledge the threat to discernment that exists within the Christian community itself. Many religious leaders and Christian communities unintentionally, and sometimes intentionally, foster the idea that we hear the voice of Jesus only through the community and particularly through the leadership of that community. They are uncomfortable with the idea that the individual Christian, with a mind informed by the Scriptures, can truly know the voice of Jesus in his or her own heart and mind. They believe that it is their responsibility to tell their fellow Christians what they should hear and how they should act.

The tragedy is that the community then does not really foster spiritual maturity. It does not enable individual Christians to hear the voice of Jesus and encounter for themselves the living bread and living water. And

---

[7]Louis Dupré, *Religious Mystery and Rational Reflection: Excursions in the Phenomenology and Philosophy of Religion* (Grand Rapids, Mich.: Eerdmans, 1998), p. 142.

so their faith becomes a derivative experience rather than a personal response to God.

In a situation like that the group identity or mentality easily disregards the boundaries of our individual lives.[8] The individual has no capacity to breathe, to make sense of what is happening in his or her own heart. And consistently what we find is that the community appeals to critical values of community itself, of duty and responsibility, of faithfulness (to the community) as a way to discourage individual consciousness. The community invades the inner life of the individual rather than supporting it.

The grace we seek, in other words, is one in which we personally experience the inner witness of the Spirit; it is our own experience—not a secondhand experience or one derivative of another's experience. However, it should be immediately apparent that we cannot learn how to discern while in isolation from the community of faith. Though we must learn discernment *for* ourselves, we do not learn *by* ourselves. Thus the tension: the community is a threat to our capacity for discernment, but to discern well requires a high level of mutual dependence within Christian community and genuine accountability to that community.

DISCERNMENT AND THE SCRIPTURES

Throughout the history of the church there have been Christians who have opposed speaking of an unmediated inner witness to the hearts of ordinary women and men. Perhaps they have feared extremism. They may have rightly been alert to the human capacity for self-deception. It has also been usual for those who have had this concern to insist that they upheld Scripture or church tradition and feared that an emphasis on a personal response to the Spirit would undermine these anchors of our faith. But fear of extremism can

---

[8]This is what Flora Wuellner called a "group mentality" and a "tribal spirit" (Flora Wuellner, "Were Not Our Hearts Burning Within Us?" *Weavings*, November-December 1995, p. 31). She went on to speak of how this is often in the ethos or ambience of a community, or how things are "done" or "not done" in a church, school or other organization. I will address this further when I speak of the convicting ministry of the Spirit and our capacity for false guilt that arises from the expectations of others (chapter five).

cause us to "quench the Spirit" (1 Thess 5:19). A wiser response is to affirm the inner witness while also emphasizing the need for discernment.

This discernment is possible only when we sustain the dynamic tensions outlined in this chapter. In turn, the tensions that undergird the discipline of discernment are kept in equilibrium by an unreserved commitment to the priority of holy Scripture. Few things are so central to the Christian perspective on discernment as the relationship between the inner witness of the Spirit and the objective, inscripturated witness of the Holy Spirit, namely, the Bible. As I hope to demonstrate through an exploration of each dimension of this inner witness, we cannot know the voice of Jesus unless we are men and women of Scripture, with our minds and hearts informed by truth. Why? Because the inner witness will never contradict the written witness of the Spirit. Further, we cannot develop our intuitive capacity to recognize the inner witness unless we are women and men who are immersed in Scripture so that the contours of our hearts and minds are ordered and enabled by the Word.

The inner witness of the Spirit is the personalization or application of the written witness to our lives. It is the ancient Word that now takes form in our lives, in this time and place, in this set of circumstances. The inner witness of the Spirit is the necessary complement to the Scriptures, without which the Bible is but an ancient book. But then it also follows that we cannot know the inner witness unless we know the written witness. Klaus Bockmühl used a wonderful image when he wrote about the relationship between the inner witness and Scripture, stressing that "Holy Scripture is the starting point and measuring rod for individual insight." He went on to suggest that Scripture is like the base line in music that keeps the score grounded and secure.[9]

We attend to both the written and the inner witness with a pure and simple objective—that we would become increasingly conformed to the image of Jesus the Son (Rom 8:29). It is clear from the New Testament that the

---

[9]Klaus Bockmühl, *Listening to the God Who Speaks: Reflections on God's Guidance from Scripture and the Lives of God's People* (Colorado Springs, Colo.: Helmers & Howard, 1990), p. 149.

ministry of the Spirit is Christocentric: the Spirit glorifies Christ and enables us to be transformed into his image. Yet when we speak of the work of
the Spirit enabling us to be like Christ, it is not just any "Jesus." The Spirit
of God will enable us to know the Christ who was sent by the Father, who
took on our humanity through the incarnation, suffered on the cross and
reigns now as risen Lord. Any other "Jesus" is not the Jesus of the New Testament, of Christian faith or—more to the point—of the Holy Spirit.

At this point, some comments about illuminism might be appropriate.
Anyone who takes discernment and the inner witness of the Spirit seriously
may be accused of being an enthusiast or a religious fanatic. Indeed,
throughout the history of the church, there has always been an affirmation
of the inner witness even while at the same time a segment of the church
has been apprehensive about any such witness. Such a reaction occurs because there has been a persistent aberration of classic Christian teaching on
this subject. Known as *illuminism*, this aberration is misguided and harmful
in many ways to the church and to Christians.

Illuminism is a teaching (and practice) that takes seriously the idea of an
inner light based on the assumption that the Spirit is present within each
person and that God teaches us through this inner illumination. However,
while affirming the inner subjective awareness, illuminists fail to give equal
importance to the outer witness—holy Scripture. Often these are individuals who insist on the importance of Scripture, but they use Scripture only
insofar as it endorses their own subjective awareness or conviction. Further,
illuminists tend to deny the critical place of the intellect and the importance of the Christian mind. True discernment, in contrast, affirms our capacity to respond to God with both heart and mind. What is particularly
perilous is that illuminists view themselves as having a privileged inner light
that cannot, and need not, be challenged by the community. They consider
their inner light to be self-authenticating; they think the counsel and wisdom of others is superfluous and unnecessary.

Sometimes we see this in religious teachers or leaders. They bristle
when it is suggested that their vision or dream or deep conviction is not en-

dorsed by others. But true humility and (as we shall see) true discernment are a knowledge of God and of the inner witness that comes in dynamic interchange with the community of faith. Truly discerning persons are conscious of their own capacity for self-deception and thus of their vital need for the encouragement, support and wisdom of others.

We need to be able to ask each other two questions. First, what do you think Jesus is saying to you at this time and in the midst of this set of circumstances? And second, how do you know this is the voice of Jesus? In the chapters that follow, I hope to provide a grammar for our conversations—something to which we can appeal in our own personal journey of faith, but also something to which we can appeal *together*. We want to be able to talk meaningfully about the experience of the Spirit, do so in a way that enables us to be discerning and, hopefully, learn to answer both questions well.

2

Three Voices,
One Tradition

 ◯)

Adiscussion about discernment is a reflection on the nature of religious experience. Experience is inherently pliable and intangible and thus hard to define. We affirm that the Spirit of God communicates inwardly to the consciousness of those who are prepared to listen. Fine and good. But what form does this take? And how is it recognized? How can we talk about it meaningfully?

It is imperative that we affirm and reaffirm that what we seek is not some vague experience or titillating encounter but nothing other than an experience of the triune God. We seek to know the Father. We believe and want to act on the conviction that it is possible to have a dynamic and personal relationship with Christ, a relationship that is mediated to us by his Spirit. The content of our experience, then, is Jesus. It is a false spiritual encounter if it fails to affirm the Jesus of holy Scripture—the human, historical Jesus who was crucified and now reigns as risen Lord. We seek an experience of Jesus that is congruent with the historic faith of the church.

Therefore, we need a language to be able to speak about this experience, not only to make sense of our own encounters with Jesus but also as a way to be in conversation with others about our experience. This does not mean a scientific analysis of our spiritual experience that essentially reduces experience to only that which is empirically verifiable. But it does mean that we have a common understanding, with terms of reference, and a grammar that authenticates and strengthens that experience. To find this, we must turn to the Christian spiritual heritage so that our experience and our conversation are informed by the Christian tradition.

THE REALITY OF A CHRISTIAN TRADITION CONCERNING THE INNER WITNESS

In Christian history and thought, the language of "tradition" speaks of a continuous witness in the life and teaching of the church that gives wisdom and guidance to succeeding generations of Christians. For the central themes of Christian thought, the tradition is clear. It is captured in the wonderful words of the ancient creeds, which arose out of the early ecumenical councils. But when it comes to discerning the voice of Jesus, we have no such creedal affirmations to which we can appeal. We turn instead to the writings of our spiritual fathers and mothers to determine if there is a pattern of thought and teaching that might point to an ongoing witness of the Spirit in the life of the church.

What we find is distinctive and compelling. There is a tradition that finds expression right across the spectrum of theological perspectives. As we explore these diverse streams, we discover a remarkable congruence that speaks, in turn, of a common heritage. In other words, as we seek to make sense of the experience of the Spirit in our day, we are not merely drawing on various bits of helpful wisdom from our spiritual heritage. Rather, an examination of this heritage points to a distinctive and specific tradition.

In the chapters that follow I will draw on a breadth of spiritual counsel and wisdom from the Christian heritage. However, in a discussion regarding discernment and the inner witness of the Spirit, and particularly the interplay between these, three names invariably stand out. For me, what highlights the reality of a distinctive tradition in the Christian heritage is that though these sources represent three different theological streams of the church, they nevertheless reflect a remarkable degree of congruency. In these three sources—Ignatius Loyola, John Wesley and Jonathan Edwards—we have witnesses to a tradition that the contemporary Christian cannot afford to ignore. Here is wisdom for life in the twenty-first century, wisdom out of our Christian heritage, and not just one contribution, or the perspective of one writer or theologian, but rather three different sources that agree sufficiently such that we have, essentially, a common historic witness to a tradition.

THE REMARKABLE CONGRUENCY OF IGNATIUS, WESLEY AND EDWARDS

Ignatius Loyola (1491-1556) was a Spanish reformer, spiritual writer and founder of the Society of Jesus, better known as the Jesuits. John Wesley (1703-1791) was an English evangelist and founder of Methodism. And Jonathan Edwards (1703-1758) was a Puritan, Congregational theologian and American preacher, highly influential in the religious revival known as the Great Awakening. These three men, through the writings they left, point to a common tradition of spiritual discernment.

For Ignatius, our primary source is the *Spiritual Exercises* (begun in rough form when he was quite young but finally published in 1548), part of which includes the "Rules for Discernment." For Wesley, his thought on this subject is available through his journal and letters, but primarily in his sermons, notably those that specifically address the matter of the inner witness. For Edwards, of particular note for our purposes is his classic work entitled *Religious Affections*. All three of these sources affirm that our point of departure is crucial: they stress the need for clarity about our ultimate allegiance. As Ignatius puts it in the *Spiritual Exercises:* "In every good choice, as far as depends on us, our intention must be simple. I must consider only the end for which I am created, that is, for the praise of God our Lord and for the salvation of my soul."[1]

We hear the voice of Jesus from a posture of attentiveness and humility. If we are to hear God and live with a confidence that we walk in the light of his will and choose wisely in response to his voice, we must be clear

---

[1]Ignatius Loyola, *The Spiritual Exercises of St. Ignatius*, trans. Louis J. Puhl (Chicago: Loyola University Press, 1975), para. 169.

about our ultimate allegiance. We need to be certain about whom we serve. This is the single most crucial issue when it comes to divine guidance and spiritual discernment.

The Christian community has always been profoundly impressed by two moments in redemptive history that capture this posture of heart and mind. First, we have Mary, the mother of the Lord, who at the announcement of the angel replied with the words "Here am I, the servant of the Lord; let it be with me according to your word" (Lk 1:38). And second, we have Jesus himself, who in Gethsemane said to the Father, "Not what I want, but what you want" (Mk 14:36). No caveats, no qualifiers.

However, it is misguided and simplistic to conclude that all we need to do is be committed and we will know the way. This world has been severely threatened by those who have great depth of commitment and even radical allegiance but who are crusaders—zealots passionate for what they perceive to be God's will, but hardly a means of grace to our world. The irony is that this zeal for God can blind us to what God is actually doing and actually saying. We must be discerning.

And herein lies the genius of Ignatius, Wesley and Edwards. For all of them, spiritual transformation comes not so much through zeal or determination as through what is happening to us affectively, the emotional dispositions of our hearts. Listening to God is a matter of being attentive to the affective orientation of one's inner consciousness. To discern, then, requires that we develop the capacity to listen with heart *and* mind. Ignatius, Wesley and Edwards each approaches this question differently, but as we will see, taken together they profile a remarkable congruency of understanding—a threefold witness to a common tradition.

IGNATIUS LOYOLA

Ignatius Loyola was a Basque soldier who, during a time of convalescence after having been wounded in battle, read a classic devotional book on the lives of Christ and of the saints. Immersed in this spiritual reading, he devoted himself to Christ and to his service.

During this time of recuperation, Ignatius also became conscious of the movements of his heart and mind, particularly his emotional ups and downs. He sought to make sense of their relationship to his newfound commitments. As he monitored his affective responses, he grew in his capacity to discern their significance.

Later, while under the influence of Benedictine monks, he was introduced to spiritual writings of the late Middle Ages, including those of the devotional masters of the Brethren of the Common Life (best known, perhaps, through the work attributed to Thomas à Kempis, *Imitation of Christ*). From this input, building on what he was learning about his own heart, Ignatius formulated an approach to the spiritual life that is encapsulated in his classic work, *Spiritual Exercises*.[2]

The *Exercises* presuppose that there is a choice to be made, what Ignatius called an "election." While the *Exercises* can be used as a "school of prayer," the original design was that through these exercises the pray-er would be enabled to make a vital life decision. The intent of the *Exercises* is to assist those who seek to discover and follow the will of God for them as individuals. This speaks, then, not of a general, moral will of God but of the particular will for one's immediate life situation. And Ignatius's approach is rooted in the conviction that this choice can be made with the assistance of the Holy Spirit through the means outlined in the *Exercises*. However, while there are exercises and disciplines through which the pray-er is led, the bottom line is that real guidance is provided by the Spirit.

A compelling phrase captures the notion of discernment in Ignatian spirituality; it is the vision of *finding God in all things*. Discernment for Ignatius and his followers is a matter of attending to, and being conscious of, the activity of God in experience. The purpose of this discernment is that

---

[2]I realize that some evangelical Protestant Christians may hesitate to learn from Ignatius. But this study of discernment arises out of the assumption that we need to learn from the spiritual masters of both the Protestant and the Catholic traditions. My own perspective is that Ignatius was one of the great masters on discernment and that no study of this spiritual discipline is complete without a consideration of his contribution.

our lives, our choices and our actions would be aligned in substantial measure to the presence and intentions of God.

Ignatius came to several notable conclusions in the *Exercises*. First, he recognized that in discernment it is our feelings that we discern. In other words, the data we use in our reflections is what is happening to us emotionally—our emotional ups and downs and inner turmoil as well as the deeper emotional disposition of our hearts.[3] This does not mean that Ignatius discounted the place of rational and critical refection. It is merely that the content or focus of this reflection is what is happening to us emotionally. He was convinced that we could take God and ourselves seriously only if we learned to take emotion and affect seriously. Emotion and feeling were for Ignatius key indicators of the work of God in our lives, for by attending to emotional dispositions we are giving attention to the media of God's influence in our lives. Feelings are the information on which we focus when we seek the mind of the Lord.

In this emphasis on affect, Ignatius made a helpful and crucial distinction, saying that the movements of the heart—our emotions—are of two kinds: desolation and consolation. "Desolation" speaks of the emotional orientation that diminishes faith, hope and love. These include the obvious negative emotional states of anger, fear and discouragement but also any emotional heaviness of heart or inner malaise by which one feels, in Ignatius's words, "listless, tepid [or] unhappy," in which one does not feel connected to God.[4] "Consolation," in contrast, is that emotional state of peace or joy in which one senses that one is in communion with the Lord and growing in faith, hope and love.[5] Consolation may be expressed in tears if our tears draw us to and enable us to live in union with Christ. But the core expression is joy that is rooted in that which is true and good—a joy that finds expression in an inner peace and quiet.

When we attend to what is happening in us emotionally, it is vital that

---

[3]This is what Ignatius called *"sentir"* in Spanish.
[4]Ignatius, *Spiritual Exercises*, para. 317.
[5]Ibid., para. 316.

we are alert to both desolation and consolation. Both, in significant ways, enable us to make sense of the movements of God in our hearts.

Second, while stressing the central place of emotion and affect in the spiritual life, Ignatius was certainly not naive. Indeed a central concern for him was the need for critical reflection because our emotions can so easily lead us astray. The solution is not that we discount the significance of emotion; such a stance, in fact, would be naive since the emotional dispositions of the heart are central to our human identity. Rather, our capacity to be misled by emotion means that we need to be discerning. And so in this regard Ignatius developed a series of "rules for discernment."

Many contemporary Christians might protest that the notion of "rules" sounds presumptuous and heavy-handed and might suggest that it would be better to offer "guidelines and suggestions" on discernment. But Ignatius provided these rules in the same spirit as a flight instructor gives the rules of how an airplane is flown. The student does not need suggestions! In learning to fly an airplane, the student needs to know the rules—the principles of flight about which there is no debate or discussion. One learns these rules of flight for the simple reason that it is a matter of life and death. Likewise for Ignatius, there were rules about what it takes to be a discerning person, and it is, in a sense, a matter of life and death.

While Ignatius offered an extended series of rules of discernment, I will highlight two at this point, particularly with respect to consolation and desolation. First, he noted that the emotional state of desolation is one in which we cannot trust our inner selves, neither can we be confident that what we are feeling is of God. We must assume that if we are in desolation, we need to wait and not choose a course of action or make a decision. The Holy Spirit leads us only in consolation—in peace and joy. The experience of desolation may be legitimate in itself. We may be angry in the face of injustice or discouraged because of a major personal setback. Conversely, our desolation may be due to our own personal negligence and lack of spiritual discipline. Either way, Ignatius would stress that a discerning person has learned the simple principle that God does not lead in desolation.

Then, as a second rule of discernment, Ignatius was quick to insist that the presence of consolation—peace and joy—means little in and of itself, for evil spirits have the capacity to masquerade as the Spirit of light. And so we must test the consolation and confirm that indeed this peace comes from God. In other words, we may feel a deep consolation or a powerful surge of joy, but it does not follow that this emotional impulse arises from the inner witness of the Spirit. If it is authentic, it will lead to faith, hope and love. True consolation, the work of the Spirit of God, will result in a life of holiness, service and generosity in response to the call of Christ.

Third, alongside these rules of discernment, Ignatius Loyola gave special emphasis to the priority of humility in the Christian life and prayer. It is no coincidence that in the *Spiritual Exercises* the section on humility precedes the explanation of the times for making a choice or decision. For Ignatius, as for the late medieval mystics who shaped his thought, humility was "seeing oneself in truth." Humility as true self-understanding means that we see ourselves for all that we are—our motives, our feelings, our weaknesses and strengths, and our limitations. It is through humility that we order our affections, and humility is a sign of ordered affections.

To appreciate this perspective on humility, we need to mention another significant contribution Ignatius made to Christian thought: the principle of holy indifference. For Ignatius, we live in truth only when our ultimate love is for Christ and for his kingdom. All creation and all created things, while coming from God, can never take the place of God and of delight in God. Thus for Ignatius, it is important that we sustain a holy indifference to these things, whether wealth or honor or career or reputation.

Indifference is not apathy or a lack of affect. It is rather an emotional posture in which we see and respond to God's creation in freedom. We experience an inner freedom from worldly goods because we have come, increasingly, to find that our lives are anchored in the love of God and trust of God's provision for our lives. Regardless of whether the Lord gives us things, we have the freedom of indifference to accept either outcome, not because we do not care or have no preferences, but because what ultimately matters is that we would live in the love of God.

It is not easy to come to this holy indifference. Indeed the great challenge in personal discernment is not so much that we know what God is saying as that we would grow into this indifference. If we are indifferent, hearing God's call will not be difficult. As I will emphasize later, nothing matters so much to this indifference as a lively awareness of the love of God.

One last note in this regard. It is important to affirm that for Ignatius this holy indifference is very much an indifference in association with Christ. Indifference is not an end in itself; rather, we seek the humility of indifference because we long to be with Christ. If we are poor, we are poor with Christ. If we live in obscurity, we live in obscurity with Christ. If we experience difficulty and setback, we are with Christ. In the words of Paul, if we suffer, we suffer as joint heirs with Christ (Rom 8:17). For Ignatius, Christian humility is the experience of being with Christ. In humility we are in association and identification with Jesus.

JOHN WESLEY

The elements of John Wesley's theology that are relevant to discernment include his understanding of the inner witness of the Spirit, his convictions regarding the safeguards that serve as parameters of discernment and his call for humility.

Few if any within the Protestant evangelical tradition have placed so strong an emphasis on the place of the Spirit's witness in the life of the believer as has John Wesley. Wesley was in many respects a typical eighteenth-century Anglican churchman until he had a unique encounter at a meeting on London's Aldersgate Street in May 1738. From that experience, this gifted and brilliant churchman was transformed into an evangelist and founder of Methodism—a movement that has had a remarkable impact on Christianity. Furthermore, Christians who are heirs to the nineteenth-century Holiness movement see Wesley as a primary influence in their thought and spirituality. In addition, many Pentecostal believers and charismatic Catholics see the roots of their own movements as reaching back to the impact of this Anglican evangelist and churchman.[6]

The experience of Aldersgate Street is captured in Wesley's well-known phrase "I felt my heart strangely warmed." He was attending a religious society meeting, and during the reading of Luther's introduction to the epistle to the Romans he was struck by the wonder of the gospel and the love of God. More to the point, Wesley experienced God's love and with it the God-given assurance that he was personally accepted and forgiven. This experience, along with his own theological formation, led him to some significant conclusions.

First, John Wesley's contribution is noteworthy because he stressed the vital place of the inner witness of the Spirit. He was convinced that the Aldersgate experience of the "heart strangely warmed" was a direct, unmediated testimony of the Spirit to his inner being. As a result, he was declared a fanatic and an enthusiast, as is so frequently the case with those who claim to have a direct witness of the Spirit. But Wesley refused to back down. He was convinced that his own experience, taken together with the testimony of holy Scripture and the historic witness of the church, confirmed the vital place of the Spirit's witness in the life of the Christian believer.[7] Wesley was deeply impressed by the ringing affirmation of the apostle Paul in Romans 8:15 and 16: "When we cry, 'Abba! Father!' it is [the] Spirit [of God] bearing witness with our spirit that we are children of God."

Wesley came to the conviction that nothing is so foundational to the Christian life as this affective awareness of our spiritual adoption and the

---

[6]Several years ago, while I was serving as the dean of Alliance Biblical Seminary in Manila, Philippines, we invited Father Herb Schneider, S.J., one of the leaders of the Catholic charismatic movement in the Philippines, to speak to our community about the movement. I found it noteworthy that he began his comments by talking about the impact of John Wesley.

[7]In response to those who denounced him and insisted that reasonable Christians did not believe in such things as an inner witness, Wesley had apt responses. Of those who might say, "But madmen, French prophets, and enthusiasts of every kind, have imagined they experience this witness," Wesley replied with "They have so, and perhaps not a few of them did, although they did not retain it long: But if they did not, this is no proof at all that others have not experienced it; as a madman's *imagining* himself a king, does not prove that there are no *real* kings" (John Wesley, *The Works of John Wesley*, ed. Albert C. Outler [Nashville: Abingdon, 1984], 1:293).

inner confidence that we are loved by God. Wesley insisted, however, that this was only the beginning. From this confidence, one develops the capacity to live in an ongoing, personal relationship with the Spirit. This dynamic of intimate union with the Spirit is, ideally, central to our Christian identity and experience.

The locus of this inner witness is the affections. Wesley affirmed the priority of the heart in Christian faith and piety based on the conviction that true Christianity is fundamentally a heartfelt response to the love and grace of God. As with Ignatius, this did not mean that he discounted the mind. Not for a moment. It is merely that he believed the primal element in human identity is found in what he termed the "heart."

For Wesley, nothing so defines the nature of Christian character as particular emotional dispositions.[8] However, this emphasis on the affections and a religion of the heart demanded discernment. As Wesley himself noted, "How many have mistaken the voice of their own imagination for this witness of the Spirit of God, and then idly presumed they were the children of God, while they were doing the works of the devil!"[9]

Wesley was no sentimentalist. For him, not just any emotional experience or expression was a sign of God's presence. He stressed that we must be discerning, and for Wesley the Scriptures were clear on the "marks, whereby one may be distinguished from the other."[10]

Wesley emphasized that there are two signs that give evidence that what we are experiencing is authentically of the Spirit. The first is a deep, heartfelt assurance that we are children of God—a confidence that is evident in our joy.[11] The second is moral renewal and reform. Joy is authentic only if it leads to integrity of life and character; otherwise, it is false and vacuous. Mean-

---

[8]See Gregory S. Clapper, *John Wesley on Religious Affections: His Views on Experience and Emotion and Their Role in Christian Life and Theology* (Metuchen, N.J.: Scarecrow, 1989), notably pp. 54-55 for a discussion on emotions and passions in Wesley's thought.
[9]Wesley, *Works*, 1:269.
[10]Wesley, *Works*, 5:277-78.
[11]Wesley spoke most of love, peace and joy, actually, but it is joy that takes pride of place in his references to the inner witness.

while, moral reform without joy is legalism or moralism, not the authentic transformation of character that arises from an encounter with the gospel.

The joy of which Wesley spoke is not a perpetual joy, such that a person never experiences sorrow or grief. Wesley acknowledged that in this world we will have times in which this joy is withdrawn. But through the gracious work of the Spirit, joy will consistently return and be the dominant emotional disposition of our hearts.[12]

Second, John Wesley affirmed not only the inner witness but also the fact that there are certain safeguards to the witness of the Spirit. Wesley was a churchman deeply rooted in his Anglican heritage, which informed his conviction that the inner experience of the Spirit is necessarily complemented by external realities that provide parameters that regulate the experience of the Spirit. They are three: Scripture, the church and reason.

The inner witness of the Spirit will never contradict the Scriptures. The Spirit's inner witness is always in harmony with the Spirit-inspired written witness. Consequently, Wesley could assert that a Christian believer matures in fellowship with the Spirit through prayer, but equally, in rigorous study of the Scripture.

In addition, Wesley maintained that the church is a parameter for this inner witness. There are two dimensions of Wesley's thought here. On the one hand, the church represents tradition and Christian orthodoxy. He recognized and appreciated the Christian tradition, which he presumed to have been led and governed by the Spirit of God. The inner witness could not, he believed, contradict the ongoing witness of the Spirit to the church. On the other hand, the church represents not only tradition but also a living community of believers. Wesley assumed that each maturing believer would become part of a band of like-minded believers. Worship, study, prayer and discipline all took place in these smaller groups. A believer's inner witness was conditioned, shaped, examined and strengthened by fellowship with other Christians. This small-group structure provided accountability and encouragement.

---

[12]Wesley, *Works*, 1:298. Wesley quoted 1 Peter 1:8 as he spoke of the Christian who "rejoices 'with joy unspeakable and full of glory.' "

The other safeguard is reason. Wesley always insisted that God does not
call us to be irrational. He believed that God does not violate prudence and
seasoned human judgment. Indeed he affirmed that reason is one of the essential elements in the formation of a Christian theology. He distinguished
between affections and passions. Passions are involuntary emotions, uninformed by either reason or the will—thus the danger of zeal without knowledge. True affections are informed and guided by reason.

The third insight that is significant in the thought and writings of Wesley
is the place of humility in Christian experience. Wesley stressed that the
"joy that accompanies the witness of [God's] Spirit, is a humble joy."[13] In an
echo of Ignatius Loyola, Wesley spoke of humility through various perspectives. On a basic level, humility includes an awareness of sin and the need
for repentance. Humility also fosters a courageous self-disclosure and honesty with God and self. And it follows that this is reflected in a deep-rooted
meekness before the mercy of God.

Further, a person of humility is disposed to the purposes and will of God.
For Wesley, without a fundamental humility or meekness, expressed in a
submission of the spirit before the holiness and goodness of God, there can
be no knowledge of God. This submission is the antithesis of self-exaltation
and self-centeredness. Only in this state of humility can we hear God in
truth. For Wesley, humility includes the awareness that we all live with a
well-practiced ability for self-deception. Knowing our capacity to live with
misguided motives keeps us humble before God and others—spouse,
friend, colleagues. We can never presume to know the voice of God.
Rather, we can acknowledge that pride is the greatest threat to authentic
discernment. We then strive for the meekness that acknowledges our capacity for self-deception and our need for others to help us recognize the witness of the Spirit.

John Wesley is usually associated with Pietism, and for some he was a
radical enthusiast or sentimentalist because of his emphasis on an affective

---

[13]Wesley, Works, 1:279.

faith. But his affirmation of the priority of the heart and the central place of joy in Christian experience does not make him a sentimentalist or an enthusiast. Wesley's religion of the heart, his call for an affective faith, found expression in submission to holy Scripture, within the context of the Christian community, and demanded the transformation of character. It was an affirmation of an inward reality that included external verification. He did not call for a denial of tradition, reason or the authority of Scripture. On the contrary, he emphasized all three. Yet he did so with a thorough conviction that the spirit of the believer could abide in fellowship with the Spirit of the living God and that we could know this, feel this and live with this union as the dynamic center of our spiritual experience.

JONATHAN EDWARDS

Jonathan Edwards was exceptional because of the unique way in which he approached the matter of discernment and for the social and religious context within which he formulated his observations about religious experience. As noted above, both Ignatius and Wesley were very conscious of their own experience as they sought to make sense of the Spirit's work. But Edwards, while acknowledging his own experience, gave focused attention to trying to make sense of the experience of others.

The context in which he wrote was revival—what is now called the Great Awakening. In the midst of a broad and powerful spiritual movement, he sought to recognize where and when God was at work. Conversely, he also sought to identify supposed "spiritual" manifestations that could not be attributed to God.

Within the revival movement, there were those who celebrated revival and viewed any emotional outpouring as a sure sign of the presence and blessing of God. This passion for emotion was matched by the resolute denial of skeptics and critics, who viewed the revivals as nothing more than emotionalism, as yet another display of what was often called "enthusiasm." Edwards defended the place of emotion in religious experience while insisting that there was the potential for illusion and deception. He was convinced that long-term renewal comes through a critical and discerning response to revival experiences.

What is intriguing is Edwards's methodology. Though a biblical scholar and theologian, his approach was phenomenological. He interviewed people, hundreds of them. In listening to their descriptions of their experience, and reflecting with them on the outcomes of the revival, he came to his conclusions about the way in which the Spirit of God works.

Edwards had a basic assumption that guided his investigation: the real test of the validity of spiritual experience is the outcome—the fruit of the experience. For example, he stressed that if we feel grief for sin, it should result in a life that moves away from sin. If we have great joy in the midst of worship, it should lead to a life in which joy is more fundamental and central to our day-to-day experience. In other words, if God is truly present, personal and corporate transformation will occur. Edwards challenged the view that dramatic emotional experience meant that God was present and that transformation necessarily followed. What mattered was not the depth of emotion or feeling; the true test was whether the experience led to genuine spiritual growth.

Under such a conviction, Edwards interviewed, listened and cataloged people's replies to his questions as a way to attend to what God was doing, to appreciate the character of the Spirit's work and then to encourage an appropriate response. To this end, Edwards called for a consideration of what he called the "distinguishing marks" of God's work. He said, "What I aim at now, is to show the nature and signs of the gracious operations of the Holy Spirit, by which they are to be distinguished from all things whatsoever that the minds of men are subject of, which are not of a saving nature."[14] He was keen to show not so much *whether* God was active in an experience but *how* God was active.[15]

---

[14]Jonathan Edwards, *Religious Affections*, ed. John E. Smith (New Haven: Yale University Press, 1959), p. 89.

[15]Edwards's insights are relevant within the context of the contemporary discussion about the character of Christian worship. One wonders if the enthusiasm for choruses is as much as anything a passion for worship that "feels good." But is this true worship? If we feel good, does this necessarily mean that God is present and active in a manner that is transforming?

Edwards came to the following conclusions. First, he said the substance of true religion is found in the affections, emphasizing that "the Holy Scriptures do everywhere place religion very much in the affections; such as fear, hope, love, hatred, desire, joy, sorrow, gratitude, compassion and zeal."[16] He affirmed that as humans we have understanding, affections and will, but he insisted that it is in the affections that we find the center point of the spiritual life. The affections represent a person's defining orientation, thus conversion is fundamentally a reorientation of one's affections. The affections, for Edwards, are the crucial indicator of the character of one's spiritual life. Though the affections are not the whole of religious expression, they are the central part, and the true orientation of the heart is toward joy and love for God and others.

Some have observed that what Edwards meant by affections does not correspond precisely with what we mean by emotions when we use contemporary psychological categories. There is some truth in this observation, in that Edwards did make a distinction between what he called "the affections" and what he called "passions." However, affections for Edwards are certainly emotions, just not emotions as shallow or transient feelings or passing fancies. Rather (much as we find in reading Ignatius Loyola), affections are the deep, inner dispositions or orientation of the heart.[17] What

---

[16]Edwards, *Religious Affections*, p. 102.

[17]One perspective on the *Religious Affections* is that of Gerald R. McDermott, *Seeing God: Twelve Reliable Signs of True Spirituality* (Downers Grove, Ill.: InterVarsity Press, 1995). McDermott insists, as a central point of his study of Edwards, that there is a distinction between affections and emotions, that emotions are fleeting but that affections really drive the engine of our lives—understanding, emotion and volition. Emotions, McDermott contends, are by nature shallow, fleeting and superficial (see p. 40, where he seeks to lay out this distinction between affections and emotions). However, he is pressing the distinction too far.

Though McDermott acknowledges that joy is an affection (p. 41), he writes, "Holy affections are not feelings, but warm and fervent inclinations that involve the mind" (p. 40). In other words, McDermott uses the language of emotion ("warm and fervent") to describe affections while insisting that they are not feelings, and then he suggests that affections involve the mind (presumably, for McDermott, this is not the case for emotions). But in response I would suggest that it is more helpful to affirm that both affections and passions have emotional content, but that for Edwards the affections were the deeper emotional dispositions of our hearts.

makes the affections noteworthy is their formative influence in our lives.

So, while Edwards made a distinction between affections and passions, they are both expressions of emotion. The whole point of the *Religious Affections* was to address the matter of emotion in worship and revival. Edwards was entering into a debate about whether emotion was valid. The skeptics were against any display of emotion, and it was precisely the place of emotion that Edwards had to defend.[18] However, Edwards defended emotion while insisting that not all emotional expression is legitimate; emotional expression in itself means nothing without a transformed life. Emotion may be fleeting, but it must be taken seriously.

The affections do reflect deep underlying dispositions. All inner dispositions or inclinations find expression in emotion, and what we need to determine is whether this inclination is authentic and true, whether our hearts are rightly oriented. We do this by an examination of what is happening to us emotionally, not by discounting emotion with the suggestion that it is fleeting or superficial. Rather, as Edwards did, we must take the affections seriously.

Second, while Edwards insisted on the vital place of the affections in religious experience, he was equally insistent that we must not be naive about what is happening to us emotionally. On the one hand, he responded to the critics of emotionalism by affirming the vital place of emotion in religious experience. But on the other, he challenged the enthusiast who viewed all emotional experience as evidence of the presence of God. He was alert to those for whom emotional experience was an end in itself, whereby they found pleasure or joy in the intense experience rather than in God.

At this point, Edwards is remarkably reminiscent of Ignatius. Edwards called us to take emotion seriously and recognize the primacy of joy—a joy that finds expression in love for God and neighbor. Edwards chided those who discount the place of affect in religious experience because, at least for the Christian believer, the affections are the focus of the Spirit's work.

---

[18]See Edwards, *Religious Affections*, p. 120.

Therefore, it is foolish to reject all affections because of the excess of some or the zeal of others (as the rationalist would do).

However, much like Ignatius and Wesley, Edwards insisted that it is equally foolhardy to accept all affections uncritically. Edwards taught that "Satan sowed tares" in movements of spiritual revival by fostering the imitation of true affections. Satan counterfeits the operations of the Holy Spirit. Therefore, we cannot be naive; we must be discerning.

Furthermore, Edwards made it clear that the ultimate criterion is one's *own* test of one's *own* heart. There is a remarkable emphasis on the individual in his thought. In the second part of the *Religious Affections* he spoke of the "approval of the godly," that is, of the need for external judgment or verification of personal inward experience. Yet Edwards was convinced that in the end the judgment of another was unreliable and perhaps even impossible. We can only discern our own hearts, not the hearts of another. Therefore, the testing of the Spirit can only be done by oneself for oneself. We can seek the counsel of others, but we cannot pronounce final judgment on any but ourselves.

Third, Edwards sought to enable and facilitate discernment. The major part of the *Religious Affections* is his exposition of "certain signs" or "distinguishing marks" of God's presence and saving work. He identified twelve signs of authentic religious affection. I have found it helpful to summarize or condense these into four critical indicators.

- Authentic spiritual influence arises from that which is spiritual. By "spiritual," Edwards did not mean "nonmaterial" but rather that which arises from a posture of being "in the Spirit," that is, oriented toward and at peace with God, as opposed to being "in the flesh." An example of this spiritual posture are the words of Philippians 4:8, where we are called to "think about these things": "whatever is true, whatever is honorable, whatever is just, whatever is pure, whatever is pleasing, whatever is commendable." In other words, a genuine spiritual influence arises when our thoughts are focused on that which is good—on that which is aligned with the work of the Spirit in the world.

- Authentic religious affections arise from an enlightened mind. Like Wesley, Edwards refused to separate or place in opposition the intellectual and the spiritual. Rather, true emotional experience comes in response to truth and the understanding of truth. It does not bypass the mind. It is at the point of this interchange between affect and the mind that Edwards made one of the most significant contributions to the discussion on the affections and spiritual discernment. In contrast to much contemporary Christianity, we see in Edwards a churchman who celebrated the life of the mind and the heart and affirmed that authentic emotional (and thus spiritual) experience is necessarily informed by truth, by the engagement of the mind and the intellect. We respond to truth with heart and mind.

- In tandem with Ignatius and Wesley, Edwards affirmed the central place of humility in Christian experience. He relied on the Beatitudes to speak of the priority of humility and the reality that pride is the single greatest enemy of the soul and of spiritual vitality. Concerning pride, Edwards wrote, "This is the main door by which the devil comes into the hearts of those who are zealous for the advancement of religion."[19] For Edwards, pride (and he spoke specifically of the danger of spiritual pride) tends to discern the faults of others rather than recognize one's own deficiencies.

- Like Wesley, Edwards insisted that true religious affections lead to the transformation of character—how we act in thought, word and deed. This is the renewal of the way we think and of our speech, behavior and practices.

Yet throughout these "marks" there remains a bottom line. There was in Edwards's review of religious experience the conviction, arising from his observations, that the one common element in all authentic religious experience is an abiding peace that one experiences in the knowledge of God and of God's love in one's heart. This is the central point of the *Affections*:

---

[19]Quoted by Richard Lovelace, *Dynamics of Spiritual Life: An Evangelical Theology of Renewal* (Downers Grove, Ill.: InterVarsity Press, 1978), p. 245. Lovelace has a helpful discussion of Edwards's perspectives on humility, pp. 245-48.

in true religion the essential experience of the heart is joy, and the fundamental expression of true joy is love for others.

AFFECT-RICH UNDERSTANDING

Evan B. Howard has recently published an important study on discernment in which he compares Ignatius Loyola's approach to understanding and discernment with that of Jonathan Edwards. He shows how these two spiritual writers, coming from different social and religious contexts, both affirmed that our capacity to discern good from evil, and particularly to discern the presence of the Spirit in our lives, rests on a focused attention on affect. What makes Howard's study doubly significant is that his examination of Ignatius and Edwards is complemented by an extensive review of experimental psychology, which, he concludes, confirms the idea that Christian discernment is "an affectively rich act of knowing."[20]

What we see from Ignatius and Edwards, as well as from Wesley, is that we do not know ourselves, much less God and the presence of God in our lives, unless we are able to make some sense of what is happening to us emotionally. We seek an understanding of our lives—our circumstances, problems, challenges and opportunities—that is illumined by the presence of the Spirit. What our spiritual heritage gives us is an appreciation that this presence is known and experienced by a critical reflection on affect. We truly understand when we know something with heart *and* mind. Discernment, then, is not merely a matter of rational analysis, of weighing the pros and cons and seeking to respond with a biblically informed mind to the options we are facing. Neither is discernment a matter of pure revelation, what some call a "word from the Lord." Rather, it is a way of knowing and seeing that is experienced as a profound interplay of intellect and emotion in which head and heart are informing and guiding each other. Discernment is a matter of attending to both the circumstances of our lives and the emotional contours of our hearts.

---

[20]Evan B. Howard, *Affirming the Touch of God: A Psychological and Philosophical Exploration of Christian Discernment* (Lanham, Md.: University Press of America, 2000).

Karl Rahner, the twentieth-century theologian who played such a critical part in Vatican II, stressed that what marks genuine knowing is the non-
conceptual experience of the love of God. Rahner's philosophical analysis
of discernment leads to the conclusion that discernment is particular—concrete, specific knowledge within the actual circumstances of life—and that
this knowing is informed by affect. Discerning is an act of knowing, but it
is knowing that is informed by what is happening to us affectively. It is by
affect that we discern if our knowing is truly the work of the Spirit. In turn,
this growth in discernment enables us to mature in faith and assures us that
our knowing is truly experiential. This kind of knowing comes in response
to the Spirit. But equally important, it is a knowing that results in generous
and courageous action in the world.[21] In other words, it is not sentimental
or pure subjectivity; it is an inner experience of the Spirit that enables us to
engage our world with grace.

And this kind of knowing requires that we attend to the affections. In responding to the critics of the emotionalism of revivals, Jonathan Edwards
sought to clarify the place of emotion and affect in authentic religious experience. In so doing, he used the language of affect to speak not so much
of the whole of emotional experience but specifically of the deeper emotional dispositions. It is these dispositions that shape the orientation of our
lives. It is here that we are able to get a sense of the inspiration and movements of God in our lives. For both Edwards and Ignatius, a Christian conversion alters these deep emotional dispositions. Through grace, the basic
affections or desires of the heart receive a new orientation. We turn from
self-absorption and grow in our capacity to love God and to desire that
which is good, noble and excellent (Phil 4).

As noted earlier, Edwards distinguished affections from passions. Passions are the more immediate and passing emotional responses that may or
may not be informed by understanding. Affections are deep-seated emotional inclinations that carry the weight of our core understandings and

---

[21]Karl Rahner, *The Dynamic Element in the Church* (Montreal: Palm, 1964), p. 135.

convictions. Edwards resisted the enthusiast who viewed all emotional experience as evidence of the presence of God, and he called instead for discernment. And Ignatius called for an awareness of our deepest heart inclinations, for herein we are able to discern the movement of God. It is in a transformed heart (renewed affect) that we are able to discern the signals of God's call and direction in our lives. And all three—Ignatius, Wesley and Edwards—would urge us to be alert to the subtle forces of pride and the priority of humility, especially when it comes to discernment.

3

WITH HEART AND MIND

❧

Christian discernment is the spiritual discipline by which we listen to God by attending with heart and mind to the presence of the Spirit in our lives. In chapters four through seven, we will consider four different aspects of the Spirit's inner witness. What is noteworthy is that each dimension of the Spirit's inner witness demands critical intellectual faculties as well as emotional vulnerability. If we are going to listen to the inner witness of the Spirit, it follows that we must not polarize the intellect and affections. This chapter will seek to examine in greater detail what we mean by the phrase "listening with heart and mind," beginning with an affirmation of the place of affect in Christian experience.

TAKING EMOTION SERIOUSLY

Ignatius, Wesley and Edwards all agreed on the priority of the heart and the place of affect in Christian experience. In reading them I am continually reminded that authentic Christian spirituality takes emotion seriously. However, it is common, at least within evangelical religious communities, to hear that "our faith rests not on feelings but on the promises of God's Word." It is also common to be shown a diagram of a train that has three cars, with the engine representing "facts," the middle car representing "faith" and the caboose representing "feeling." Unfortunately, this is a woefully inadequate portrayal of the place of emotion in Christian experience, partly because it fails to even begin to capture the relationship between reason and emotion or that which exists between faith and feeling.[1] What has left the strongest impression on me and many others in religious communities where this has been taught is the conviction that feelings are secondary at best. In this picture, emotion is incidental to our Christian experience, something that tags along as an extra, like the caboose of a train. Some have taken this image even further and suggested a more sinister perspective in which feelings are viewed as dangerous—not to be trusted and definitely not a critical indicator of the character of our souls. Rather than being vital to faith, feelings are portrayed as a threat to true faith.

However, the writings of John Wesley and Jonathan Edwards suggest that this dismissive perspective is not congruent with the evangelical Christian heritage. When we add Ignatius Loyola to the discussion, we appreciate that this kind of teaching is not consistent with the entire scope of the Christian witness. The Christian spiritual heritage takes emotion very seriously, particularly the interplay between the mind and the heart. What we learn is that we cannot think clearly and deeply, and thus cannot have "faith in facts" (to refer again to the train image), unless there is a definite emotional content to this faith, a faith that then ultimately rests not so much on facts as it does in a person.

"Lift up your hearts" is a classic liturgical phrase found in many worship traditions. The appropriate response, of course, is "We lift them up to the Lord." This call-and-response captures well the recurring theme within holy Scripture that our response to God is never solely a matter of placing intellectual confidence in certain facts or promises. It is a reminder that affect is indeed the engine that drives our spiritual experience.

We are thinking, feeling and acting beings. Descartes got it wrong when he stated, "I think; therefore I am." What a distorted, one-dimensional view of the human person! Worse, it missed the center of who we are. We learn from our spiritual heritage that the core of who we are is found in our affections. Accordingly, the affections are the most critical indicator when it

---

[1]The image of the train is often presented with the assumption that the train would run with or without the caboose since a caboose does nothing to keep the train moving. The obvious implication is that emotion, or affect, is not essential to Christian faith and experience.

comes to discernment. What is happening to us emotionally is the telling sign of who we are and what is happening to us spiritually. Philosopher Robert C. Solomon put it this way: "Emotions are not just disruptions of our otherwise calm and reasonable experience; they are at the very heart of that experience, determining its focus, influencing our interests, defining the dimensions of the world."[2]

James Fowler echoed Solomon when he wrote that "deep emotions determine the values, the purposes, and the ends for which human intelligence and energy will be mobilized."[3] Emotions are not transient but formative. The true weight of a person's convictions is reflected in emotions that, in turn, shape those formative convictions. Emotion, then, is not an incidental aspect of our experience. Our emotions define our experience and give weight to our convictions. They give meaning to our lives. They reflect our fundamental values. They color, if not actually determine, each judgment or decision we make.

What we learn from Ignatius, Wesley and Edwards is that the inner witness of the Spirit in our lives will not be known and appreciated merely by the application of intellect to facts or phenomena. By its very nature, an intentional response to the inner witness of the Spirit of God requires that we develop the capacity to be attentive to what is happening to us emotionally. This is so in large measure because affect is the vital sign of our spiritual health and well-being. What is happening to us emotionally does not correlate perfectly with the will, word and inner witness of God. Yet as we mature in faith, hope and love, our emotions will increasingly reflect the intentions of God.

All of this is a reminder that emotion is central to God's purposes in our lives. In the Scriptures the language of "heart" speaks of the central part of human identity. In its broadest sense, "heart" speaks of the volitional, cognitive and affective aspects of a human person. I am using the language of "heart"

[2]Robert C. Solomon, "Some Notes on Emotion, 'East and West'," *Philosophy East and West* 45, no. 2 (1995): 171-202.
[3]James Fowler, *Becoming Adult, Becoming Christian: Adult Development and Christian Faith* (San Francisco: Harper & Row, 1984), p. 118.

to focus more narrowly on the emotional dimension of our identity. However, following the biblical usage, this is closely aligned with, and cannot be divorced from, the intellectual and volitional dimensions of our inner lives.

It is beneficial to highlight the place of affect in the purposes of God. To begin with, Jesus stated explicitly that through his mission in the world the joy of his disciples would be made complete. For the joy that was set before him, Jesus endured the cross (Heb 12:2). Though his disciples experienced the grief of a broken world, their grief would be turned to joy (Jn 16:20). Joy is not incidental to our salvation. Rather, what strikes one in reading the New Testament is that the hope of humanity is consistently captured in the language of affect. In the kingdom that is yet to come humanity will know a joy that we cannot lose (Jn 16:22). And so we read in 1 John that the biblical author was writing expressly "so that our joy may be complete" (1 Jn 1:4).

Jesus has now ascended to the Father and has sent the Spirit to dwell among us. The church, filled with the Spirit, celebrates the risen Christ. The joy of the church is but a foretaste of the joy the Christian community will experience when Christ returns. However, this present joy is a key indicator that the church lives now in anticipation of the consummation of the reign of Christ on the earth. In other words, joy is the sign that indeed the Spirit dwells among us and in us. In the chapters to follow, I hope to show that joy is linked to a deep awareness of the love of God, the forgiveness that is experienced in Christ and the reality that we hear the truth in the power of the Spirit (1 Thess 1:6).

By the Spirit we love one another and serve Christ with generosity, in the church and in the world. If we love one another, it is because our fears have been overcome (there is no fear in love). By the Spirit we have learned how to live with hope in a broken world. And by the Spirit we have learned to do all that we have been called to do with a joy that cannot be taken away, knowing that if we do not do our work with joy, it will be of no benefit to those whom we serve (Heb 13:17).

In John 14 we read how Jesus assured his disciples that he would leave his peace with them and, further, that he would send them the Holy Spirit.

The close connection between the Holy Spirit and the peace Jesus gives is not coincidental; the two are intimately linked. We cannot have the one without the other; and peace is a key sign that we have the Holy Spirit. Elsewhere St. Paul insisted that the kingdom of God is about righteousness, peace and joy in the Holy Spirit (Rom 14:17). Peace and joy are the critical indicators of the presence of the Spirit in our lives.

In Philippians 4, for example, we are reminded that we cannot live with anxiety and fear, but rather through prayer we are called to experience the peace of Christ. St. Paul, in 1 Timothy 2:8, stressed that we cannot worship with anger in our hearts. To do so is an affront to God. It is the posture of nonfaith. It is a violation of the humility that is essential to true worship. More to the point, if we are in anger, we are not worshiping in the Spirit.

All of this is consistent with the great prayer book of the Old Testament and of the church: the Psalms. The Psalter is essentially a collection of prayers that have, as their distinctive characteristic, the expression of the heartfelt longings of the people of God. Indeed the whole spectrum of human emotion is captured in the Psalms. And the Psalter demonstrates that the evidence of faith is a steadfast heart: "My heart is steadfast, O God, my heart is steadfast," we read in Psalm 108:1, which continues, "I will sing and make melody."

So it should come as no surprise that spiritual writers from such diverse traditions as those represented by Ignatius, Wesley and Edwards conclude that we must recognize the important place of affect in human experience generally and in Christian spirituality specifically. Our Christian spiritual heritage suggests to us that our emotions are telling, indeed primary, indicators of the grace of God in our lives. And notably, contemporary studies on emotion confirm the insights of these spiritual writers and the central place of emotion in our experience.[4]

---

[4]See Paul E. Griffiths, *What Emotions Really Are: The Problem of Psychological Categories* (Chicago: University of Chicago Press, 1997); Antonio R. Damasio, *Descartes' Error: Emotion, Reason and the Human Brain* (New York: Grosset/Putman, 1994), particularly chapter seven; Antonio R. Damasio, *The Feeling of What Happens: Body and Emotion in the Making of Consciousness* (New York: Harcourt Brace, 1999); and Robert Solomon, *The Passions: Emotions and the Meaning of Life* (Indianapolis: Hacket, 1993).

I find the observations about the interplay between intellect and emotion particularly significant in this regard. It is not that if we are depressed or deeply discouraged we cannot know the grace of God. It is, rather, that what is happening to us emotionally is not incidental but central both to our identity as human beings and to the conscious and intentional response we have to the grace of God in our lives.

THINKING CRITICALLY

The French philosopher Blaise Pascal has this brief line in one of his *Pensées*: "All reasoning comes down to surrendering to feeling."[5] Most of us are so deeply influenced by the rationalism of our culture that we are immediately perplexed by such a statement. But Pascal was convinced that a full awareness of our feelings, that is, attention to what is happening to us emotionally, becomes the determining factor that informs and shapes our lives. This is but one more reminder that discernment requires that we be attentive to our emotional state.

This is not an easy proposition. We are complex creatures emotionally, and sometimes our emotional responses do not make sense to us. That is, we see no direct link between our understanding and our emotion. For example, there are people who fear garter snakes, knowing full well that they are harmless. We can feel fear, desolation and perhaps other emotional lows without there being a clear cognitive correlation between cause and effect. We can be discouraged and know we are discouraged yet still acknowledge to a friend that we are not entirely sure why we are feeling this way. Conversely, many who smoke know the dangers they face yet seem to have no fear. In similar fashion, many who speed while driving are not afraid of losing control of their vehicles even though a degree of fear would lead to a safer lifestyle. What we see in this is that if affect does inform understanding, we actually behave irrationally.

Our feelings may not correspond to our understanding of our world and

---

[5]Blaise Pascal, *Pensées*, trans. A. J. Krailsheimer (New York: Penguin, 1966), p. 216.

may not enable us to act in truth. Another side of our dilemma as human beings is that we are not always able to speak meaningfully about our emotions. We do not necessarily know what we are feeling, or better put, what emotion we are experiencing. We all have emotions, but we do not necessarily all have feelings. An emotion is something that is felt; we *feel* an emotion. But not all people perceive clearly what they are experiencing emotionally. Some are angry, discouraged and fearful but do not know this and cannot name the emotions. They cannot live in the truth of what they are experiencing emotionally because they are disconnected from their own emotion. And so Antonio Damasio has observed that we need to make a distinction between "having a feeling" and "knowing a feeling."[6] It is one thing to have a feeling and quite another to know the feeling such that our emotional experience informs our lives. And, I would add, so that what we are experiencing emotionally can inform our experience of God.

This means that we will not be able to truly "lift up our hearts" in prayer and worship unless we think critically about our lives and what is happening to us emotionally. In this, it is helpful to distinguish between primary and secondary emotions.

Primary emotions are those that are triggered by immediate sensory input. For example, we are angry in response to some occurrence, and our emotional response is linked to that event or development. The emotional response may or may not be cognitive. The main feature is that it has the character of an immediate response to an identifiable circumstance or situation.

A secondary emotion is rooted in understanding and cognitive perspective; it is the fruit of careful thinking. While it is very much an emotion, a secondary emotion reflects deep underlying values and commitments. This distinction suggests that we need to learn how to be attentive on both levels: to know what we are feeling in response to the immediate, namely the circumstances that have been part of our recent past, but also to appreciate what

---

[6]Damasio, *Feeling of What Happens*, p. 284.

is happening in the deep, underlying emotional orientation of our lives.

This careful reflection, then, requires both experience and honesty. Over time we come to know ourselves and our own emotional capacities and propensities. It takes time. It requires honesty. Nothing is gained by denying our anger, for example. It is a subtle form of pride when we say we are not angry when in fact we are sulking over having been ignored or offended. The outcome can only lead to inauthenticity, as happens when we worship with anger rather than with joy in our hearts (1 Tim 2:8).

It is helpful in this regard to consider a classic spiritual exercise, the *examination of conscience*. For many Christians, this is nothing more than a consideration of one's errors, mistakes and sins, finding where one has broken the holy law of God. Former generations have viewed this exercise as a focused examination on wrong behavior and indicators of guilt. But recent theologians are recognizing that although acknowledgment of our failures needs to be part of our prayer experience, it is much more helpful to see these failures within the context of our whole emotional life.

I have found it profitable, when in conversation with a friend or my spouse, for us to ask one another when in the last days or weeks we have each experienced joy and when we have experienced sorrow, frustration or anger. Such an exercise fosters my capacity to be honest about my emotional responses to my world. John Carmody suggests that this is the best way to approach the examination of conscience, making it a careful reflection on what we have experienced in the recent past. We focus, Carmody suggests, on the tender places—sadness and joy—which are important indicators of the inner person.[7] It requires a basic honesty to accept the ways that sorrow, frustration and grief have intersected our lives, but also the multiple ways in which we have experienced joy and the blessing of God. Carmody writes, "In starting to examine our consciences, we do well to fix our attention on the things that count, on the projects, persons and episodes that have left an emotional trace."[8]

---

[7]John Carmody, *Reexamining Conscience* (New York: Seabury, 1982), pp. 3-5.
[8]Ibid., p. 18.

The examination of conscience is then a careful and selective review of our recent past. This assumes that, in the words of Carmody, "God tends to move us, to want to teach us through our emotional gains and losses. He wants, as well, slowly to move us to some purchase on our emotions, some freedom from their dominance."[9] In facing up to our joys and sorrows, we can come to grips with our responsibilities, because we have considered our own lives and fostered the self-knowledge that is a basic ingredient of growth in wisdom and spiritual maturity. Few things are so critical to self-knowledge as to know what one is feeling.

However, a vexing problem muddies the waters—the reality that we are sinners; our hearts can so easily deceive us. While we can affirm our *desire* for good and our longing to act in love and truth, we also must recognize inner propensities that are fueled by nothing other than fear, greed, lust, sloth, pride or any number of other inclinations that undermine good intentions. We are filled with conflicting longings and desires. And so we can legitimately ask, how can I know if what I long for is truly the will of God? The answer, quite simply, is that we need to learn how to *discern*.

And discernment is learned over time, as we come to recognize the movements of God in our hearts. We discover that we must learn to trust our emotions and our inner intuition while simultaneously acknowledging our capacity for self-deception. Discernment calls us to attend to the heart in a way that is informed by our critical faculties so that we are not easily misled.

On the one hand, we must reject the way of the rationalist, who believes that emotion is inherently excessive and unreasonable. Those who suggest as much do not understand the nature of the human person. On the other hand, we must not be susceptible to every passing feeling. Ignatius, Wesley and Edwards would call us to use our heads, think critically and consider what is occurring emotionally, discerning what is truly of God. In humility we must recognize our capacity for self-deception, self-absorption and self-gratification. Those who love depths of emotion and

---

[9]Ibid.

heights of feeling but resist the need for sober-minded discernment are naive about the propensities of the human heart. They fail to see, for example, that some forms of emotional experience in worship are nothing more than self-indulgence.

The call to "lift up your hearts" is a direct challenge to the suggestion that intellect is primary in personal experience. However, we must also stress that while Ignatius, Wesley and Edwards (three intellectual giants, it should be noted) called for a recognition of the central place of affect, they did not in any way disparage the mind. They were not sentimentalists. They affirmed the vital place of understanding and reason in Christian experience. They affirmed that affect is, properly speaking, informed by truth, and they recognized that we can be led astray by misguided emotion. Ignatius, Wesley and Edwards confronted both the rationalist, the intellectual skeptic who denied the vital place of affect in Christian experience *and* the sentimentalist who refused to engage affect with a critical mind.

True emotion is the fruit of an enlightened and informed mind; if our emotions are confused and in turmoil, then our thinking is just as confused and potentially dangerous. There are two dangers that need to be avoided: a cerebralism that discounts the central place of affect and a sentimentalism that fails to appreciate that the affections be informed by our understanding. We must listen with heart and mind.

SPIRITUAL MATURITY AND EMOTIONAL MATURITY

If what I have observed so far is true, then it has a significant implication: we do not mature in our Christian experience unless we mature emotionally. What happens to us emotionally is not peripheral but central to our religious experience. To put it bluntly, people who are out of touch with their emotions are out of touch with God, for God speaks to us through the ebb and flow of our emotional lives. We must, then, learn to face our anger, our fear and our discouragement honestly. We need to learn how to grow in joy and live not in anger or fear or anxiety but in the peace that transcends all understanding (Phil 4:6-7). Joy and peace are the real tests of whether we

are women and men of faith who walk in the Spirit. We act in faith only
when we act in joy.

We live in a discouraging and broken world, so we must learn to be encouraged on the slightest provocation, coming back again and again into
communion with him who told his disciples, "I have said these things to
you so that my joy may be in you, and that your joy may be complete" (Jn
15:11). We must learn to be an emotionally resilient people who know how
to be angry without being consumed by anger, because we have learned
how to let our anger go down with the sun (Eph 4:26). We must be honest
with our fears but also learn how to cast our cares on God. We must be attentive to the subtle ways in which discouragement and depression can infiltrate our hearts and foster a cynicism that is deadly (yet easily rationalized
as wisdom). Yes, we will mourn, but our mourning will be turned to joy.

In other words, the affirmation of joy and peace as the critical indicators
of the presence of the Spirit does not mean that the only legitimate emotional expression is joy or peace. Anger, fear, mourning and discouragement might each be an appropriate response to the brokenness of the world
in certain situations.

Consider anger. Anger is the emotional response to an injustice committed against us or someone we love. As such, it is the appropriate response. In a case like that, to deny anger would be to be untruthful. And it
would be unhelpful, if not actually harmful, to suppress or ignore our
emotional response. We have been given the capacity for anger much like
our physical bodies have been given the capacity for pain. To ignore anger
would be comparable to ignoring a fire on the stove when you reach your
hand for a pan, or as foolish as putting a carpet on an ember that has
strayed from the fireplace.

However, we must also recognize that anger is not always legitimate; it can
be petty and childish. Furthermore, the great danger in anger is that it can
become not only the immediate justifiable response to some event but also
the molder of our deep-seated emotional disposition. If we do not recognize
and account for our anger and then intentionally let it go down with the sun,

we may easily accumulate a store of unresolved emotion, so that we are no longer just angry at what has happened but, subtly and insidiously, have become angry people. And for an angry person there is no longer a one-to-one connection between their anger and specific events in their world.[10]

Our emotional response to the world, then, reflects both our fundamental values and our personal vision, and it determines the contours of our lives. Thus we are mature only if we have learned to be angry when there is wrong in the world that justifies moral indignation, only if we have learned to mourn when there is loss, only if we have learned to experience fear that enables us to live in truth. In the end we are mature, walking in faith and in the Spirit, only if the fundamental disposition of our hearts is joy.

Of course, for some the call to joy will seem like an impossible challenge. There are those who live daily under the dark cloud of depression. If they experience joy, it is only fleeting. Many are those who live with emotional disorders in which depression and pervasive anxiety are the norm. And often these are intelligent and creative individuals who genuinely want to love God and grow in faith, hope and love. For them, any discussion of joy is often only a reminder of the dark cloud under which they live. A call like this, to an honest encounter with affect, is a call to walk into darkness, and it almost appears as though they have no hope of becoming discerning people.

I acknowledge this. Those who suffer from depression face a considerable struggle. They need the support and encouragement of their friends and of the Christian community as well as of skilled professionals who can help them find healing. However, I also acknowledge that an emotional disorder is a *disorder*. Those who experience depression know this better than

---

[10]A constructive response to anger, whether it is petty or legitimate anger, is one in which we acknowledge the anger and then consider what it means. What is it saying to us? For one thing, anger can help us identify what is most important to us—our values, passions and commitment. For another, anger can give us insight into how we need to act to change the circumstances or patterns of our lives (not to fix others but to see how we ourselves are acting and reacting). If I am always angry at work, for example, I need to ask what it will take for me to live with joy in this set of circumstances. Or if I am angry because I am unappreciated, I need to choose to live at peace without this affirmation. Finally, anger can help us see what really matters to us, and this may give us insight into our vocation.

any of us; that is why they long for emotional health and do not take it for granted when they experience it. The principles that will follow for the exercise of discernment are no less true for them than for the rest of us.

Our daily prayers and our weekly public worship are, essentially, an opportunity to order the affections—to return to a posture of faith that enables us to respond in truth, emotionally, to God, to one another, to our world and to ourselves. We order our lives, and thus our emotions, around the reality of the crucified and risen Christ, a reality that both calls us and enables us to live in joy. And then the encounter of our prayers and our worship enables us to see and respond to the world in truth: to be angry, but not to sin; to be afraid as appropriate, but not to be consumed by our fear; to be discouraged when there is setback, but not to become cynical.

Emotion, then, is not merely a sensation. It has meaning; it is an informed response to our world. Therefore, what we are feeling must be guided by reason. If we are angry or afraid, it is because there is a genuine wrong or something that truly threatens us. Another way to put this is to say that emotion must be fitting. What we long for is the ordering of our affections so that what we feel is congruent with our world, so that our emotions are the appropriate response, in due proportion to our world. When emotion is guided by reason, we can engage reality in a manner that not only enables us to live truthfully but also enables us to be transformed by the truth.

A discerning person, then, is one who has come to terms with two seemingly incompatible perspectives. On the one hand, we have learned to trust our hearts, for this is the core of our being. But on the other hand, we see how easily we are self-deceived. Discernment requires that we affirm the priority of the heart and also that we turn from any kind of mindless credulity about what we are feeling.

JOY AND HAPPINESS

Some Christians insist we make a distinction between joy and happiness. Happiness, they suggest, is circumstantial and in a sense superficial, and anyone can be happy in response to positive circumstances. Joy, by contrast, is experienced in response to the presence of Christ in our lives. A variation of this is the suggestion that joy is not even a feeling. Happiness, it is said, is a feeling, but because joy is a matter of faith, an assent to propositions, one does not actually need to *feel* joyful in order to *be* joyful.

The idea that happiness is circumstantial is partly true, but it is also partly false. It is more accurate to recognize that joy and happiness, even if there is a distinction between them, are both circumstantial. The question is one of determining which circumstances will shape our emotional dispositions. If people are unhappy, they cannot claim that despite the apparent unhappiness, they are really living in a joy that comes from Christ. Rather, to live in joy is to choose to live in the light of the resurrection as one's fundamental emotional disposition. This means that we will respond with integrity to a broken world—with anger, mourning, discouragement and fear, as appropriate. We will refuse to accept the posture of some who suggest that Christians are always joyful if they live in truth.

We do not need to accept the call of some to always put on a cheerful disposition because only then do we have an authentic witness to Christ. This can only lead to a superficiality that denies what we are really experiencing and, in the end, what is really happening in the world. But though we will feel the pain of the world and will experience anger, fear and mourning, we will not live there. In other words, while it is appropriate to speak of a surface response to an immediate event or circumstance that brought happiness, we must also recognize that there is an intimate link between these experiences and our response to them when it comes to whether we live in joy.

Can non-Christians have true and authentic joy? Certainly! For we are all created by God, and God does not allow sin to so break down our lives that we cannot be glad in his creation. They can live, unwittingly, in the light of Christ's reign and enjoy his gifts even if they do not acknowledge the Giver.

The Hebrew and Old Testament perspective on joy should inform our Christian perspective. In particular, it could challenge any propensity we might have to distinguish between joy and happiness out of a false dualism between the body and the soul. And it can challenge the inclination of some to present a Christian veneer, whether of the appearance of happiness or not, in the belief that what really matters is internal and that the physical and external experience is not so significant (that is, it is temporal happiness). Further, the Old Testament challenges the false idea that true joy is spiritual and inner and that psychological joy is by definition suspect and likely fueled by a misguided search for pleasure.

The description of the Old Testament people of God suggests that, without reservation, and indeed with deep abandon, we should find joy in the common and ordinary, the physical and tangible. For the Old Testament people, the reasons for joy were both the wonder of God's great redemptive work and the simple pleasures of daily life. And so, for example, they would find joy in remembering the Exodus each year on the Passover, but they also would find joy in a good meal and in good wine (Judg 9:13, Ps 104:15). Music and dancing were the tangible expression of this joy (Job 21:12; Lam 5:15). The people's reasons for joy were many, but they included the birth of children, the love of one's spouse (Prov 5:18), a good harvest and the prosperity it represented (1 Chron 12:40; Is 16:10) as well as victory in war (1 Sam 18:6; 2 Chron 20:27). And, of course, joy found expression in their worship and in the religious feasts, through processions and in the offering of tithes. While the sense of joy was surely an inner experience, a sense of spiritual well-being that came to the one who delighted in God, in the law of God and in the truth, it was not and could not be divorced from the physical dimensions of life.

There is certainly such a thing as false joy, that is, anything that brings pleasure at the expense of others or in violation of the law of God. But this in no way discounts the genuine, meaningful and truly spiritual experience of joy and delight in the gifts that come from the hand of God. And that leads us to the heart of the matter.

While joy is certainly linked with the circumstantial and tangible blessings of God, the essence of faith is found in the deliberate decision to rejoice even when these external sources of joy are not present (Hab 3). However, this does not make joy a different emotion or experience. It is a joy that is still linked to the tangible expressions of God's goodness, but it is a joy that resides in a confidence that these will come in the future. That is, it is still joy in a good harvest, but not in a harvest that one is currently experiencing. It is a joy of confidence that one day the harvest will be plentiful. It is a joy that is rooted in faith, not in what is seen and experienced immediately, but in what is not seen yet expected to be fully visible and tangible one day. It is the joy we have in anticipation of the eschatological kingdom when all things will be made well. And thus faith is the only basis for this joy, a confidence that one day justice and peace will embrace in an earthy, tangible reality. It is the joy of redemption, of the restoration and renewal of all of God's creation.

This is the joy of which Jesus spoke during his earthly ministry. Joy was announced by the angel to Mary at the birth of Christ. And it was *good* news; this was the reason for the Magi's joy when they encountered the Christ child (Mt 2:10). Throughout the course of his ministry Jesus continually pointed to that day when all will be made well and when, in a grand meal, we will celebrate the consummation of his kingdom.

In other words, this does not mean that we are always happy or always joyful. When there is loss or reason for fear, anger or mourning, we will respond accordingly. But we will not camp there (emotionally, that is). We will come back to an emotional center of joy even though what brings us joy is not immediately present. And we do so because we have faith and know that one day all will be well. We can live with good cheer and with lighthearted happiness, even when we are fully conscious of the brokenness of our world and even in the midst of the multiple ways this brokenness intersects our own lives.

This whole discussion about heart and mind suggests that we need to attend to those practices that enable us to find this inner integration, this capacity to be heart-and-mind people. To this end, I would suggest three practices that foster this integration: (1) participation in the arts; (2) the singing of hymns of the faith in the context of worship; and (3) manual labor, which is an activity that embodies what we are feeling. But I also need to mention humor—not joke telling per se but simply recognizing that we cannot take ourselves too seriously. Of course, it must always be humor that is fitting and that sees the comic side of life without denigrating another or demeaning ourselves.

THE CHARACTER OF HUMILITY

What we seek, of course, are *ordered* affections—emotions that reflect a genuine and authentic response to God and to the world. The key to this ordering is humility. As I examine the different dimensions of the Spirit's witness to our hearts, I will stress that each dimension is known as we are able to grasp and experience this humility. The emphasis on humility in the writings of Edwards, Wesley and Ignatius is a reminder of the importance of this quality in Christian spirituality. Roberta Bondi, for example, has noted that for the early church fathers there was a recurring twofold teaching: (1) the goal of the Christian life is to love God and neighbor; and (2) humility is the means by which this goal is attained.[11]

In our reflection on discernment we will see that humility means living in the conviction that we are loved. Yet it also means an awareness that we are sinners in need of forgiveness, though never in a manner that puts into question the assurance or confidence that we are loved. Humility also includes the refusal to judge one's neighbor. Humility is letting go of the need to impress others. Humility refuses to compare oneself with others and celebrates their gifts, abilities and accomplishments.

Humility, thus, is an inner disposition, a cultivated attitude of the heart, very different from a certain type of temperament or personality. And the operative word here is "cultivated." We can *learn* this fundamental posture of the heart. Learning discernment is, in effect, learning humility, and as I hope to show, humility in turn is the posture in which we

---

[11]Roberta C. Bondi, *To Love as God Loves: Conversations with the Early Church* (Philadelphia: Fortress, 1987), p. 32.

are most able to attend to the voice of Jesus.

So as we examine each dimension of the Spirit's inner witness, along with the task and art of discernment, it is appropriate to consider at each step of the way what it means to respond to the voice of Jesus with humility. It is as we walk in humility, however feeble our efforts, that we grow in our capacity to attend to the Spirit with heart and mind.

It is helpful to think of the inner witness of the Spirit as having four distinct expressions:

- the inner witness that assures us we are loved

- the inner witness that convicts us of sin

- the illumination of the mind

- guidance in times of choice

Each of these four is a vital dimension of the Spirit's ministry to us and a critical means by which we know and live by the voice of Jesus. Each will be the focus of an entire chapter in this book. Each is known and experienced as we learn to listen with both heart and mind.

The first is the most critical and is necessarily our point of departure.

4

THE ASSURANCE OF GOD'S LOVE

Nothing is so fundamental to the Christian journey as knowing and feeling that we are loved. Nothing. This is the basis for the whole of what it means to be a Christian. There is no other foundation on which we can build. It is from the experience of God's love that we know the grace of God and live out every other dimension of our Christian faith.

In stressing this, though, we must also highlight how the apostle Paul made a direct link between this experience of the love of God and the presence of the Spirit in our lives. The force of this is apparent from the flow of his prayer in Ephesians 3. He prayed that his readers would be strengthened in their inner being through the power of the Spirit (Eph 3:16), then complemented this by praying that Christ would dwell in their hearts through faith (Eph 3:17). It is vitally important to see that these are not two different things for which he was interceding: first that the Spirit would empower them and second that Christ would dwell within them. Rather, they are but two ways of expressing the same reality. To have Christ within us, dwelling in our hearts, is one and the same with being empowered in our inner being by the Spirit. Christ abides within us by the Spirit. We cannot have the one without the other.

Yet what captures our attention in this prayer is how this happens—how we are empowered by the Spirit and indwelt by the second person of the Trinity. It comes through a conscious awareness of, and experience of, the love of Christ. And Paul used wonderful language to capture this, as he spoke of his longing that we would be rooted and grounded in love (two different metaphors) and then that we would appreciate its all-encompassing character. There is a direct correlation, in other words, between experiencing the love of Christ and being filled with the fullness of God.

The Bible makes it clear that God loves us and that to be a Christian is to live in God's love. However, though God's love is the obvious message of Scripture, it can never be assumed that we comprehend this love. Again and again we must call one another back to the wonder of this love. What we seek is to live lives that are surrounded by a conscious awareness that we are loved. And thus surely one of the priceless gifts we give one another is an increased awareness of God's love for the other.

THE LOVE OF GOD IN CHRIST

This emphasis on a conscious awareness of God's love can be found in the writings of Edwards, Ignatius and Wesley. But in Wesley we have the particular emphasis on this principle as the point of departure for his whole theology of the inner witness. And rightly so.

I will describe four dimensions of the Spirit's witness to our hearts. While each is vital to the spiritual life, that is, to what it means to walk in the Spirit, this aspect of the Spirit's ministry is foundational and primary. It is captured in the words of St. Paul when he wrote, "All who are led by the Spirit of God are children of God. For you did not receive a spirit of slavery to fall back into fear, but you have received a spirit of adoption. When we cry, 'Abba! Father!' it is that very Spirit bearing witness with our spirit that we are children of God" (Rom 8:14-16).

This text in Romans 8 is a primary reference for this aspect of the Spirit's ministry. But I find it helpful to consider this text in the light of what St. Paul had stated earlier, particularly the reference in Romans 5:5, where he wrote of the love of God poured into our hearts by the Holy Spirit. But we need to consider this verse within its context, and thus I quote a more extended section from this chapter (I include the verse numbers as well, for ease of reference in my comments that follow):

3We . . . boast in our sufferings, knowing that suffering produces endurance, 4and endurance produces character, and character produces hope, 5and hope does not disappoint us, because God's love has
been poured into our hearts through the Holy Spirit that has been
given to us.

6For while we were still weak, at the right time Christ died for the
ungodly. 7Indeed, rarely will anyone die for a righteous person—
though perhaps for a good person someone might actually dare to die.
8But God proves his love for us in that while we still were sinners
Christ died for us. (Rom 5:3-8)

The first half of this chapter from St. Paul is anchored, grammatically
and theologically, in the words of Romans 5:8. Central to the gospel is the
principle that God has loved us, and this is evident—indeed proven—by
the act of God in Christ Jesus: "Christ died for us." This defining statement
captures the reality of the good news. What was most noteworthy in the
mind of the apostle was that Christ died for the ungodly (Rom 5:6). This
makes the love of God distinctive—unique and worth celebrating. It also
suggests that this event merits close scrutiny; something is happening here
that must not be missed.

God loves those who do not deserve to be loved—the ungodly. The text
speaks of those who reject the love of God, those who are enemies of God.
We do not appreciate the extraordinary reality of God's love for us unless
we see that this love has always been there, even while we were still in a
posture of rebellion against God. And this is at the heart of what we celebrate in the gospel.

This means that there is nothing we can do to make God love us more,
for the full extent of God's love was shown to us when we were God's enemies. God loves us. We cannot earn this love, manipulate things to make
God love us more or in any way make ourselves more lovable. Nothing can
make this love increase; we are already loved to the full.

Many struggle to believe that God loves us just as we are. For some, their
own experience as children persuaded them that if they were going to be

loved, they would have to meet parental expectations.

Every year during the Christmas season we do our mall shopping and are forced to listen to the piped-in Muzak that filters through the stores. We hear winter songs and Christmas carols, and invariably we hear "Santa Claus Is Comin' to Town." This is a particularly insidious piece of music, since it cuts at the heart of the gospel. It may sound like an innocent song that we can teach children, but consider the words.

> You better watch out, you better not cry,
> Better not pout, I'm telling you why:
> Santa Claus is comin' to town.
>
> He sees you when you're sleepin',
> He knows when you're awake,
> He knows if you've been bad or good,
> So be good for goodness sake.

What is the message? The song tells us that if we want to receive the benefits of Christmas, then we had better be good. If we are not good, then Santa Claus will know, and if he knows, there will be negative consequences.

That message is the very opposite of the message of Christmas. The glory of Christmas is that Christ loved us while we were yet sinners. That is the whole point of Christmas; we celebrate the love of God. But "Santa Claus Is Comin' to Town" turns this on its head and thereby undermines the gospel.

One may think the song is innocent and meaningless, except for this: the perspective of this song resides deep in the heart of each person who has not learned to accept God's love. God loves us, and there is nothing we can do to make God love us more. All we can do is accept, as a principle of faith, the fact that we are loved by God. We believe this because Christ, the Son of God, died for us while we were yet his enemies.

For many (if not most) of us, our experience while growing up was just the opposite of unconditional love. Our homes were settings in which the fundamental assumption was that we would be loved if we behaved appropriately.

How many children have assumed that if they wanted the love and blessing of their parents, then they had to behave according to their parents' expectations?

As a parent, I know how difficult it is to love unconditionally—to love and accept my children and not demand that they change before they know my love and blessing. It is easy, if either of my sons fails to fulfill some expectation of mine, to show my displeasure by standing aloof, withholding my blessing, making him feel as badly as I possibly can. But my call as a father must be to love unconditionally, that is, to express sorrow and perhaps even anger when something wrong is done, but to do so in a manner that never violates my first call to love my children. And knowing how difficult it is to do this only highlights for me the wonder of God's love. The bottom line remains: I must strive to love my sons unconditionally and to assure them of this love regardless of their behavior, for this is how God loves each one of us.

Some Christians believe this is dangerous teaching. They are inclined to think that if people know God will love them even if they are bad, then nothing would motivate them to be good. However, this is faulty theology when placed beside the clear message of Scripture. It is not for us to decide the terms or conditions of God's love, and the Word of God clearly states that God loved us while we were yet sinners.

But more to the point, what this perspective fails to see is that the only possible basis for growing in faith is the love of God—a love that we are sure and certain of. However much we may want people to be holy, the way to encourage them to grow and mature in their faith is not by hanging a carrot (the love of God) just out of their grasp. We can find the wholeness for which we long only if we know, first, that we are loved. If this is taking a risk, it is a risk that *God* will take. And there is no other foundation for spiritual growth and vitality than the confidence that we are loved. This is the gospel: God loves us. Nothing can shake this or undermine this reality. God loves us, delights in us, takes pleasure and joy in each life. God calls each one by name and as Creator celebrates what he has made. This love is never utilitarian; God does not love us for what we accomplish or do. We are, quite simply, loved.

Our greatest need is to know this truth and to anchor our lives to it, living in a profound inner confidence of God's love. This is truth. This is freedom. This is our point of departure for everything we are and hope to be. In some form or another, we all probably wish that others would love us, indeed that *everyone* would love us. But obviously this will not happen. Nevertheless, we can be confident of this: the Creator of the universe loves us. Each of us.

If we do not learn to live in the love of God, we will always be vulnerable to the opinions of others. We will, unwittingly, crave their affirmation or fear their criticism. Somewhere I read that Martin Luther King Jr. expressed a longing that he would not crave the affirmation of others (which would only inflate his head) or fear their criticism (which would crush his spirit). This is a grace that wisely balances the opinions of others, but it will be known when we are confident that we are loved by our Creator.

We need to explore this truth further, for there are many people who believe in principle that they are loved and yet do not sense God's love.

THE MINISTRY OF THE SPIRIT

Many believe that God is a God of love who has acted on their behalf. They believe that Christ died for them. Yet how many times have we heard it said (or even said ourselves), "I know in my head that God loves me, but I do not feel it"?

Of course, there are many who do not see this as a problem. They suggest it is not necessary that we *feel* God's love; it is sufficient to *know* it intellectually. Yet imagine how disheartened I would be if I overheard either of my sons tell someone that he knows I love him but he does not feel it. For unless my sons know affectively that they are loved, my love for them has not really made a difference.

God's love will make a difference in our lives only if we feel it. If we are going to love others as we have been loved, if we are going to worship with abandon and serve with generosity, then it will be because we feel in the depth of our being that we are loved. Everything in our lives rests on the confidence we have in this love. And this is why we must see the words of verse 8 in this text alongside the promise of verse 5 in Romans 5.

Romans 5 makes two points about the love of God. In verse 8 we have the affirmation that God proved his love for us in the death of his Son. But there is more. The second point, found in verse 5, is that God poured his love into us through his Spirit. According to Douglas Moo, what Paul asserted here is the reality that the love of God is conveyed to our senses by the Holy Spirit and that this is the assurance we need. In commenting on Romans 5:5, Moo writes, "The confidence we have for the day of judgment is not based only on our intellectual recognition of the fact of God's love, or even only on the demonstration of God's love on the cross . . . but on the *inner subjective certainty* that God does love us."[1]

Verse 8 speaks of history: Christ has acted on our behalf. Verse 5 speaks of the experiential: the Spirit enables us to live in God's love. The first is cerebral—a question of conviction, understanding and belief. It's great as far as it goes, but tragically, many Christians never get beyond this. The second accounts for what is just as critical: the affective, subjective and experiential awareness of this love. We read, "God's love has been poured into our hearts through the Holy Spirit" (Rom 5:5).

The grace we seek is a deep confidence in the love of God. And thus, in the language of Paul in Ephesians, if we are strengthened in our inner being "with power through his Spirit," it will only be as we are "rooted and grounded in love"—a love "that surpasses knowledge" (Eph 3:16-17, 19). And so he prayed that we would know the breadth, length, height and depth of this love. What we long for is the grace to believe that God does not love us reluctantly but absolutely and with generosity. Through the ministry of the Spirit, we experience this love as the anchor and inner strength of our lives, in much the same way that the love of parents is fundamental to the emotional health of a child.

And so we lift up our hearts to let the Spirit do what the Spirit is intent on doing—overwhelming us with the love of God. We allow the Spirit to enable us to experience the crucified love of God (Rom 5:8)—or what some

---

[1]Douglas Moo, *Romans 1—8*, Wycliffe Exegetical Commentary (Chicago: Moody Press, 1991), p. 312, italics added.

aptly call "the cruciform love of God"—so that this love prevails in our lives, takes root and is established in our hearts. We *know* we are loved.[2]

The spiritual tradition in which I was raised, the Christian & Missionary Alliance, is typical of many denominations that stress the work of the Spirit in our lives. As I look back, I appreciate the teaching I received, but what is noteworthy is that when it came to the ministry of the Spirit, two aspects of this ministry were emphasized: strength in the face of temptation and empowerment for ministry. While both of these are vital aspects of the Spirit's ministry, what we so easily miss is that the assurance of God's love comes prior. The *first* references to the ministry of the Spirit in the book of Romans (in 5:5 and then in chapter 8) speak of the inner assurance—the witness of the Spirit confirming that we are children of God—and the love of God poured into our hearts.

This is the foundation from which we need to begin and from which the whole ministry of the Spirit proceeds. It is imperative, then, that we attend to this ministry and respond favorably to the prompting of the Spirit of God. We cannot walk in the Spirit unless we accept the love of God poured into our hearts by the Spirit. When we resist this, we resist the Spirit.

Why would anyone resist this? To begin with, we must never underestimate the power of self-pity—one of the first signs of self-centeredness. We may resist the Spirit because we know that he will always call us to peace and hope, to gracious acceptance of difficulty and disappointment, even to blessing those who curse us (Mt 5:44). This is not necessarily welcome news, and so some would rather remain in self-pity than accept the humbling reality that God loves them.

Others resist because accepting the ministry of the Spirit requires a radical vulnerability. Looking at the language of Romans 5:5, it is clear that to welcome the Spirit we must open our hearts. Surely this is the basis of the ancient liturgical call to worship "Lift up your hearts to the Lord" and the

---

[2]Surely this is what St. Paul intended to emphasize, at least in part, by his statements in Ephesians 1:13 and 14 when he spoke of the seal of the Holy Spirit. This Ephesian reference would seem to be the equivalent of what he affirmed in Galatians 4:6 when he declared that because we are children of God, God has sent the Spirit of his Son into our hearts, a Spirit by which we cry, "Abba, Father."

response "We lift them up to the Lord." To accept the ministry of the Spirit can be humbling, bringing us down from our false posture of self-sufficiency and self-dependency.

However, there are others who for very different reasons find it difficult to believe that God loves them. They long to believe, have sought to be vulnerable before the Spirit and have long since moved beyond self-pity, but they still struggle to accept and experience the love of God. I am thinking of those who have been hurt often. Perhaps as children they were abused by authority figures whom they should have been able to trust. Perhaps as adults they have had a spouse who was repeatedly unfaithful. Or perhaps they have belonged to religious communities that have reinforced the picture of a God who is always unhappy with them for their failures. Their hearts are tender and receptive, but it is hard for them to accept the fact, proven in the death of Christ, that not only does God love others but also God loves *them*.

In Romans 5:9-11 the apostle looks to the abiding hope that we have as Christian believers. In verse 9 he speaks of being saved in the day of God's wrath and in the day of judgment. This confidence is hinted at in verse 10 as well—a confidence that even as we have a foretaste of God's love now, how much more will we know God's love and life in the kingdom to come?

It is important to highlight this, for many struggle to believe that God loves them. They have 1,001 doubts, and it is vital to affirm that these doubts will one day pass away. The measure we have now of the love of God is but a drop in comparison to the outpouring of God's love that we will know in that day. If we have not known the love of parent or spouse, or if we have been let down by a friend or betrayed by a lover, we may be certain that the love of Jesus can sustain us now. We can have hope in that day when we will know, without any doubt and in full measure, the love of God. And so we pray, "Come, Lord Jesus!" (Rev 22:20).

This is not to discount the possibility of experiencing the fullness of God's love in this life or even the vital role that others can play in enabling us to know that God loves us. Many will experience the outpouring of the Spirit's ministry of love into their hearts precisely because they have known the love of God's people shown to them again and again. They have a window through which they can see that they—yes, even they—are loved by God. But though we celebrate, and even in a sense depend on, the love of others to help us experience the love of God, there is still nothing that can sustain us like the conscious, affective awareness that the Creator loves us.

Henri Nouwen has suggested that we consistently experience the love of God against the backdrop of what he calls a "second love"—the love we experience through parents, teachers, spouses and friends. The problem is that while we have all experienced this second love, we have also had, to greater or lesser extents, the feeling of frustration with others. Along the way, someone who ought to have demonstrated the love of God to us instead let us down and betrayed that love.[3] We have been hurt, and the consequence (entirely understandable) is that we are not inclined to "lift up our hearts." Nouwen suggested that, actually, there is always an element of rejection, disappointment, ambiguity and ambivalence in this second love. Consequently, it is all the more crucial that we learn to open our hearts to the ministry of the Spirit, who would pour the love of God into our hearts—a love that is secure and strong and dependable.

SUFFERING AND THE LOVE OF GOD

To know the love of God demands radical receptivity to this ministry of the Spirit. We are called to lift up our hearts to the Lord, and this means that we tear down the fences that we have set up in our hearts, the protection that we have placed around our emotions.

But the apostle Paul did not make light of the pain we have experienced along the way. To the contrary, having summarized the terms of our salvation in the opening verses of Romans 5, he then began a new section with a reference to suffering. He placed the discussion of the love of God in the context of our experience of pain and disappointment. Thus the challenge. Our experience of difficulty makes it hard for us to open our hearts to the Spirit, yet

---

[3]Henri J. M. Nouwen, *In the Name of Jesus: Reflections on Christian Leadership* (New York: Crossroad, 1989), p. 25.

(paradoxically) nowhere in our experience is it more crucial that we do so.

It is no coincidence, therefore, that the matter of suffering is raised right from the beginning as the context in which Paul discussed the love of God. Suffering—hurt, difficulty and setbacks—establishes the context in which we either open our hearts and know the love of God or turn away in hardness, anger and self-pity. How we handle difficulty makes all the difference in the world and is the determining factor in how we respond to the ministry of the Spirit.

In discernment, then, we cannot conclude that a lack of suffering is a sign of God's love. We must not decide that if all is going well for us, if we are comfortable, wealthy and successful, it must mean that God is pleased with us and that these benefits are a demonstration of God's love. To the contrary, the love of God is known and discerned in the context of difficulty and pain. In fact, the time when it is most critical to discern and know (affectively) the love of God is the time of suffering.

The suffering that is spoken of here represents all difficulty—the pain we experience physically, emotionally and spiritually—explicitly because of our identification with Christ, but then also implicitly in all suffering that comes as a consequence of evil in our world. The apostle indicated that we should actually boast in our suffering. By this he meant that we should embrace suffering—accept it, walk into it and choose that through suffering we will grow in grace and hope.

In Romans 5:3-4 St. Paul outlines a progression within the experience of difficulty. We read that suffering produces endurance, which leads to character, which leads to hope. He describes this as though it were a simple progression with the one necessarily leading to next. However, we know full well that every time we experience pain, suffering and disappointment, we are at a Y in the road. While suffering can certainly lead to endurance, character and hope, it can just as easily lead us down another road. Our response to suffering can lead to anger, then bitterness and finally cynicism, hardness and self-pity. We cannot be naive about our response to difficulty; it can so easily darken our spirits and leave us disheartened.

Pain cannot be avoided. We live in a broken world, and the pain we experience will, in many respects, either make us or break us. If we are going to grow in grace in the midst of the pain, it will only be as we walk the difficult road with a profound awareness that the Lord of glory loves us. It is not that we make light of the pain or deny that we are suffering; it is rather that we choose to walk in the grace of God *through* the pain. We choose to walk this road in the light of God's love, which is poured into our hearts by the Holy Spirit.

The paradox, then, is that if we embrace suffering, rather than causing us to doubt the love of God, it becomes the context in which we come to learn, know and appropriate God's love as our own. The very thing that might cause us to doubt the love of God (namely, suffering) is the context in which it is most crucial and in which we are most capable of seeing and appropriating the love of God. This, surely, is what it means to live by faith—believing that God loves us, despite the contrary evidence.

AN INTENTIONAL RESPONSE TO THE MINISTRY OF THE SPIRIT

Whether in good times or bad, we come back to the simple spiritual exercise of lifting up our hearts to Christ so that the love of God might be poured into our hearts by the Holy Spirit. But how to we do this?

First of all, it important that we not overstate our difficulties. There is no value in saying that things are worse than they really are. Thomas Merton made a pointed aside when he wrote, "I have a peculiar horror of one sin: the exaggeration of our trials and our crosses."[4] His words are a good reminder, for we easily complain when in fact we have it remarkably good. This is not for a moment to suggest that we do not suffer; it is merely to emphasize that we must not overstate our suffering.

Next, as every Christian spiritual tradition affirms, the most basic discipline of the spiritual life is that of giving thanks. Gratitude is fundamental for the Christian believer because through thanksgiving we open up our hearts to the Spirit of God.

---

[4]Thomas Merton, *The Sign of Jonas* (New York: Harcourt Brace Jovanovich, 1953), p. 6.

In the *Spiritual Exercises*, for example, Ignatius knowingly placed the act of thanksgiving early in the examination of conscience, so that those whom he guided in prayer would know the grace of lives lived in humble, joyful thanksgiving. And my experience of the *Exercises* has led me to believe it is wise to focus our attention on what is concrete and specific, notably those gifts of God and those reasons for thanksgiving that we have personally experienced. This would include, of course, the significant moments, relationships and gifts from God that anyone looking in on our life would recognize as a sign of God's goodness toward us. But it can also include those seemingly insignificant things that perhaps only we recognize.

Wise and discerning Christians have learned to be continually alert to the signs of God's grace and goodness. We see indicators not only right in front of us but also out of our peripheral vision, as it were, as we seek to be ever conscious of the wonder of a good God. We remember that the way is never so dark or discouraging that there is not always some indicator of the goodness of God. And this awareness of the goodness of God is Spirit-guided and inspired. It is by the Spirit that we see our lives in light of the goodness of God. It is by the Spirit that we see with thanksgiving.

Quite simply, when we give thanks, we open our heart and let down our guard. We cannot live in self-pity and gratitude simultaneously. Through thanksgiving we dwell in the truth, for we live in the confidence that God is good and that, more specifically, God has been good to *us*. Further, the act of thanksgiving humbles us before the reality of this goodness. We know that we have all goodness as a gift, not as something we have earned or that we merit. It is a sign of God's love toward us.

Thanksgiving, then, is the most basic act of our spiritual lives, whether in our daily prayers or our worship with the people of God on Sunday. Many have found it valuable, perhaps in connection with their daily prayers, to actually write out the reasons for thanksgiving. Perhaps in a spiritual journal, as a regular act of faith, they list the signs of God's goodness. Initially we might find that such a list comes easily, as we state the obvious and identify what is squarely before us. But as our list continues, we can be attentive to those elements or events or people who are in our peripheral vision, that which we so easily take for granted. And, as we list, we give thanks.

This does not mean that we deny pain, suffering and disappointment; it is rather that in the midst of the pain we refuse to turn our backs on God. Our posture is always one of discernment, of a heart that is attentive to the love of God. Does this mean that as soon as we give thanks the love of God is poured into our hearts, and in this moment we gain an affective awareness of God's love? Oh, that it were so simple! While I certainly do not want to underestimate either the significance of thanksgiving or the power of the Spirit, for most this awareness will come over time. Thanksgiving is learned and practiced bit by bit, and in the same way we learn to recognize the movement of God in our hearts, becoming increasingly conscious of God's love for us. And as we are grateful for the particulars in our lives, what we essentially do is foster our capacity to live lives of deep gratitude for all of God's gifts—those that are obvious and those that are seemingly insignificant. They all stand out to us as indicators of God's gracious love.

As an additional suggestion, consider the following. After you have made a list of those things for which you are grateful, go back over that list and give particular thanks for the people you have identified. While we can usually remember and identify those persons who have failed us and hurt us, this list of those things for which we are thankful will invariably include individuals who were faithful signs of the grace and goodness of God. Some will fail us, but others will love us and be a kind of aqueduct through which the Spirit can pour God's love into our hearts. Delight in the love of others when it is there—the love of spouse, of friend, of parent, of child, of the community of faith. Let the love of others keep you from self-pity, from fear of vulnerability and from anything that would make you resist the ministry of the Spirit.

Discerning the Inner Witness to God's Love

It is important, in the euphoria of celebration and thanksgiving, that we be discerning. How do we know that what we experience is truly the witness of the Spirit to our hearts, a witness that empowers us with the love of God? There are two critical signs in this regard: humility and a love for others.

The first sign is that the love of God leads not to pride but to humility. We are enlivened and awed by the wonder of God's love, humbled by the reality that the Creator of the universe loves us and that this love was demonstrated at Calvary. And thus it is a false witness if we think we are loved because we earned it or because we are better than others.

Humility, among other things, is living in the conviction that we are loved. And yes, it also means living in the truth that we are sinners in need of forgiveness. However, this recognition of our sin never puts in question the assurance and confidence that we are loved. Humility is the posture of awareness that we are loved by God. Humility enables us to move beyond self-pity and self-absorption. One form of self-absorption is that of being consumed with all that other people have done wrong, either in general or to oneself in particular. However, as Roberta Bondi put it, "Humility . . . does not indulge itself in the luxury of disillusionment."[5] Further, humility includes self-acceptance, as we refuse to compare ourselves with others and refuse to try to be other than who we are.

The second sign that we have genuinely experienced the love of God is that we begin to love others as we have been loved. We are no longer absorbed with ourselves but instead can give ourselves in gracious service to others. We learn how to listen more and speak less. We serve with generosity rather than calculation. We free and empower others rather than trying to control the lives of others, particularly their behavior.

These two signs are but a reminder that the affective awareness of the love of God is not optional or incidental. This is not the soft side of Christian faith and ministry. It is, rather, the fundamental posture from which we live, the rock on which we stand, the roof over our heads, the integrating point for all that we are and hope to be.

---

[5]Roberta C. Bondi, *To Love as God Loves: Conversations with the Early Church* (Philadelphia: Fortress, 1987), p. 56.

5

THE SPIRIT CONVICTS US OF SIN

I tell you the truth: it is to your advantage that I go away,
for if I do not go away, the Advocate will not come to you;
but if I go, I will send him to you.
And when he comes, he will prove the world wrong
about sin and righteousness and judgment:
about sin, because they do not believe in me; about righteousness,
because I am going to the Father and you will see me
no longer; about judgment, because the ruler of this
world has been condemned.

JOHN 16:7-11

John 16 speaks of two ministries of the Spirit, both of which Jesus identified in the context of his declaration that the Spirit would come to glorify
him (Jn 16:14). The action by the Spirit to convict us of sin is the first. The
second is the way in which the Spirit illumines our minds with truth (Jn
16:12-15). Taken together, they speak of the twofold converting ministry of
the Spirit—the grace that enables us to turn away from sin and into a life
informed and governed by truth. But it is helpful to consider them sepa-
rately, at least for the moment.

The Spirit brings conviction for sin. This is essential if the Spirit is to glorify Christ in us. Our sin is incompatible with the presence of Christ in our

lives and his purposes for us. Christ is glorified as we mature in our faith, continually recognizing and turning from sin. This suggests, then, that we cultivate a relationship with Christ through our response to where and how the Spirit is calling us to turn from sin. We are alive in the Spirit when we have a sensitive conscience.

For so many, after they have been Christian believers for a time, it is easy to go from one day to another or one week to another scarcely conscious of the convicting ministry of the Spirit. They may even be quite consistent in fulfilling what they believe to be God's law in what they do and in what they refuse to do. But sin is far more subtle. We never graduate from this dimension of the Spirit's ministry, for there is always sin in our hearts. Pride and self-centeredness shape the deep impurity within each of us. As we grow older, different circumstances at different points in our journey expose us to new temptations and reveal other dimensions of the darkness of our hearts.

I wonder if part of the reason that Paul urged Timothy to leave behind the sins of youth (2 Tim 2:22) was that the sins of his middle years and of his senior years would be enough to contend with! We wrestle with different temptations as we grow older. Different aspects of our hearts come to light as we face new circumstances. Pride reveals itself in other ways when we are not as young and when opportunities are not as many. It is for this reason that we should never cease from praying the prayer of the psalmist: "Search me, O God. . . . See if there is any wicked way in me" (Ps 139:23-24). For the inner witness of the Spirit is always there if we are but willing to listen—and then, of course, to turn.

THE DEADLY CHARACTER OF SIN

It is helpful to think of temptation—the inclination to sin—as arising from doubt about the goodness and love of God. But then the temptation to sin has within it an implicit question: is sin a matter of life and death? We cannot appreciate the urgency of this dimension of the Spirit's witness to our hearts unless we recognize the deadly character of sin.

The reason the Spirit convicts us of sin is because sin is death. Our only hope for life is to recognize that sin has the capacity to destroy us. This is the message of St. Paul in Romans 6—8, where he urges us to see and feel what sin really is. It is not only that the wages of sin is death; it is also that we are slaves of sin, and thus of death, and that if we live in sin, we walk the way of death.

The crisis of sin originated in the Garden of Eden. God advised the first human parents that there are consequences to sin: obedience leads to life, while disobedience leads to death. And so when temptation came through the words of a snake, as portrayed in Genesis 3, the woman rightly countered by saying that sin would have consequences. The response of the snake was brazen: "You will not die" (Gen 3:4).

There is a sense in which every time we are tempted we are once more encountering the suggestion that sin is not a matter of life and death. We believe and act as though sin will not really destroy us. As often as not, we are inclined to think that God is merciful and will forgive us. But this misses the point: God is calling us away from sin, from that which is not life but death, from that which undercuts our capacity to hear the voice of Jesus and be all that we are called to be.

We seek, then, the grace of the Holy Spirit, who makes us aware not only of sin but also of the deadly character of sin and our potential for both forgiveness and life. This is a massive undertaking because our whole self is bent on denying the presence and power of sin and on resisting the thought that sin really is sin. Our inclination is to see the sin of others and not our own. We are blind to and caught up in our own sinfulness, so that we resist seeing our predicament. This mental habit keeps us from a genuine, heartfelt response to the convicting ministry of the Spirit.

But we cannot see our sin except by the gracious work of the Spirit. And thus we rightly pray that the Spirit would penetrate our propensity to live in self-deception and apathy, that the Spirit would disturb us where we live in false comfort and enable us to have eyes to see our own self-righteousness. This convicting ministry of the Spirit enables us to see the deadly character of sin, sin's power apart from the grace of Christ, and the genuine possibility of living in the freedom of righteousness.

Complacency regarding the wrong and injustice in our world, but also regarding the lack of consistency and integrity in our own lives, is an ever-present danger. Many prefer not to take notice of their sin; they do not like to be confronted with their responsibility for their own actions. But this acknowledgment is an essential means by which we respond to the God who loves us and calls us to follow him. Christ has loved us and died for our sins; thus if we choose to live in his love, it means that we must come to terms with the reality of our sin and our responsibility for it. But we can face the darkness of our hearts honestly only because we know we are loved. Without the awareness of God's love, the darkness would overwhelm us.

In the awareness of God's love the Spirit bids us acknowledge our sin, confess and repent, and move from death to life. Some suggest that the Christian does not need to repent and make confession because sins have been forgiven at the cross, past, present and future. But such an idea misses the point. While we are certainly forgiven and accepted by Christ, we are simultaneously saints and sinners. We are saints in that we have been accepted by God and justified through Christ. We are forgiven. But we are also sinners who need to take seriously the multiple ways in which sin has the capacity to rob us of life. To suggest that we are saints and therefore do not need to make confession fails to admit this dual identity of saint and sinner. Such a perspective also overlooks the call to spiritual growth that comes, in part, as we face up to the presence of sin (as death) in our lives, take responsibility for this sin and grow in righteousness.

And one of God's gifts to us is an active awareness of the character of the human predicament, the reality of sin and its deathly character and the reality of God's mercy and empowering forgiveness. Our only hope regarding sin, then, is that we would both acknowledge and feel that sin is sin, and that we would appreciate our own culpability. The gift that is given to us by the Holy Spirit is the conviction for sin, that is, that we would *feel* guilty, or that our conscience would be (in the words of Acts 2:37) "cut to the heart."

The convicting work of the Holy Spirit is not only that we would have an understanding of sin, of how what is wrong is wrong, but that we would feel the force of this in our own conscience, knowing it affectively.

The feeling of guilt is a gift much as is the pain we experience when we touch a hot stove. It is certainly painful, but it keeps us from self-destruction. The feeling of guilt is essentially an awareness of truth that merits our attention. To feel guilty is to know and feel truthfully. It is to acknowledge both the reality that something is wrong and our personal responsibility and accountability for that wrong.

THE FEELING OF GUILT: LEARNING TO DISCERN

The grace that we seek, when we lift up our hearts to the convicting ministry of the Spirit, is the grace to see ourselves in truth, that is, to see ourselves as God sees us. We know this through an affective awareness of our guilt. The catalyst for the convicting ministry of the Spirit may come from any number of sources, but as often as not, it comes through the Word when it penetrates and lays bare the intentions of the heart (Heb 4:12-13).

However, there is a danger: we may conclude that if we feel guilty the Spirit of God must be convicting us of sin. We could easily conclude that all feelings of guilt come from God. But this is not the case. It may well be that *most* of the times when we feel guilty the guilt is not from God. Therefore, the matter of the convicting ministry of the Spirit demands discernment.

Just because we feel guilty does not mean the Spirit of God is convicting our hearts regarding sin. And the key test or indicator in this regard is any feeling of condemnation. False guilt is burdensome. False guilt condemns us. True guilt—that which is the fruit of the Spirit's ministry—is liberating; it leads to freedom. St. Paul, then, made a distinction between "godly grief," which by its nature leads to life and salvation, and "worldly grief [which] produces death" (2 Cor 7:9-10). The convicting ministry of the Spirit does not condemn us but rather is life giving, liberating and empowering. Indeed, as we read in 1 John 3:21, a key sign that we are living in the truth is that our hearts do not condemn us.

If our hearts condemn us, we know that what we feel and experience does not come from God. This is so for two reasons.

First, we can always assume that the convicting ministry of the Spirit rests on the basis of an assurance that we are loved. That is, the assurance of God's love precedes (logically, if not experientially) the convicting ministry of the Spirit. The Spirit convicts us of sin precisely because we are loved. Thus any sense of guilt that puts in question this love is, by its very nature, flawed. It does not find its source in God.

Second, the ministry of the Spirit leads to freedom. And it is specifically the freedom of humility. The convicting ministry of the Spirit is one that, through the experience of healing and forgiveness, sets us free, empowers us and enables us to embrace life—the very life that we have through the work of Christ on the cross. In other words, the convicting ministry of the Spirit is always but one side of the overall leading of the Spirit into life. Through Christ, the Father is drawing us to himself. If we are convicted of sin, it is not so much because we are bad people as that we are being drawn into life! We are brought into an awareness of our sin for the simple reason that our sinful nature is luring us away from the life to which the Father is calling us.

Consequently, we must be alert to false guilt. We need to be discerning and learn how to recognize the guilt that is not from God and does not lead to freedom. It is helpful to think in terms of three forms of false guilt.

First, there is the guilt we feel that can only be attributed to the evil one. In Scripture the demonic angelic host is spoken of as a force that accuses and condemns. That we have known forgiveness in Christ does not mean that we no longer need to be alert to this form of false guilt. Many Christians, it seems, live perpetually doubting whether they have truly been forgiven. They have not really embraced the wonder of the gospel, the reality that in Christ there is no condemnation (Rom 8:1). In some cases this may be because they never experienced real forgiveness in their family of origin, and for others it may be that even within their Christian religious communities they have not experienced the gospel as the unequivocal forgiveness of sins. They do not really believe that God forgives.

This form of false guilt finds ready expression: we feel guilty for that which we have already confessed and found forgiveness. Our hearts, under the influence of evil, condemn us and subtly (and sometimes less than subtly) proclaim that God has not really forgiven us. This is not the witness of the Spirit. The best recourse is to declare to oneself and to the heavens, "In Christ there is no condemnation!"

We experience a second form of false guilt in response to the expectations and emotional manipulation of others. Discerning people learn to recognize both the ways in which others seek to make them feel guilty and the ways in which their own hearts respond to the expectations (or perceived expectations) of others. Sadly, we must acknowledge that there are many people who seek to make others feel guilty so that their own expectations are met. They may be parents who subtly suggest that if expectations are not fulfilled, it must mean that the child is no longer good and lovable. Or they may be religious leaders who use emotional manipulation to get people to fulfill their vision and expectations. Or they may be bosses in the workplace who say that if you are a "team player," you will comply with their agenda. And it is a sad fact that some people know of no other way of relating to others than by manipulation and emotional blackmail, ensuring that others fulfill their expectations by making them feel guilt when these expectations are not fulfilled. They may even couch their expectations in spiritual terms, implying that this is what God desires as well. That is perhaps the worst form of emotional manipulation.

We certainly need to hear from others. And as I will note below, the genuine convicting ministry of the Spirit could come through the words of another. We need to be open to what God has to say to us through others—Christian sisters and brothers as well as those with whom we live and work. Indeed the church often needs to recognize the prophetic voice of others in the world, perhaps individuals of other religious traditions, whom God is using to call the church to be consistent with its own confession. But we also need to distinguish the voice of Jesus from the challenge or expectations of others. And this ability will come only when we manage to give up our fear of others' judgments.

However, we cannot always blame others. While emotional manipulation is surely a violation of the integrity and dignity of the human person, sometimes when we feel guilty for failing to fulfill the expectations of others, it may be that those expectations are merely *perceived* expectations. Our hearts condemn us, but no one else is condemning us! Yet our desire to please others and to feel that they approve of us often leads us to a constricted pattern of life. We are perpetually wondering what others are thinking of us and just as frequently are assuming that they are not happy with who we are and what we do. Of course, this is a burden we are not designed to bear. It is a false guilt; it does not come from God.

Third, another form of false guilt is the guilt we feel when we have failed to live up to our own expectations and personal aspirations.[1] Our discouragement with ourselves is often an oppressive burden; we condemn ourselves and rehearse again and again our failings. But sin has nothing to do with discouragement with ourselves and our own failure to live up to our personal ideals. This is not true sorrow for sin, but rather another expression of pride.

Not all Christians are prone to this sort of self-imposed guilt. But some of us are quite capable of driving ourselves with certain ideals or expectations that, while good in themselves, are either unrealistic or unnecessary. I, for example, am capable of leaving my office at the end of the day and feeling disappointed with myself for the things I failed to do. I am inclined to think that I was not as diligent and disciplined as I should have been with my time. But if I pause long enough to ask God to help me see my day, it is more than often the case that something else comes to mind. I may not

---

[1]For this insight, I am indebted to John English, who first helped me to see this distinction between the Spirit's ministry and our expectations for ourselves. He wrote, "Often I am discouraged because I have failed to live up to some ideal that I have set for myself" (John J. English, *Spiritual Freedom: From an Experience of the Ignatian Exercises to the Art of Spiritual Guidance*, 2d ed. [Chicago: Loyola Press, 1995], pp. 74-75). The danger is that we might confuse this with the ministry of the Spirit.

have been as patient as I should have been with someone. I may have spoken a strong word to one of my sons when I should have listened. I may have rushed out of house that morning, and now that inattention to my family comes back to mind as I drive home at the end of the day.

I am not suggesting that our ideals are wrong in themselves. It is merely that we cannot confuse these with the witness of the Spirit and the voice of Jesus. The danger is that we might hear only these personal expectations and miss the convicting ministry of the Spirit. We must be alert to the subtle ways in which these ideals may crowd out the still, small voice of God, who is quietly calling us from sin to life. These self-expectations are usually burdensome as well. They do not liberate. They do not enable us to live in the freedom of the Spirit.

Thus what we long for is a conscience that is informed by the truth and sensitive to the inner witness of the Spirit of God. And, as with each dimension of the Spirit's witness, we are called to lift up our hearts to the Lord and be attentive to the voice of Jesus that calls us from sin. This inner posture is well expressed in the heartfelt prayer of the psalmist:

> Search me, O God, and know my heart;
> > test me and know my thoughts.
> See if there is any wicked way in me,
> > and lead me in the way everlasting. (Ps 139:23-24)

This is a position of extraordinary vulnerability before the Creator of the universe. Yet we cannot possibly respond eagerly to the exhortation to "lift up your hearts" and open ourselves to the convicting witness of the Spirit unless we know that we are loved. Indeed our capacity to experience the Spirit's ministry with regard to our sin is in proportion to our capacity to experience an affective awareness that we are loved.

GUIDING PRINCIPLES

When we consider the convicting ministry of the Spirit, it is helpful to keep three guiding principles in mind.

1. *Avoid the temptation to look at others rather than yourself.* We cannot discern for another. This is fundamental and basic. The common temptation, especially with this dimension of the Spirit's ministry, is to look at others rather than to open up one's own heart to God.

It is easy to compare. We all have an eagerness to see how the Spirit needs to convict others—an eagerness that is, of course, matched by a blindness to our own inclinations. We happily discern for others, and we likely have a verse or two from the Bible to substantiate our "objectivity" in this regard.

But we cannot know how God is convicting another; we can only know our own hearts. And so we will not mature in our capacity to discern unless we resolve that we will not judge others or determine for others what God is saying to them. It is challenge enough to know our own hearts.

We are most likely to see the "need" of others at those times when we are eager to see their behavior change. When we look to the actions of a co-worker or someone with whom we live or a fellow member of the church, we are convinced that life would be easier if *that person* would change. And our emotional energy is devoted to our complaint against another rather than to our response to the Spirit. We should be asking, "O Spirit of God, where in this relationship are you calling *me* to change?"

And for pastors, missionaries and others within a religious vocation, it is all too easy to see our call as that of enabling *others* to grow, to come to terms with *their* shortcomings and their need to become more mature disciples, while we fail to recognize our own sin. Our prior call before God is to respond to the convicting ministry of the Spirit to our own hearts.

Most of all, we recognize that though we travel this road together, we each have a different path and the call of God for each is unique. The imperative for me is to learn to be attentive to the witness of the Spirit to *my* heart.

This does not mean that there is never an occasion when we challenge one another and even confront one another in the face of grievous sin. I am not suggesting that if a brother is beating on his child we are not to speak to such behavior. Paul made it clear (note his words in Galatians 6:1-5) that our life in community includes a gentle confrontation and restoration of one who "is detected in a transgression" (v. 1). But as he went on to stress, each must test his or her own work and "all must carry their own loads" (v. 5). Only as we each take responsibility for our own lives will we be able to mature in faith, hope and love. We can challenge and encourage one another, but we cannot live the Christian life or respond to the convicting ministry of the Spirit for one another.

2. *Respond in one area of your life at a time.* Generally speaking, the Spirit addresses only one area of our lives at a time. In the section of Scripture where Jesus described the ministry of the Spirit—first, the ministry of convicting the world of sin, and second, that of teaching the disciples the truth—he also made an intriguing statement. Jesus said, "I still have many things to say to you, but you cannot bear them now" (Jn 16:12). Note the pastoral sensitivity of the Lord to the disciples; he only told them as much as they could bear. And while this statement has as its primary link the words that follow and the description of the Spirit as the Spirit of truth, the same principle clearly applies as well to the convicting ministry of the Spirit.

This suggests that when we open up our hearts to the Spirit and pray the prayer "Search me, O Lord, and see if there is any wicked way in me," the response is not one in which the Spirit lays bare our hearts and all the darkness that resides within us. It is likely the case that if the Spirit were to disclose the full extent of our sin, it would decimate us. It would, in other words, be more than we can bear.

And this is why I suggest that usually God is calling us to leave sin and embrace life in only one area of our lives at a time. Some may think that this is not good enough. They are conscious of their many failings and think that God takes a multiple-agenda approach with us. But can we bear that much? Further, we must not underestimate the real transformation that occurs when we attend to one area of our lives at a time.

What we most need when we lift our hearts up to the Spirit is not a laundry list of our sins but rather the one thing from which we now are being called to turn. Sometimes we might have the grace to see what some have called "our basic disorder," that which at this moment or in this chapter of our lives most threatens us. And so we would strain to see as much as the Spirit would show us, where it is most imperative that we give our attention, but also where we most urgently need to allow for the gracious work of God.

This is easier said than done. Many of us are convinced about how God should make us better and more gracious people, but a genuine response to the Spirit seeks to turn from sin where the Spirit is calling us to turn. Our question, then, is this: "Spirit, where are you calling me to turn at this time?" When the Spirit puts his finger on a matter in our lives, we might then protest and identify something else—something that from our perspective clearly needs an infusion of God's grace. But at those times it is good to think of something that was first mentioned to me by a spiritual director: "Clearly the Father's response is to suggest to you that he has all of eternity to deal with those other concerns, but for now, for this time in your life, *this* takes priority and reflects the call of the Spirit." The issue at hand, then, is not where we would wish for change; it is rather a resolve to know and respond to where the Spirit of God is calling us to turn.

3. *Take into account the full range of human sinfulness.* One of the ways in which classic liturgical prayers express the confession for sin is as follows:

> Most merciful God,
> We confess that we have sinned against you
> in thought, word and deed,
> by what we have done
> and by what we have left undone.
> We have not loved you with our whole heart.
> We have not loved our neighbors as ourselves.

We are truly sorry and we humbly repent.
For the sake of your Son Jesus Christ,
have mercy on us and forgive us,
that we may delight in your will,
and walk in your ways,
to the glory of your name.[2]

A prayer of confession like this opens us to the full range of the Spirit's convicting ministry. Sin is not merely bad deeds. Rather, we are wise to be attentive to how the Spirit of God may be convicting us with respect to our speech, the attitude of our hearts, our mental propensities as well as what we have actually done. On all scores we must be attentive not only to what we have done but also to what we have neglected to do.

Furthermore, it is good to attend not only to the specific things about which the Spirit might convict us but also to the call of the Spirit concerning the *bent* of our hearts. Perhaps the specific details are only symptomatic of a larger pattern, which in turn reflects an orientation of our hearts. And the Spirit may draw to our attention our habit of impatience or our propensity to live in anxiety or the presence in our hearts of an anger that once may have been good and true but that has now taken on a life of its own. But the bottom line remains: "Lord, where are you calling *me* to turn—not the person next to me in the pew on Sunday, not my colleagues at the office or family members, not anyone else but me?"

We seek the grace to know the convicting ministry of the Spirit that calls us from death to life, that empowers us to embrace the life of God. In the chapter that follows, I will speak of the illuminating ministry of the Spirit to our hearts and minds, as the Spirit enables us to know and walk in the truth. However, a wise truth bears repeating: the Spirit cannot lead us into new light unless we live in the light we have already received. And that is precisely what conviction of sin is. It is the Spirit calling us to live in a manner

---

[2]This edition of the classic penitential prayer is found in *The Book of Alternate Services of the Anglican Church of Canada* (Toronto: Anglican Book Centre, 1985), p. 46.

consistent with what we already know.

As a sobering note, it is also important to mention that the convicting ministry of the Spirit can be ignored or rejected. In other words, we can resist the Spirit. The Spirit does not coerce but persuades with quietness and gentleness. And so we have the warning and the encouragement in the book of Hebrews: "Today, if you hear his voice, do not harden your hearts" (Heb 3:7-8).

We need a sensitive conscience. This means that we avoid the hardened heart of the person who refuses to hear and resists the prompting of the Spirit. But we must stress that this is not something we fear, and we certainly do not threaten either children or church members with the possibility of a hardened conscience if they do not respond as we think they should. We are sobered by this possibility, but we do not live in fear. The Spirit's work is one of freedom and empowerment, not of threat or anxiety.

If we live in fear of a hardened conscience, we may unwittingly fall into another error, that of an overly scrupulous conscience. This is the fastidious conscience that nags us and grants us no inner freedom in the Spirit. I wonder if we cannot speak of this as but another form of the false guilt already mentioned, wherein one lives feeling perpetually condemned rather than in the joyful freedom of a child of God. The overly scrupulous conscience leaves us feeling that we never quite get it. It speaks of perfectionism, a moral imperative that is more burdensome than liberating. And an overly scrupulous conscience often means that one burdens others with one's own conscience.

A key sign of a genuine response to the convicting ministry of the Spirit is humility. What we long for is captured in the words of the Beatitudes: poverty of spirit, mourning, meekness and a hunger and thirst for righteousness (Mt 5:3-6). From this posture we live in the truth. This is the condition of heart that enables us to respond to the convicting ministry of the Spirit. And a primary expression or evidence of this humility is joy, as we see so clearly in Luke 15, which speaks of a joy both in heaven and on earth when a sinner repents. This is not, then, the false humility of a broken or an abused spirit or even a broken will.[3] It is, rather, the genuine humility that enables us to know the Spirit's empowering forgiveness, and a key sign of this is joy.

THE SPIRITUAL DISCIPLINE OF CONFESSION

As noted in the last chapter, gratitude is the spiritual discipline that enables us to respond intentionally to the Spirit's witness assuring us that we are loved. As a complement to this, confession is the spiritual discipline that enables us to respond intentionally to the convicting ministry of the Spirit. It is important to note, then, that just as we need to learn how to give thanks, so we need to learn how to make a confession of sins. Confession is a critical means by which we lift up our hearts to the Spirit and respond to the Spirit's call on our lives.

The spiritual discipline of confession is a series of acts, none of which stands alone. What follows is a summary of these.[4]

The prayer of humility. To confess is to acknowledge in general terms that one is a sinner in need of mercy. We know as we open our hearts that there are multiple expressions of disorder, self-centeredness, envy, selfishness, petty irritation, misguided motives and confused affections within us. Our only hope is that God is a God of mercy. And so we pray, "O Spirit of God, you know my heart and my way of life. Where, in your holiness and mercy, are you calling me to turn?"

---

[3]Some readers might wonder about Psalm 51:17: "The sacrifice acceptable to God is a broken spirit; a broken and contrite heart, O God, you will not despise." It is important to see these words in their context. The objective of confession is not humiliation but joy and gladness (v. 8) and the joy of salvation (v. 12). Further, the point of this section of the psalm is to contrast burnt offerings and sacrifices with the primacy of an internal posture of contrition and awe before a holy God. See Marvin E. Tate, *Psalms 51—100*, Word Biblical Commentary (Dallas: Word, 1990), p. 28. I would also note that to the degree that we are humbled in the awareness of our sinfulness, this is the work of the Spirit, in contrast to the approach of many who think it is their responsibility, whether as pastors or parents, to personally humble those in their care if there is a problem with sinful behavior.

[4]Christians of all generations and cultures have found guidance and encouragement in the great prayers of confession found in Psalm 32 and Psalm 51 as well the words of 1 John 1:8-10.

Acknowledgment of wrong. Then, in response to the ministry of the Spirit, we can with honesty and inner conviction acknowledge that the matter that the Spirit brings to mind is indeed wrong. It is inconsistent with the character of God and contrary to what we know to be true and good. We agree with the Spirit that we are not living in truth and freedom. Central to this recognition, though, is that we seek the grace to see ourselves as God sees us.

Acknowledgment of responsibility. Confession necessarily includes the acknowledgment of responsibility. We read in Genesis that when God came to Adam and asked whether he had eaten of the tree, Adam acknowledged that indeed he had, but then immediately he pointed to the woman! And Eve in turn acknowledged that wrong had been done, but like Adam, she refused to take responsibility for her actions. In her case, she pointed to the snake. But true confession both acknowledges wrong and admits the reality of personal responsibility. There are no excuses, no extenuating circumstances. We cannot blame another, blame God, blame our upbringing or blame the traffic. We knew better. And so we pray, in the words of Luke 18:13: "God, be merciful to me, a sinner." *Kyrie eleison*—Lord have mercy.

Repudiation and turning from sin. True confession includes grief and remorse for our sin; we feel badly about what we have done or about the attitude of our hearts. But true confession is not so much remorse as it is a turning. It includes both contrition and the resolve to take adult responsibility for our lives. And thus confession includes a conscious repudiation of the way of sin, of the pattern of speech, thought or behavior from which we are being called to turn. We acknowledge that sin is the way of death and we are embracing the way of life. We take responsibility for how we will live in the grace of God.

Acceptance of forgiveness. The confession of sin has a twofold objective: that we would know the forgiveness of God and that we would experience genuine reformation of our lives. Consequently the assurance of forgiveness cannot be taken for granted; it is a necessary aspect of the discipline of confession. It should be conscious and intentional. We accept the reality that we are forgiven, mindful of the promise of God that if we confess our sins, we can be assured of God's mercy (1 Jn 1:9). In addition, it is important to stress that forgiveness is given freely; it is not earned or merited. Nor is forgiveness granted on the basis of our level of sincerity. It is a gift.

Reformation and accountability. Finally, confession includes an orientation of our lives toward the truth and light into which we are being called. On the one hand, this means that there is purposeful action—we do that which is consistent with our confession. We turn from sin. But many spiritual masters counsel that we are wise to go a little further.

For example, I once heard a colleague observe that when driving a car in the Canadian prairies, one always has to take account of the crosswind that might blow the car off the road. One drives, then, continually turning into the wind, not straight ahead, or the wind will push one into the ditch or into the oncoming traffic. In much the same way, my colleague suggests, in the spiritual life we do not always move straight ahead but take account of the buffeting wind. We turn (to reverse the image) away from that which has the propensity to undermine our spiritual lives. If our sin, for example, correlates with a pattern of television watching, then we might choose to get rid of the television. If our sin involves a pattern of speech, we choose to observe a period of silence each day. What we seek is a reformation of life and character, and this way of reformation calls us to recognize our propensities and adjust the pattern of our behavior accordingly.

Sometimes the reformation of one's life, through confession, includes the determination to provide restitution or to seek the restoration of a relationship. As much as possible, confession should find concrete expression in our lives, where we choose to act in a way that makes things right and establishes our lives on a path that is characterized by justice, truth and peace.

Further, there is great value in a pattern of intentional accountability to another—a friend or spiritual adviser, or even perhaps to a small group of fellow Christians. Such a relationship is a recognition that we do not walk the Christian road alone. Indeed, apart from the encouragement of others, we will likely not be able to withstand the force of temptation and trial. And so there is value to a pattern of accountability for our lives in which we can speak openly about temptation and allow others to hold us answerable for our actions.

This raises a question: is it appropriate and fruitful to confess one's sins to another?

CONFESSING OUR SINS TO ONE ANOTHER

Many Christians who have chosen to define their faith as other than Roman Catholic have assumed or been taught that confessing one's sins to another is neither necessary nor helpful. They contend that this is a priestly function and that there is but one mediator between people and God: Christ Jesus.

This perspective might be challenged at two points. First, we have the explicit exhortation of James 5:16, where we read, "Confess your sins to one another . . . so that you may be healed." Second, we find that the New Testament declares all Christians to be priests who serve with the High Priest, Jesus Christ. And the role of a priest includes the act of mediation—not in a manner that supplants that of the High Priest but specifically as part of the ministry of Christ to the church and to the world. So just as the Word of God is mediated through the preacher, and just as the governing authority of Christ is mediated through those in leadership, so the priestly work of Christ is mediated to us through the community of Christians of which we are a part.

This does not mean that there is no forgiveness if we do not confess to another. However, it does mean that we should take seriously the possibility and potential of mutual confession. Dietrich Bonhoeffer suggested that the act of confessing our sins to one another is one of the fundamental elements of true Christian community. He noted that when we confess our sin in the presence of a fellow Christian, the sin loses its power as it is brought into the light. And often this is the only thing that will undercut a recurring habit of sin.[5] What we experience in baptism is renewed through the act of

---

[5]Dietrich Bonhoeffer, *Life Together*, vol. 5 of *Dietrich Bonhoeffer Works*, trans. Gerhard Lüdwig Müller and Albrecht Schönherr, ed. Geffrey B. Kelly (Minneapolis: Fortress, 1996), p. 113. See his whole chapter on the importance of confession, pp. 108-18.

confession. For in confessing our sins to another, we also have renewed opportunity for the other to assure us that we are forgiven.[6] And Bonhoeffer suggested that we need this, lest we only fancy ourselves to be forgiven rather than truly experience the forgiveness of God.[7]

Finally, we should consider the offering of confession in a public forum. It is noteworthy that all classic liturgies of the Christian church have included the formal act of confession, repentance and assurance of pardon. However, in the last century or more, it has become increasingly common that services of public worship do not have an intentional act of confession as part of the order or worship.

One of the reasons given for eliminating public prayers of confession is that formal prayers lack sincerity and authenticity and that the only true confession is spontaneous. But hymns and spiritual songs are written prayers, and no one suggests that if a prayer is sung it is inevitably void of meaning. Thankfully, many churches are recognizing the value of formal prayers of confession as a way to guide the prayers of God's people and as a way by which we acknowledge together that we are sinners in need of grace. A simple prayer of confession that we read together is a way by which we stand as sinners and then accept the wonder of God's forgiveness—we know we gather as forgiven sinners.

Of course, there is also a practice in which people attending revivalist meetings will make public confession of their sin. By "public," though, I do not mean the company of God's people who together confess that they are sinners in need of grace. Rather, this is the practice whereby an individual will stand before those assembled and confess sins as a way to identify with the revival that is taking place. Is this a good idea?

---

[6]The "assurance of pardon," as it is often called, is precisely that: it is the declaration for the one who has made confession that in Christ he or she *assuredly* is forgiven. It is not so much the granting of forgiveness as it is the expression of confidence that God forgives. But Thomas Aquinas suggested that this act also involves a prayer that the one making confession would be forgiven, insisting that the one who hears the confession does not grant absolution but rather joins the penitent in asking God to forgive (*Summa theologica* 84/3).

[7]Bonhoeffer, *Life Together*, p. 113.

There are certainly circumstances when an individual has wronged a group of people, whether coworkers, colleagues, friends or family, or potentially a whole church community. In such a case it may well be appropriate for the sinner to acknowledge the wrong, offer reparation and seek forgiveness from the entire group. But it is quite another matter for an individual to confess his or her personal sin before a whole group.

The kind of confession seen in revivalist meetings easily becomes a form of exhibitionism and voyeurism. We might reasonably question whether anyone is being edified by this practice. Furthermore, a public assembly is not a setting in which sin, in all its complexity, can be disclosed and also find resolution.

While the longing for resolution of one's sin and guilt is understandable, it is far wiser to confess in the privacy of a relationship with a spiritual guide or friend. This should be someone who can bear the responsibility of confidentiality and bring an assurance that one has been forgiven. But the main point in all of this is that confession is a spiritual discipline that enables us to open our hearts to the convicting ministry of the Spirit and appropriate the grace of Christ—both the experience of forgiveness and the enabling to grow in faith, hope and love.

6

THE SPIRIT ILLUMINES OUR MINDS

I still have many things to say to you, but you cannot bear them now.
When the Spirit of truth comes, he will guide you into all the truth;
for he will not speak on his own, but will speak whatever he hears,
and he will declare to you the things that are to come.
He will glorify me, because he will take what is mine and declare it to you.

JOHN 16:12-14

The Spirit is the *Holy* Spirit, and so it follows that through the witness of the Spirit we are convicted of sin and called from death to life. Likewise, the Spirit is called the "Spirit of truth," and thus we should fully expect that there is a distinctive and important relationship between the Spirit and truth. We need to clarify how our minds and lives are shaped by truth and how the Spirit plays a primary role in this formation of our understanding.

THE PRIMACY OF TRUTH

Central to the Spirit's ministry is the reality that the Spirit transforms us into the image of Christ, specifically through the truth. Such is the transforming and redemptive power of truth! The Spirit does not make us anew through some illusory force or sheer energy; rather, truth is the very means by which we are transformed.

We must, then, be alert to any hint within our Christian communities that would discount the importance of truth and the life of the mind. Some Christians, for example, are heirs to revivalism, a spiritual movement that unfortunately fostered the idea that intelligence and scholarship are potential threats to the Christian life. And some contemporary Christian communities practice an approach to the Christian life, worship and community that downplays the importance of study and learning. Others insist that "people are more important than truth," as though truth is somehow a threat to genuine human life.

The outcome of this disregard for truth, however subtle, is an inevitable denial of the ministry of the Spirit. For the Spirit works in and through the truth. We become fully alive and free when God's truth informs, forms and reforms our lives. Truth matters. And the Spirit and the truth function in tandem.

We see this in the initial work of God in our lives, the experience of coming to faith. In the letter of James we are urged to receive the Word with meekness (Jas 1:21), specifically because it is through the Word of truth that we have new birth (Jas 1:18). And we find the same connection in 1 Peter, where the call to spiritual growth through the Word (1 Pet 2:2) is based on the reality that we have been "born anew . . . through the living and enduring word of God" (1 Pet 1:23).

In other words, the transformation of the Christian, through spiritual maturity and growth, comes through the truth that engages us and enables us to live in freedom and strength. We come to faith through the truth and we mature in our faith through the truth. Thus Jesus reminded his disciples that the Spirit is the Spirit of truth who would guide them into the truth. The followers of Jesus, then, are sanctified by the truth (Jn 17:17).

We may wonder, as we face up to a negative habit of thought or behavior or some aspect of our speech that we so long to see transformed, *What has the capacity to change me?* If we are going to be made new, what precisely will enable this to happen? And the answer is, quite simply, the truth.

So it comes as no surprise to discover the emphasis in the New Testament on the importance of teaching. In the call to make disciples, Jesus specifically stressed that a disciple is made through teaching (Mt 28:19-20). We read that the early church devoted themselves to the apostles' teaching (Acts 2:42). And it is noteworthy that in the pastoral exhortation within the epistles of 1 and 2 Timothy and Titus we have the recurring emphasis and call to teaching as a central element of pastoral ministry. The assumption that lies behind these calls is this: the community of faith will mature in faith, hope and love only as the community engages the truth. There is no vital congregational life without teaching. It is truth that sets us free (Jn 8:32), that empowers us to fulfill our calling as Christians. We do not fear the truth, and we certainly do not discount it, for in so doing we would discount the ministry of the Spirit. If we take the Spirit seriously, we take truth seriously.

TAKING OUR MINDS SERIOUSLY

Taking the truth seriously necessarily means that we take our minds, and the life of the mind, seriously. Our encounter with the truth is specifically through our minds. It follows, then, that truth is of little worth unless we value what it means to have minds that are capable of learning, understanding and critical thinking.

It is remarkable how frequently people say they do not have good minds. For many, it is a result of an upbringing in which their parents or their siblings continually ridiculed their capacity to think and understand. In my own case, I can still remember the deriding comment of a first-grade teacher who was impatient with me when I seemingly could not grasp something, and I often think this setback in my own development was not overcome until I had an eleventh-grade teacher who helped me to see my intellectual capacities. When our ability to think and use our minds is questioned, especially at a young age, it strikes at something central to our identity and our potential for personal development. The deriding words of those who are older, or of our peers, can easily leave a lasting mark. Critical to the formation of children and young people is the affirmation of their capacity to think deeply and to engage truth.

One implication of respecting our minds is that we are attentive to the intake, that is, to what fills our minds and informs our thinking. Surely an essential Christian discipline is that of being intentional when it comes to what we see and hear and where we focus our thinking. The apostle Paul urged his readers to "think about these things," namely, that which is true, honorable, just, pure and worthy of praise (Phil 4:8). There is likely nothing that determines who we are and what we become so much as the content of our minds.

Our behavior is the fruit of our thinking; our actions and reactions, our inclinations and propensities, are all the result of what is happening in our minds. It follows, then, that the Christian should take the mind seriously and appreciate that it is essential for us to seek, with passion and determination, to know truth.

THE ART OF MEDITATION

Thanksgiving is the spiritual discipline by which we respond intentionally to the witness of the Spirit assuring us that we are loved. Likewise, confession is the discipline by which we accept the convicting ministry of the Spirit. Even so, there is the spiritual discipline by which we respond intentionally to the ministry of the Spirit that would illumine our minds with truth: meditation.

Meditation is the spiritual discipline by which we engage truth with both heart and mind. We are attentive to the tangible, physical realities that we engage with our senses and that we examine with our minds as well as the spiritual dynamics that represent the presence of God in our lives and in our world. We both learn and practice this fundamental exercise. The primary focus of meditation for the Christian is engagement with Scripture, in which we use our critical faculties to read the text yet also learn to open our hearts to the communication of the Spirit. The practice of meditation can and should be applied to every manner in which we engage truth and seek understanding.

"Slow down, you're moving too fast." The art of meditation requires that we appreciate two critical realities: first, that we learn how to learn, which is

slowly; and second, that we learn how to listen with heart and mind.

As Paul Simon has put it in one of his classic tunes, "Slow down, you move too fast. You've got to make the moment last."[1] And we only learn when we slow down to make the moment last. We live in what some have called the "information age," and there is no doubt that data, information and (one might even say) truth are available like never before. Lack of information is not our problem. But abundant information does not make a person either wise or even necessarily inclined to live in the truth; there has never been a time in which this has been more clearly the case. Still, the challenge is not just for this era. The temptation has always been there to approach learning and study as though it were nothing but the acquisition of information, to seek to become a master of one's field and to demonstrate one's accomplishment by the extent of one's knowledge (often measured by academic degrees).

However, the spiritual discipline of meditation calls us to slow down and appreciate that, as often as not, the Spirit is seeking to teach us one thing at a time. We do not receive more light until, as it is said, we learn to walk in the light we have already received. And so, in the *Spiritual Exercises*, Ignatius cautioned retreat directors not to give their retreatants too much material for their reading and meditation, "for, what fills and satisfies the soul consists, not in knowing much, but in our understanding the realities profoundly and savouring them interiorly."[2]

I was impressed with this early in my pastoral ministry through a memorable story I heard from one of my parishioners. It was our practice then

---

[1] These words occur in Simon's tune "59th Street Bridge Song (Feelin' Groovy)," *Parsley, Sage, Rosemary and Thyme* (New York: Columbia Records, 1966).

[2] See Ignatius Loyola, *The Spiritual Exercises of St. Ignatius,* trans. Louis J. Puhl (Chicago: Loyola University Press, 1975), para. 121-26, 133-34. As Ignatius put it elsewhere, in the introduction to the *Exercises*, "It is not the quantity of food, but a healthy digestion which nourishes the body; so it is not the great amount of knowledge communicated, but the manner in which the heart receives it, and is nourished by it, that satisfies the needs of the soul. Moreover, experience proves that the heart will receive with delight, and with greater real profit, what it discovers for itself, either by its own reflections, or by the light shed upon it by Divine grace, than what is present to its intelligence by lengthened discourses."

to hold two services each Sunday, including an evening or vesper time of worship. As a young preacher, I always found it a challenge to come up with two sermons to be preached each Sunday—one for the morning and another for the evening. One Sunday evening a dear church elder was with me at the door to the church helping me welcome those who were coming in for the service. And when there was a break in the flow of arrivals, he joined me on my side of the doorway with a sparkle in his eye as he announced that when he heard my sermon of that evening, it would be the eighth sermon he would have heard that day!

Well, he must have noticed my surprise, for he went on to tell of a typical Sunday in his life: rising early to catch a favorite radio station and the sermon of a well-known radio preacher, timing his breakfast so that he and his wife could watch their favorite television evangelist give his weekly sermon on the air from a church in California, planning their drive to the church so that they could hear another radio sermon during their commute. My Sunday morning sermon, then, would be their fourth sermon of the day.

In the afternoon, his wife (probably thinking that she had had her fill) would leave him to continue his routine as he took in another television program with its weekly sermon and usually a taped sermon that he would pick up from his storehouse of sermons on cassette. But she would join him at supper as they heard together his seventh sermon of the day. My sermon on Sunday evenings was their eighth, and then before retiring in the evening, there was yet another radio preacher whom they never missed!

I listened in amazement, and as the elder spoke, what came to mind was the well-known parable of the seed and the sower (Mk 4:1-20). In this parable Jesus told of a sower who went out to spread seed. Some seed fell on the hardpan of the path, and it was quickly eaten up by the birds. Of course it did not grow to bear fruit. Other seed fell on rocky ground, and the result was that the plants grew up quickly but then were easily scorched by the sun. The seed had no depth of soil and did not bear fruit. Some seed, in turn, was dispersed among thorns, and again there was no fruit—this time because weeds choked it out. And finally some seed was scattered on good

soil and produced plenty of grain. Jesus used this parable to alert his followers to the importance of listening to the Word. He compared the different
soils to the different kinds of response to the Word and urged them to listen
carefully and to be hearers in whom the Word is established in their hearts
and minds and bears fruit in their behavior.

I wonder, if Jesus had told this parable in our day, whether he would
have added a fifth category to the parable. Maybe he would have taken note
that ours is a time in which we are inundated with data and can easily confuse having much information with having much wisdom. He might have
said something like this: "And as she went, the sower took a large handful
of seed, and it fell in a clump, and so it was that nothing grew and no fruit
was born because the seeds crowded each other out!"

From that point on, as long as we had the vesper service, I thought that
I should provide a sermon that would continue or echo the theme of the
morning sermon. I began to appreciate that we are simply not capable of
hearing and genuinely responding to two sermons on a Sunday (let alone
nine!). For my dear brother, listening to sermons was a hobby. Perhaps this
has its place, but it is not genuine spiritual learning. It is not the spiritual
discipline of meditation and response to the Spirit's ministry of illuminating
our minds with truth.

To meditate is to "slow down," as the song says. If there is one thing that I
need to know, one thing that the Spirit is drawing to my attention, what is it?

Some time after my experience with the elder, I was in the Philippines as
a theological educator, and for several years I was not in the pulpit but in the
pew on Sunday. And during those years, I had opportunity to sit under the
preaching ministry of Alex Aronis at the Union Church of Manila. He is a
fine preacher, and on many a Sunday I made it a point to take copious notes
from the sermon, eager to take down as much as possible of the insights that
had arisen from his study of the text and his application to contemporary life.
He apparently noticed this, and after one Sunday service, he asked me about
it. I told him how much I appreciated his preaching and that I was trying to
get as much as I could from it. His response was apt (for me at least, at that

point in my journey of faith). He suggested that perhaps a wiser course of action would be if I were to listen for the one thing that the Spirit was saying to me through the sermon. He wondered if I would miss the main thing that the Spirit was saying to me by trying to absorb everything I was hearing.

And since then I have often been reminded that each time I sit in the pew and hear a sermon, this is what I am being called to do: to hear what the Spirit is saying to me, not to those around me, not to the whole world, but to me in particular. Not all the preachers I hear are as eloquent or careful in their exegesis as Alex is, but I have found that again and again so much depends on my response, on the posture of my heart. If I but ask the question—"Spirit of the living God, what are you saying to me through your preacher for this moment in my life?"—I consistently find that there is remarkable clarity about what I am to see.

To listen with heart and mind. When it comes to the spiritual discipline of meditation, not only do we need to learn how to listen slowly, but more, we need to learn what it means to listen with heart and mind. Jonathan Edwards stressed that true understanding is not merely cerebral. He made a helpful distinction between "notional understanding" and "the sense of the heart, wherein the mind doth not only speculate and behold, but relishes and feels."[3]

Such language is foreign to most of us. Edwards wrote of a manner of listening and learning that runs contrary to what we have ordinarily been taught. As children of the Enlightenment, we tend to be one dimensional in our listening and learning. Our contemporary school systems, whether we have grown up in the East or the West, have not taught us how to listen with heart and mind, to attend to both affect and intellect in our learning. We have actually been taught the opposite, that education means that we discount affect and learn to engage the facts with as little emotion as possible. Our university systems have been built on the premise that scholarship is objective and detached. We have been taught to engage information cerebrally and dispassionately because, as we "learned" again and again, our

---

[3]Jonathan Edwards, *Religious Affections*, ed. John E. Smith (New Haven: Yale University Press, 1959), p. 272.

emotions are messy and complicated and undermine "true" learning.

Of course, Ignatius, Wesley and Edwards would challenge this. But it is heartening to see that many contemporary voices are also questioning this standard approach to learning. Parker Palmer, for example, stressed that true learning necessarily involves the interplay of intellect and emotion. He recalled the story about Barbara McClintock (1902–1992), who was perhaps the premier biologist of the twentieth century.[4] Palmer built on the biography of McClintock written by Evelyn Fox Keller, who noted that the genius of McClintock was that she refused to objectify and analyze from a distance. One naturally wonders what enabled McClintock to see further than her colleagues. The answer that Parker quoted from Keller is this: "Over and over again she tells us one must have the time to look, the patience to 'hear what the material has to say to you,' the openness to 'let it come to you.' Above all, one must have 'a feeling for the organism.' " And this phrase — "a feeling for the organism" — then became the title of the biography.[5]

Keller and Parker emphasized that McClintock was a brilliant thinker, capable of precise analytical thought. However, her real genius, her ability to process data and use logic, was due to another reality: she *loved* the corn plants that were the focus of her study.[6] And thus Palmer concluded, "Intellect works in concert with feeling, so if I hope to open my students' minds, I must open their emotions as well."[7]

Yet none of this should be new to the reader of the New Testament, where we regularly observe the connection between intellect and affect, between understanding and emotion.[8] Two examples suffice for the moment,

---

[4]Parker Palmer, *The Courage to Teach: Exploring the Inner Landscape of a Teacher's Life* (San Francisco: Jossey-Bass, 1998), p. 55.
[5]Evelyn Fox Keller, *A Feeling for the Organism: The Life and Work of Barbara McClintock* (New York: Freeman, 1983), p. 198.
[6]Palmer, *Courage to Teach*, p. 55.
[7]Ibid., p. 63.
[8]I suggest that it *should not* surprise the contemporary reader of the New Testament, but it is my experience that in fact it usually *does* surprise those with whom I read the text. It would seem that the Enlightenment/Cartesian split between intellect and affect establishes a grid so that, as often as not, this intimate link is missed.

both from the letters of St. Paul. In the first recorded description of a Christian conversion, Paul celebrated the conversion of his readers (1 Thess 1:4-6). He specified that the ministry of the Spirit had brought into being this new life. It was the Spirit that did this! And he highlighted that the definitive evidence of the Spirit in their midst was that the word of God was received with joy, despite persecution. For post-Enlightenment readers, this joy is, as often as not, read as a nice extra—great if you have it, but not essential to understanding. But the Christian heritage, and indeed the whole tradition with respect to discernment, suggests that they received the Word *because* they received it with joy; there is no other way. This joy is the sign of the authenticity of their conversion.

Another example of this interplay between understanding and affect is an interesting parallel that Paul brought out when he called his readers to "let the word of Christ dwell in you richly" (Col 3:16). What he clearly longed for was that their minds, indeed their entire beings, would be thoroughly and deeply informed by the Word of Christ. And what is noteworthy is the context in which he stated this. He first urged them to "let the peace of Christ rule in your hearts" (Col 3:15). While this is not strictly a case of Hebrew parallelism, there is an obvious link.[9] Just as the peace of Christ cannot rule in our hearts unless we receive the Word, so also the Word of Christ cannot dwell richly within us unless the peace of Christ rules in our hearts.

We listen with heart and mind or else we do not listen. And the particular concern needs to be what is happening to us emotionally. What ultimately prevents us from hearing the Word is not a lack of intelligence but a hardness of heart, or pride. Conversely, humility enables us to hear with joy and receive the Word with hearts ruled by peace. James, too, was concerned that his readers receive the truth, for they had received new birth by the truth, which has the power to save the soul (Jas 1:18, 21). And with this in mind, he spoke of anger (Jas 1:19-20). When he reminded his readers that

---

[9]Hebrew parallelism is the literary device, most commonly found in poetry, in which a second line is an echo of the first, reinforcing the meaning of the first line or affirming and building on what has been said.

they needed to be slow to anger, he was acknowledging that we live in a broken world and we may well have good reason to be angry. He acknowledged, in other words, the legitimacy of anger. But we must not be easily stirred to anger or easily lose our temper; we must appreciate the inherent danger that resides in anger, which is why the apostle Paul stressed that we must not sin in our anger and that we must not let the sun go down on our anger (Eph 4:26). If we fail here, Paul stated, we make room for the devil. Hence the need for vigilance! However legitimate the anger, however right our response may be to some circumstance or development, we cannot stay there. Anger is not the emotional disposition in which we can live in the Spirit. As James put it, "Your anger does not produce God's righteousness" (Jas 1:20). And so he urged us instead to welcome the Word with meekness.

There is a similar emphasis in 1 Timothy 2. In this important discussion about the character of Christian worship, the text first speaks of how men worship and then of how women worship, but the point for both is essentially the same. Men are urged to pray without anger or argument; women are called to learn with a quiet spirit. Both are being called to worship and learn with meekness.

We see then that the spiritual discipline of meditation requires that we learn to slow down and attend to the one word that would represent the illuminating ministry of the Spirit. And in our slowing down, it is equally imperative that we learn to be attentive to what is happening to us emotionally. We cannot be naive or negligent regarding the place of emotion in spiritual experience or our own emotional posture of heart. It matters. In fact, it makes all the difference.

In Psalm 119:36 we find the well-known phrase that in the King James Version reads, "Incline my heart unto thy testimonies." This suggests that we engage truth (the decrees of God) only if our hearts are inclined to do so, and this requires a fundamental humility, a meekness evident in joy and peace.

Our response to the illuminating ministry of the Spirit requires that we learn how to lift up our hearts, for the human mind cannot engage truth except in tandem with the heart. As has been stressed, few things are so crucial to our capacity to attend to the inner witness of the Spirit as to know and appreciate what is happening to us emotionally.

LEARNING TO LISTEN

Learning to listen as the Spirit calls us to truth means that we do more than read what lies before us in Scripture. Reading is good, but it is not the same as listening. And to listen, we must engage both heart and mind. To read, and listen with heart and mind, requires that our inner posture before the truth be one of faith, humility and receptivity. We engage the truth with an eagerness to live in it, not as judges of the truth but as those who long to be mastered by it. It is then that we open our hearts and lives to the transforming power of the Word. This is not an option, unless we want to be content with merely engaging the Word cerebrally. Then the Scriptures will remain only a body of information and principles that we might mine for information and helpful tips for living the Christian life. The Spirit does not and cannot renew, empower and transform us through the ancient text unless we learn to read differently, to listen with both heart and mind to the truth.

This kind of learning is applicable regardless of what we seek to learn; it applies to scientific analysis as much as it does to the study of the Scriptures. What we urgently need is a union of heart and mind. Whether it is in the sciences, engineering or the skills of an artisan, it is imperative that we move away from the propensity to divorce thinking from feeling. We simply do not learn and do not understand unless we have a love of the subject being pursued, a joy in the encounter with truth and a humility before its truthfulness. If our inner disposition is one of anger, for example, our understanding is inevitably distorted. We cannot separate thinking from feeling. If our emotions are muddled, our understanding is muddled as well.

This applies equally to the study one might do at a university as to the learning that comes as we attend to a sermon during Sunday worship. But nowhere is it more critical than when we read a text of the Bible, with the desire that the Word of Christ would dwell in us richly and that the Spirit would illumine our minds with the truth. That is, all learning requires that we attend to truth with heart and mind, but this dynamic is heightened, a matter of life and death to us, when it comes to our response to the Spirit, as we seek to have minds illumined by the power of truth through the Scriptures.

We listen with heart and mind. We read the Bible with our intellects, taking the text seriously—honoring its form, its genre, its historical setting and the intent of the human author. But we are also reading with an open heart that is attentive to the voice of Jesus, who speaks to us through the text by the ministry of the Spirit. An ancient term describes this exercise; it is called *lectio divina*.

THE *LECTIO DIVINA*

The *lectio divina* is a form of prayer that has as its intent that we would hear, for ourselves for this day, the Word of God.[10] The question is not, what is God saying here for others? If we are teachers and preachers, for example, we do not approach the text wondering how this will preach. Our agenda is rather God's *personal* word to us through the ancient Word.

This kind of reading possesses four noteworthy features that enable it to have this highly personal character.

First, the *lectio divina* honors the historical and human character of the Bible. It is important to stress that this kind of reading of Scripture takes the nature of the Scriptures seriously. While this certainly is a devotional reading, it would be false to suggest that it is an approach to the text that denies or downplays our intellect and reason. Not for a moment. Neither is *lectio divina* a way of reading that bypasses the exegetical study of the Bible. On the contrary, true devotional reading of St. Paul's letters, for example, reads them precisely as ancient letters to ancient communities; it respects their particularity. A truly devotional reading of Jesus' parables seeks first to comprehend how these parables would have been heard in first-century Pales-

---

[10]See Ignatius, *Spiritual Exercises*, para. 249-57. This practice is what Ignatius called the second method of prayer. I commend two guides to the *lectio divina* and the praying of the Scriptures: Evan B. Howard, *Praying the Scriptures: A Field Guide for Your Spiritual Journey* (Downers Grove, Ill.: InterVarsity Press, 1999); and Basil M. Pennington, *Lectio Divina: Renewing the Ancient Practice of Praying the Scriptures* (New York: Crossroad, 1998).

tine and how Jesus sought to reveal the wonder of the kingdom through them. History, grammar, syntax and cultural background all enable us to read the text and then, through this ancient text, to hear God speak to us today. We do not honor the Scriptures when we do not honor the way in which God brought them into being. Scripture has a fundamentally human character that must be respected if we are to appreciate its divine character.

And thus true devotional reading respects our critical faculties and the hard work of learning to interpret the Scriptures. There is an important distinction that needs to be made. Meditation is not asking the question, what does this verse mean to me, personally? Rather, it is first asking, what *did* this verse mean? and then, how is God speaking through it to me today?

Second, *lectio divina* disciplines us to read slowly. Our goal is not to master the text or know the text per se but rather to be mastered by the truth, to slow down enough that we are humbled before the ancient text. In other words, this is not the kind of reading where we are encouraged to read through the Bible in a year, however valuable that approach to the Scriptures might be.

We desire that the Word of Christ would dwell richly within us (Col 3:16), a process and an experience that takes time. It cannot be rushed. By its very nature, meditation is a discipline that enables us to slow down and respond with intentionality to the truth. We might compare this kind of reading to an extended meal that lasts through an evening, where each morsel and course is savored without hurry. We pause, consider, ruminate and take it in at a moderate pace, realizing that if we move too quickly we will miss something important.

I must add, though, that we do not move so sluggishly that we lose the sense of text. We do not read in such a way that we do not honor the flow of the message. But we do slow down enough so that we are able to attend to the text itself as well as to the personal word that we would hear from God.

Third, since the *lectio divina* requires that we read with heart and mind, we always read with attention to what is happening to us emotionally. We are seeking not only understanding but also transformation. To grow in wisdom and experience the transforming power of the Scriptures through the ministry of the Spirit, we must learn to open heart and mind. And for this we must be aware of our emotional disposition as we read. When we meditate on Scripture we are learning, but it is a learning that includes a consciousness of our affections.

And what we seek, of course, is affections that are ordered, where we come to love and relish the good, the noble, the excellent and the true (Phil 4:8), where we come to experience what it means to have the peace of Christ ruling in our hearts (Col 3:15) and where we are able to hear the Word of God with joy in spite of difficulty or persecution (1 Thess 1:6). The spiritual discipline of meditation, in other words, presumes that the Bible will inform our minds and enable us to think Christianly as it simultaneously orders our affections.

And for this, we read and attend to the ancient Word with humility. Hans Urs von Balthasar described this kind of reading well when he spoke of Mary, Martha's sister:

> The attention which Mary gave to Jesus, sitting at his feet, was by no means a personal indulgence or a pleasant daydreaming. Nor was it a selective groping for those ideas which suited her, which she "felt able" to translate into reality, let alone pass on to others as her ideas. It was entirely open-ended readiness for the Word, a readiness to participate in it, without preferences, without picking and choosing, without a priori restrictions. It was an alert, sober attitude, attentive to the slightest indications, yet ready to embrace the widest panoramas.[11]

I would note particularly Balthasar's phrase "open-ended readiness for the Word." Such a readiness recognizes that mere "knowledge puffs up" (1 Cor 8:1) and that humility bends the knee, quiets our hearts and calls us to obedience. This kind of humble response is possible only if we are attentive to what is happening to us emotionally. We long to hear the Word of God

---

[11]Hans Urs von Balthasar, *Prayer*, trans. Graham Harrison (San Francisco: Ignatius Press, 1986), p. 91.

with love and not fear, with joy and not anger, with hearts that are ruled by the peace of God. What we seek is the grace that is alluded to when two followers of Jesus, rehearsing their encounter with the risen Jesus, said, "Were not our hearts burning within us while he was talking to us on the road, while he was opening the scriptures to us?" (Lk 24:32).

We may need to relearn how to learn and how to open heart and mind as we engage truth. Something that can assist us in this endeavor is music. We often think of music as a form of entertainment and overlook it as a powerful medium for learning. Luther and Wesley, and the whole Evangelical revival along with them, appreciated the fact that when we sing, we open our hearts and minds to the truth we are singing about. Therefore, worship songs and hymns must have theological depth and we must sing with vigor, for when we do, we open our hearts.

This is not to suggest that we should use music to manipulate emotions—to stir up a crowd and get them ready for the truth to be delivered in a sermon. The fact that this is possible reminds us of the close connection between affect and intellect, and the potential of music to set a mood. But this is not what I mean here. What I speak to is simply the vital place of song and hymnody in public worship as well as our private prayers, the wonder of truth that is sung with an eager heart.

Fourth and finally, it is important to stress that the outcome of the *lectio divina* is the encounter with Christ Jesus himself. Our ultimate longing is not to know the text so much as it is to know the one who speaks to us through the text. For many Christians, it would seem, their devotional lives are a "quiet time" in which they meditate on the Bible and pray in a manner that suggests that their encounter is really with the Bible and not with Christ. However valuable this might be, what the Christian really seeks is to meet *Christ*. True devotional reading anticipates this encounter. As Paul put it, we "are being transformed . . . from one degree of glory to another" because we see Christ (2 Cor 3:18).[12] And our daily prayers are opportunities for union

---

[12]Mystical theology would suggest that true meditation necessarily leads to contemplation of Christ; see 2 Corinthians 3:18 as a biblical reference in this regard.

with Christ, a union that is facilitated by the ancient text of the Bible. In our public worship, what we long for is that we would see Jesus. The holy Scriptures are read and preached so that this encounter is possible. The goal of our pursuit of understanding and wisdom is that we might know Christ experientially, that we might meet the One who is the very embodiment of truth.

This is a crucial reminder because many of us can be content to so relish one insight that we do not allow a new understanding to enable us to know, love and serve Jesus—the very purpose of Scripture. In the end what brings true joy and consolation is that we delight not in *our* insight into the Scriptures but in *their* power to transform us into the image of Christ. What matters is not our mastery of the text but the wonder that the ancient text enables us to know Christ and be known by Christ.

This attentiveness to our hearts is but a reminder that we must be alert and discerning. We must be aware that we cannot presume upon the illuminating ministry of the Spirit or presume that whatever insight we receive necessarily comes from God. The evil one can distort this illumination; we can read the Bible and receive false comfort. All of us are capable of a self-serving reading of the text. We know that many who read the Bible do not know the truth. Their own reading, ironically, blinds them to the truth, and their fanatical or sectarian religious posture is one that discounts any other reading of the Scriptures. And so we are wise to never presume that we have special insight into a text of Scripture or that our understanding of the text cannot be challenged by others. Our humility before the text is necessarily complemented by our humility before and with others who read the Bible with us.

We must be ever alert to the subtle and insidious pride that would infiltrate our hearts and lead us to take joy in how much *we* know or any inclination to use our understanding as a tool by which we judge others. When we sense any of this in our hearts, we have a sure indication that we are not discerning the inner witness of the Spirit. It should raise a red flag if we think we have an insight that no one has ever had before. But a more prevalent danger is reading with a fixed grid of interpretation and application that limits the Spirit's word to us. And this is why some choose not to underline their Bibles, as but one way they can foster their capacity to read the Bible without having a sign of their earlier reading catch their eye and inspire any thought that they already know this text.

CONCLUSION

While the primary focus of my comments has been the spiritual discipline of meditating on Scripture, it is important to reiterate that while this may be the primary means by which the Spirit witnesses to our hearts, it is surely not the only way that the Spirit brings truth to our attention. The Spirit does not work solely through the Bible. The apostle Peter received an illumination from the Spirit through a dream. In our daily lives we might find a new insight through the words or actions of others, such as our children, non-Christian neighbors or the daily newspaper, or through the visual arts or a good novel. All truth is God's truth, and the Spirit is capable of illuminating our minds through any number of means—if we are open.

As we go through our days, whether the daily routine of home, work and leisure or the special occasions when we travel, the key is always the same: openness and receptivity. The ideal is that we would approach our day with a childlike eagerness to listen and learn, to hear and consider, open to surprises. God may speak to us through a child or a young person. The wise know that they must listen more than they speak, and a truly wise person knows there is much to learn from those who are young.

Surely we should also be attentive to the way in which God may speak to us through his created order, through the wonder of flora and fauna, the breadth of sky, land and sea (Rom 1:19-20). And this is but a reminder of the wonder of all of God's creation. How sad I feel when I hear people speak of being bored with any part of what God has made! They might visit the great expanse of the prairies, for example, and say they saw nothing and were bored, and I ache that they missed the marvel of what God had made and the ministry of the Spirit to their own hearts and minds.

Some cannot live unless they are titillated, entertained and comforted. But the illuminating ministry of the Spirit is one that will not entertain us.

There is certainly great joy in learning and often a deep comfort in the engagement with truth in both the text of holy Scripture and the created order. But God's ministry to us is often subtle. This means that some of the most significant things that God is teaching us are known only in retrospect. John of the Cross suggested that it is important that we remember that God often teaches us this way. He wrote, "God usually affirms, teaches, and promises many things, not so that there be an immediate understanding of them, but that afterwards at the proper time, or when the effect is produced, one may receive light about them."[3]

He then went on to note that this was the way of Christ with his own immediate disciples; he taught them many things they did not understand until much later (Jn 14:26). And so I am reminded that in travel as well as in reading, whether it is through formal learning in a sermon or a lecture or the "learning" that comes on the way in daily life, much that we come to know through the witness of the Spirit is learned over time. It is learned in retrospect (which is why there is such value in keeping a journal of our learning). Surely this is what was intended, at least in part, when the Gospel writer spoke of Mary as one who "treasured all these words and pondered them in her heart" (Lk 2:19). And surely this is a reminder to all of us that when we hear a sermon, the word of God to us may not be clear until much later. We are wise, then, not to insist on an immediate relevance or application but to learn to ponder and wait to see what God is saying to us through what we have seen, heard and encountered.

Most of all, we are reminded that we only listen, only attend to the Spirit when we come with open hearts and open hands before the truth; this is the posture of life-giving humility, the disposition that enables us to truly engage the Spirit of the Living God.

---

[3]John of the Cross, *The Ascent of Mount Carmel*, vol. 2 of *The Collected Works of St. John of the Cross*, trans. Kieran Kavanaugh and Otilio Rodriguez (Washington, D.C.: ICS, 1979), p. 170.

7

THE SPIRIT GUIDES IN
TIMES OF CHOICE

❧

We live with two simultaneous realities: first, the fact that we have the capacity to choose, and second, the fact that we long to choose *well*.[1] A person is a volitional being; we each have the power to choose, to alter the course of our own life and the lives of others. Our decisions make a difference.

The good news is that just as we can speak of an inner witness that assures us that we are loved, that convicts us of sin and that illumines our minds with truth, so we can also speak of an inner witness that guides us in times of choice. We choose, but in our choosing we are not alone. We have with us the presence of the Holy Spirit, who guides us in our decision making. To appreciate this aspect of the Spirit's ministry in our lives, we need to highlight the critical act of choosing.

CHOOSING WELL

We are not predetermined beings; we are choosing and acting beings. The glory of our human identity is that God has brought into being *persons*, and

---

[1]For a more complete study of this theme, some readers may wish to consult my earlier book on this subject, *Listening to God in Times of Choice: The Art of Discerning God's Will* (Downers Grove, Ill.: InterVarsity Press, 1997). It provides a model for decision making and discusses at more length the place of affect when we are discerning the Spirit in times of choice.

a person by definition is one who is capable of choosing.[2] And so we have throughout Scripture a reminder of this reality and its implications. "Choose this day whom you will serve" (Josh 24:15) is but one such example. It presupposes that our choices make a difference. We have the capacity to shape our future and that of others for good or for ill. God takes our decisions seriously, honoring our capacity to choose.

This would be a terrifying reality were it not for the complementary fact that God providentially cares for all and that we live under divine mercy. This does not excuse our misdeeds or mean that we take our decision making less seriously; it merely means that we do not need to fear the responsibility that comes with learning to choose well.

Choosing well is an art. But it is first of all a burden that is accepted. We cannot choose well unless we first, willingly and without bitterness, accept the reality that choices are a part of life and that we will not live in truth and freedom unless we act. Sometimes this means that we accept the reality of a Y in the road, a decision that is forced upon us. We can resent this or graciously accept it as part of life. We cannot go in both directions. And sometimes our choosing is a matter of courage. We choose even though no decision is forced upon us and the easier option would be to let the expectations and social inertia of our environment carry us along. But we choose, as an act of life and as an intentional response to the call of God on our lives.

We long to choose well, to accept that indeed this is *our* life and our responsibility. We want to act with integrity, in a way that is congruent with the particular call of God on our lives. We long to know when to act and when to wait, to know when our waiting is pathetic fatalism or procrastination and when it is an act of faith and patience. We long to know when to move forward and when to back off, when to sit still even though we would rather act and when to act when our inclination might be to wait.

We long to know when we are being called to respond to matters of

---

[2]I perhaps need to stress that the definition of a human being certainly includes more — much more — than this volitional definition, but it is the volitional component that I am highlighting here.

injustice or problems in the church or the workplace and when we are being called to pray, study and wait. And when we do act, we want to be confident that this is truly what we are called to do. We know, perhaps, of our own potential to take on too much or to act according to the expectations of others. We know, perhaps, that we are capable of doing things only to be noticed and long to act in a way that is not driven by misguided motives.

In other words, we know that our capacity to choose means that we are capable of choosing well and also of choosing poorly. We can make mistakes. Indeed there is no doubt we that have made poor decisions in the past and we will make poor decisions in the future. But this does not for a moment discount the need to learn how to choose well and responsibly, to make choices that as much as possible reflect what is best.

Those who learn how to choose well recognize a fundamental principle of life and of discernment—that good is not good enough. What we seek is the best, and the good is often the enemy of the best. Discernment means seeking the best in the face of competing options, all of which may be good in themselves but some of which are not the best to which we are called.

On any given day, or in any chapter of our lives, we are faced with innumerable ways in which we might invest our time. And they might all be good things to do. A Christian, then, recognizes that when faced with the alternatives of good and evil, there is no real choice; one *must* do the good. But the greater challenge comes when we are faced with multiple alternatives that are all morally good. The question then becomes, which is the good to which God is calling me? And the good then becomes the enemy of the best, since it is quite possible for us to fill our days doing good things but neglecting the one thing that we must do and to which we are called. Many, for example, neglect their personal prayers, or fail to give appropriate attention to their children, and excuse the error by claiming that they were doing other good things. But doing a good thing does not justify neglecting that which is central to our call. Both Mary and Martha were doing good things, but Mary was assured that she was doing what mattered most. It is not that Martha needed to leave the kitchen and join her sister; it was simply that she needed to do what she was doing.

Having used the Martha and Mary example, I should stress that we must beware of assuming that religious activities are always better than other kinds of activities. For example, for men to neglect their responsibilities as fathers and to defend this because they were doing religious work is simply unconscionable. We must always be alert to the temptation to turn from that which matters most and justify ourselves because we were doing something that we determined was good. Therefore, we are wise to be alert to those who appeal to the good as though this settles a debate. It may be good, but will it deflect us from what is best for us? And it is particularly important that we keep alert whenever religious activities and motivations are used to justify the good.

Many fail to embrace the best for a number of reasons—out of ignorance or fear, for example. And thus the grace we seek is the courage to go for the best, and this, of course, requires that we learn how to *discern* the best. Indeed St. Paul wrote, "This is my prayer, that your love may overflow more and more with knowledge and full insight to help you to *determine what is best*, so that in the day of Christ you may be pure and blameless" (Phil 1:9-10, emphasis added). In other words, what we seek is an *informed* love. We seek for our lives, and in our service for one another, not merely the good but the best. We are content with nothing less than doing what is right. It is not acceptable to us merely to do the good; we seek for ourselves and for one another that which reflects *all* that we are called to be.

Every choice is then both a yes and a no. If I marry this person, it means that I do not marry someone else. If I take on this assignment or this job, it means I say no to other opportunities. If I choose to spend my day in this way, it means I am saying no to other activities that might have filled my day. And surely this is what makes decision making a challenge: we cannot be everywhere and we cannot do everything. There are many good things that we might do, and we cannot do them all.

Again, this would be a terrifying and impossible burden were it not for the providential care of God. He is a God who is present and alive in all that is—the land, the sea and the sky—but also a God who is personally present to each one of us.

We are not alone! This is exceedingly good news. It is true for the whole of our lives, whether in joy or sorrow, whether in success or failure, and it is deeply and profoundly true when it comes to our decision making. When we make a choice, the Spirit is with us. Indeed we speak of God as Shepherd, that is, as one who guides (Ps 23). And we experience this guidance most keenly in our times of choosing.

Still, our decision making is our responsibility; it is our act of choosing in response to the options, problems and opportunities that are placed before us. God does not choose for us, and we cannot expect others to make our choices for us, not if we want to accept adult responsibility for our lives. Indeed, the capacity to discern well and make wise decisions is a critical sign of spiritual maturity. And further, it is something that we learn as we mature in faith and grow in wisdom. God is good and gracious and often keeps us from experiencing the full consequences of foolish choices. But this is no excuse for not learning to decide well. The whole tone of the New Testament suggests that it is imperative for us to grow in our capacity to discern. The author of the letter to the Hebrews chides the readers for their failure to mature as discerning people. By that time they should have been mature believers, able to discern. They should have been teachers and not merely infants in the faith (Heb 5:12-14).

Taking responsibility for our choices and decisions is part of becoming an adult and maturing in our faith. As noted, we are not alone, so when in our choosing we seek to be attentive to the Spirit, we are not escaping from the world or evading the act of choosing. Rather, recognizing our capacity to choose poorly, and longing to choose not only the good but the best, we approach our decision making with a posture of discernment. We seek to make our choices in a way that is informed by our personal encounter with Christ and the inner witness of the Spirit to our hearts. And what we find is that where the Spirit is, there is freedom, and thus choices and decisions lie before us not as burdens but as challenges and opportunities to grow in faith, hope and love. We can act with courage, grace and generosity.

The grace we seek is to discern and embrace the life to which we are called by God, to act with integrity, to see and appreciate how God is active in our world. Moreover, what we seek is not just awareness of the general way in which God is at work in the world but the specific way in which God is calling us to act. God's call on our lives is specific and unique. There is no set formula for our lives. Rather, as women and men in Christian community who live in active engagement with the Scriptures, we seek the best for our lives, particularly in the choices we make.

I would also add that we should each be able to speak with clarity in response to the question, how do you make decisions? There should be, for each of us, a self-conscious awareness of how we work our way through the choices that will inevitably come our way. And we should be able to speak about this with others, particularly those who care about us or are affected by the choices we are making. Even though we speak of decision making in the same breath as discernment, and even though we recognize the presence of the Spirit of God in our choosing, this act is never so mysterious that we cannot speak with clarity of how we make decisions.

Something else needs to be stressed in this regard. In what follows I wish to address the act of decision making in response to the prompting of the Spirit. I write this in the consciousness that we make a multitude of decisions, ranging from big, once-in-a-lifetime choices to ordinary, day-to-day choices. What we need are some helpful guidelines for choosing well. However, it is important to highlight that this reflection on decision making has application not only to the life-altering choices of our lives but also to the fundamental way in which we go about our daily lives. We make decisions constantly, daily and weekly. Making choices is part of the fabric of life, a part of being human at work and in relationships. The capacity to make choices is therefore inherent to the capacity to live. If we cannot choose well, we cannot live well.

Since decision making is so much a part of the fabric of life, we need to see that our greatest need is not so much that we would learn guidelines to make the big decisions of life as that we would cultivate a context—a pattern of life, work and relationships—that is conducive to good decision making. Rather, we need to foster an orientation of life that enables us to choose well. We do not want merely to discern in times of choice; we seek to become discerning women and men. Having said this, it is most helpful to think about the patterns of our lives by using our decision making as a lens through which we consider the whole.

THE POWER OF INTENTIONALITY

God is fully present to us in our times of decision, but we will learn to appropriate this reality and respond to the inner witness in times of choice only if we learn, in turn, to be present to God. And this requires that we be intentional, not impulsive. We can learn not to trust the moment or what feels good or right but rather approach our decisions with thoughtfulness. Good decision making is the fruit of a choice that is well considered.

Wise Christians are not impressed by the common notion that spontaneity is more life giving, more fun or a greater reflection of the presence of the Spirit in our lives. To the contrary, they recognize that the Spirit is very much present to us, but that we cannot trust the impulses of our hearts. We cannot trust spontaneity but must be discerning.

There are, of course, times when we just need to go with the impulse of the moment. On the spur of the moment we may buy flowers for a loved one or say yes when invited to dinner. Sometimes we should just do what strikes us as a good thing to do! But when it comes to the decisions that shape the contours of our lives, we are wise to pause and consider the implications of our choices. And this means, more than anything, that we learn to interpret the movements of our heart.

As much as with any other dimension of the Spirit's witness, effective decision making and discernment require the engagement of both heart and mind. Discernment requires attentiveness to what we see and observe as well as to what is happening to us emotionally. Our capacity to discern is not merely a matter of rational analysis of our environment and of the strengths and limitations of a particular situation; it is also an intuitive response that is informed by our encounter with Christ and by our own emotional response to the world and to Christ.

We choose purposefully. Wise people recognize the foolishness of impulsiveness, but they also recognize that there are times in which a choice *must* be made. They are alert to inclinations toward procrastination and refuse to rationalize delays in choosing. Furthermore, they know that life includes change and that both wisdom and courage are called for when we respond to the inevitable changes that come our way, whether at home or at work. Changes in our environment and our circumstances are but another way in which we are called to choose. The issue becomes one of intentionality.

Part of the reason why intentionality is so crucial is that our lives are messy and complicated. The choices we need to make are also complicated and, as often as not, colored by our own emotional turmoil as we are torn between alternatives or confused about what we are feeling and thinking and what we really want. Often we are alert to the ways in which we might disappoint others or let them down, and so this emotional content clouds the choice and, seemingly, undermines our capacity to choose well. Intentionality in decision making enables us to see through the complexity and find clarity, purpose and hope. This does not ever mean that all the inner turmoil of our hearts is eased or that all ambiguity in life is erased. But it does mean that we are able to say, with simple confidence, that we know as well as anyone can know that this is what God is calling us to do.

Intentionality in decision making requires that we are attentive on two levels: first, that we use our minds to understand the issues at hand, and second, that we attend to what is happening to us emotionally.

Understanding the issues and the decision to be made. A decision is a choice that determines what course (if any) we will take or what practice we will adopt in response to the particular circumstances we face. As such, it is a conclusion that shapes how we will think about the past, the present

or a future situation. It is a judgment about reality, about facts as we perceive them. This judgment comes through assessing alternatives in anticipation of potential consequences. Therefore, effective decision making
requires that we are clear about what is happening around us. It means using our heads to understand our options, our potential problems, the issues
as they present themselves and the resources available to us (if the consideration of resources is pertinent to the decision we are making).

There is nothing in the history of Christian spirituality to suggest that in
discernment we do not use our minds. To the contrary, a basic assumption
in discernment is that God speaks into the particularity of our lives. Consequently we will be able to hear God only if we are alert to those particularities. And thus we do not serve others well when they are facing a critical
choice and we say to them, "Just pray about it and God will show you the
way." This is unnecessarily burdensome and, frankly, not helpful. Good decision making and discernment require that we be alert to circumstances.

Accordingly, one of the most basic elements of decision making is that
we frame our decision well.[3] This requires at least two things.

First, we must do all we can to understand our circumstances. We need
to be sure of our options, recognizing our potential difficulties and obstacles (honestly, without romanticizing one alternative over the other) as we
consider the options in the light of our resources as well as our limitations.
Further, the better we know ourselves, the greater the possibility that we
will be able to choose well. The more illusions we have about ourselves, the
greater the chance that we will not choose well.

Second, framing the decision well requires that the issue at hand be
made as simple as possible. The decision itself may be a very complicated
matter, but we cannot choose well within the complications of our life situation unless we find some measure of simplicity. Simplicity is a matter of

---

[3]I am not addressing all decision making here but rather those decisions that shape the contours of our lives—what might be called "basic" decisions. In this respect I am following a
helpful distinction that Tad Dunne made between basic and instrumental decisions in *Spiritual Mentoring: Guiding People Through Spiritual Exercises to Life Decisions* (San Francisco: HarperSanFrancisco, 1991), p. 167.

removing the clutter, setting aside all that is not essential to the decision at hand. In this regard, I recommend the following steps.

1. We should frame the decision at hand as a clear yes-or-no choice between two alternatives. This is because, if we are faced with more than two alternatives, we will as often as not find that the issue is too complex for us to effectively consider it.

In my own experience, for example, I have found that I cannot effectively choose between whether I should stay at my current place of work or accept an offer of employment elsewhere. This is too complicated. I must first decide if it is time for me to move on. If I decide it is not the right time, then there is nothing else to consider. But if it is time for me to move on, I will first make that choice and then consider what I should do next.

2. We should subdivide complex decisions into manageable choices. What needs to be decided first? Is there one decision that sets the tone for everything else that is before us? Where can we begin to choose, even if we do not resolve all the issues right away?

We can subdivide a complex decision, for example, by making a distinction between *what* we are to do and *when* we are to do it. Often when these two qualifiers are confused, decision making is overly complicated and difficult. I may discern, for example, that God is calling me to resign from my place of work, but then, as a separate act of discernment, I can ask the Lord for clarity about *when* I should resign.

When David was anointed king of Israel, he surely discerned that this was what he was supposed to do. However, David did not assume the throne until it was given to him, after a delay of many years. What this biblical example teaches us is that God often grants us a vision or an idea or a conviction that something is to happen. But then we need to discern and wait with patience. Our eagerness for something to happen may not correspond with the timing of God.

Further, it is important to stress that God leads us one step at a time. We are not being asked to decide what we will do with the rest of our lives but only to discern what God is calling us to do in the following stage of life.

We make the choice unnecessarily complicated when we overstate the significance of the decision. When it comes to marriage, we are certainly deciding "until death do us part." But on just about everything else, we are not making a lifelong commitment; we are merely seeking to discern what God is calling us to do next.

3. We should frame the decision as something over which we have genuine influence. The choice must be something about which we can properly decide and that does not depend on what others do. We can take responsibility only for our own actions and reactions and not the actions and reactions of others. We can only ask, what is God calling *me* to do in this situation, quite apart from what others do or how others respond?

For example, if I am considering marriage to someone, I cannot properly choose if we should marry; there is someone else who has a say in this! Rather, what I can do is decide if I will make a proposal of marriage. This then frees the other, to whom I might make this proposal, to choose as well and to discern if it is right for her to accept my offer of marriage.

To discern well, we need to think clearly and carefully. Once we have framed our decision, we are in a position to consider how the Spirit of God might be prompting our heart in response to the choice that lies before us.

Attentive to the presence of desolation. As with each dimension of the Spirit's witness to our hearts, we know the voice of Jesus by attending to what is happening to us emotionally. And it is at this point that the classic spiritual wisdom of the *Spiritual Exercises* of Ignatius Loyola is so pertinent. The *Exercises* were developed specifically as a means to help individuals make a choice, to align their lives with the purposes of God for them. This resource has great relevance as we explore this dimension of the Spirit's inner witness.

In the "rules of discernment" that are summarized in the *Exercises*, we are reminded that our emotions are generally of two kinds: desolation and consolation. These are rich terms that capture a whole range of emotional response.

Simply put, *desolation* is an emotional response to the multiple ways in which we experience a broken world. We usually experience desolation as a negative range of emotions, including anger, fear, mourning and discouragement. Sometimes our reactions are self-indulgent and hardly reasonable. We are irritable and impatient and easily angered. Or we are consumed with a worry that has been fueled by our unwillingness to accept the peace of God in our hearts. However, our desolation may be a true and authentic response to injustice, disappointment or loss. After all, we do live in a broken world. An authentic Christian response to the world means that we feel its pain. And sometimes that pain intersects our lives.

In contrast, *consolation* is our emotional response to a set of circumstances that reflect the power and goodness of God. Whether it is the joy of the sunrise, the satisfaction of a job well done or the pleasure that comes in human friendship, consolation speaks of our experience of joy and peace, consciously or unconsciously, in response to the rightful rule of Christ in our world.

As a fundamental rule of discernment, the *Spiritual Exercises* urge us to act on a decision only in consolation. Conversely, if our hearts are in desolation, we do not act, for then we cannot trust ourselves to act rightly and truthfully. And thus our best course of action is either to wait or to continue in a previous decision that we made in consolation.

Few things are so basic to the act of discernment as the resolve that we will respect the presence of desolation in our lives, regardless of how reasonable or unreasonable that desolation may be. We may be profoundly angry as a result of a deep injustice we have experienced. The anger may be quite legitimate. However, it remains as a basic rule of discernment that we must not make a decision at that point, acting out of our anger. We must only act in consolation.

The emotional posture of consolation is crucial in making a choice because we can trust ourselves and act in confidence only when we know that our hearts are in tune with the Spirit. Or to put it differently, we can choose well only when we choose from a fundamental posture of faith and trust in God. If we are in a posture of faith or trust, if we are in tune with the Spirit, it follows that our emotional disposition is one of peace and joy. We can choose well only when peace rules in our hearts (Col 3:15). When we are in desolation—discouraged or angry, fearful or discontented—we cannot trust ourselves to act well. Even if we choose to do the right thing, we are in danger of doing it the wrong way or of doing it prematurely. It will be an action that arises out of our fear or anger; it will not be an action that is informed and energized by joy.

Again, I must stress that desolation may be the right response to something that one has experienced. We may well feel desolation because we see the world as God sees the world. We may rightly feel the full force of anger when we encounter a major expression of injustice. Yet, however justifiable our anger might be, it is not the emotional terrain on which we can stand when are seeking to choose well.

Consider four different emotional responses to our world. Each may be, and often is, a legitimate response, but none is an emotional posture from which we can choose in confidence.

We may experience anger, the emotional response to injustice committed against us or against those whom we hold dear or against that which is true and good.[4] When anger is justified, we are urged in Scripture not to lose our tempers and to appreciate that anger is not something from which righteousness will come (Jas 1:19-20). We are not to sin in our anger and not to let the sun go down on our anger (Eph 4:26). The great danger, if we hold on to our anger, is that there is no longer a one-to-one connection between our anger and our circumstances. Instead we become angry people, with anger and bitterness, not joy, as the fundamental disposition of our hearts.

We cannot trust ourselves in anger, for anger distorts our thinking and taints our whole emotional response to our circumstances. We cannot live (and choose and act) from anger. Rather, we act in faith and in tune with the Spirit when we learn to let go of the anger, leave it with God and accept

---

[4]Many of us are too easily angered. Yet in the case of others, one wonders if they do not need to learn how to be angry. If nothing makes a person angry, maybe this person needs to reconsider the multiple ways in which our world is broken and people are used and misused.

the consolation and peace of God. This is easier said than done, of course. But it is no less necessary. When we act in anger, we cannot be sure that we are acting in truth and freedom.

Consider also the emotional response of fear. Fear is the emotional response to a threat against ourselves or against those we care for. Again, fear may be understandable and appropriate if we are threatened, though it is also true that many live with a perpetual fear and worry and have lost a sense of connection with actual peril. Yes, fear is the natural expression of our vulnerability as creatures living in a broken world. Yet if our emotional disposition is one of fear, we cannot be confident we are choosing and acting in faith. Only as we observe the call to "not worry about anything" but to respond to God with prayers of intercession and thanksgiving, and receive God's peace, can we begin to act with integrity and freedom (Phil 4:6-7). The fear may be legitimate and make sense, but we cannot choose from a posture of fear.

Two other examples of desolation are discouragement and mourning. Each is an entirely understandable emotional response to setback and disappointment. But if we act out of discouragement, we are not acting in faith and hope. We are not in tune with the Spirit. And if our heart is filled with the pain of mourning, our heaviness of heart coincides with what we have experienced, but it is still not an emotional disposition from which we can act in freedom.

One way to think about the need to act only in consolation is to compare it to the ancient ways of navigation at sea, when sailors were dependent on the stars to guide them across vast unmarked stretches of ocean, using the science of nautical astronomy. On a clear night sailors would accurately fix their position using the stars, then use their best measures of course and speed to keep track of their position by "dead reckoning," sometimes for several days and through cloudy or stormy nights when no stars were in view. There was nothing wrong with a cloudy night; sailors simply knew that they could not get their bearings on such a night. And so they continued to reckon based on what they had established on clear nights. In similar fashion, Ignatius suggested that this rule of discernment calls us to stay the course in desolation, to "remain firm and constant in a resolution and decision which guided us the day before the desolation, or in the decision to which we adhered in the preceding consolation."[5]

Desolation will come. We should assume it will be part of our experience. We will no doubt experience the pain of loss and the ache of mourning, whether the loss of a loved one at death or a lost opportunity or a farewell to a family member or friend. An expression of grief or sorrow is possibly the right and true response to an experience of loss. We are even urged to mourn with those who mourn. However, the emotional response of mourning is a posture that is aligned with the brokenness of the world; it is not the emotional posture of faith. It is necessary to mourn our losses, but we are not wise to choose or act from the disposition of a mourner, any more than an ancient sailor would try to get the ship's bearings on a cloudy night. We must, if we are wise, learn to act out of joy. And even as our heart remains in a cloud of pain and loss, we need to be aware of our mourning and, as it passes, to act only as we can confidently say that we are choosing in consolation.

Naturally, this simple rule of discernment—do not decide or act out of desolation—raises many questions. For some, it raises a theological question: Why do we experience desolation? In some respects this is part of the dilemma of evil and our experience of pain in this world. For our purposes here, it is important to stress that God does allow suffering and that as Christians we are not preserved from pain but are actually called by God to experience with Christ the brokenness of the world. We suffer with the Lord because we are heirs with him (Rom 8:17).

It must be acknowledged, though, that we are often prone to overstate the extent of our pain and suffering. We must be alert to our self-indulgent propensity to bemoan our situation, when in fact we may be doing quite well. Sometimes our desolation is nothing more than the feeling of frustration we have when we are held up in traffic or did not get our way at the

---

[5]Ignatius Loyola, *The Spiritual Exercises of St. Ignatius*, trans. Louis J. Puhl (Chicago: Loyola University Press, 1975), para. 318.

office or were irritated by someone coming to the door on a marketing campaign. We need to be aware of our reactions and not give in to them or allow self-pity to cloud our hearts and rob us of joy. In other words, sometimes our desolation has little to do with our experience of a broken world and much to do with wanting others to feel sorry for us. And even when the pain we feel is clearly not something petty or self-indulgent, we must be alert to any propensity we might have to stew in our desolation rather than accept into our hearts the peace of God—a peace he so longs to grant us.

While some wonder about the theological issues arising from the presence of desolation, for others this rule of discernment raises an obvious practical question: What about urgent decisions? This is an especially important question if desolation persists. Life is filled with all kinds of decisions and questions and, some people insist, it is unreasonable to wait for consolation.

Several things could be noted in response. First, it is often the case that we overstate the urgency of our decisions. Our pressure to respond to a situation may actually be nothing but our desire to meet another's expectations or the propensity to hurriedly seek the comfort of closure in a decision. We need to realize that some things are not resolved easily or quickly. We live in a social environment that often demands resolution when there is simply nothing to be gained by such haste. We need to be able to slow down and assure ourselves and others that we will address the issue at hand. We will not delay, but neither will we be rushed into a response. And sometimes our feeling of urgency does not correspond to the facts. We have the time we need to choose well.

Second, when we are feeling pressed to make a decision under duress, this is precisely when we most need time and space to choose well. And so, when there is urgency, we can develop the ability to cancel an appointment, clear some time in our daily routine, find a quiet space where we will not be interrupted and come to some clarity about what is happening to us emotionally.

And third, when desolation persists, it is sometimes helpful to make a preliminary decision as a way of buying time. For example, perhaps you have had a car accident and you know that you are simply not in a good frame of mind to go shopping for a replacement vehicle. One alternative is to rent or borrow a car for the meantime, until you can find some time to make this choice in peace and not out of the frustration over losing a car.

For others, the questions that arise about desolation are more psychological. They ask, what about the person who is in depression (a kind of perpetual desolation)? Even for those who are not depressed per se but whose desolation persists, the question naturally arises as to whether this rule of discernment is reasonable.

Here is where it is imperative that we be in discussion with a good counselor or spiritual friend or guide, ideally someone who can help us process our emotional circumstances and begin to address the cause of our desolation. In the meantime we can act in a way that is congruent with whatever measure of peace we *have* been given.

What then do we do in response to desolation? First, as noted above, we must respect the presence of desolation in our hearts. Nothing is gained and much harm can result from a denial of desolation, whether anger, fear, mourning or discouragement. This does not mean that we announce to the world that we are in sackcloth and ashes, but it does mean that we know ourselves well enough that we recognize when we are in desolation. And we respect that desolation; we take it seriously.

Second, it is important to identify as much as possible the source of our desolation. If our desolation is due to physical fatigue, then we must find time for rest and personal renewal. If the desolation is due to unresolved anger or discouragement or persistent fears, we can choose an intentional course of action that takes seriously what we are feeling but also appreciates that we do not want to remain there. And if our desolation is due to the neglect of our routines and spiritual disciplines, we can turn and seek once more to live in a manner that is congruent with our conscience.

And third, it is important that we learn to wait. In response to the presence of desolation, we can choose to lie low, to recognize that haste can only hurt us and others. One benefit of waiting is that we allow the desolation to teach us about ourselves. If we are in anger, it may tell us something about what matters to us, what we are prepared to contend for. It can also tell us that we are too easily irritated or resentful. Mourning is always an important time of reflection. All loss is but a "small death," as I once heard it put, and so we are wise to slow down, to be attentive to our hearts and to see and feel in truth. And discouragement for many is an opportunity to come to terms with disillusionment—to face up to the fact of their illusion and to put their hope, once more, not in their own dreams and aspirations but in Christ and his work in the world.

Desolation can be humbling. It is a reminder that the joy we experience in this world is all gift. But on the other, it is also humbling that desolation frequently illumines or discloses more of ourselves, something about our character that we might not otherwise notice—our vulnerability, our pride, the weakness of our faith and our need for spiritual growth. And consistently we find that desolation teaches us patience. In other words, desolation is not wasted time. It is, rather, an honest experience that merits our attention and respect.

However, the bottom line remains the same: we are wise if we do not choose or act in desolation. We never so respect it that we choose to stay there. Rather, we respect desolation because we long that our hearts would once more be ruled by peace and that we would know the joy that is the fruit of the Spirit's presence in our lives. We choose to walk in faith.

This walking by faith is, then, the crucial issue. As long as we are fully engaged with our world, we will always experience both joy and sorrow. Indeed when St. Paul wrote in 2 Corinthians 7:4 that he was "overjoyed in all [his] affliction," he was highlighting this very tension: we engage our world and feel its pain, but we are also people of the resurrection. However, though our lot is always one of both joy and sorrow, we must still insist that not all reality is equally influential in the shaping of our affective dispositions. While we respond with integrity to both the fragmented character of our world and to the reality of our hope in Jesus Christ, one of these has the final word. One of these will ultimately determines where our hearts rest. The last word is not Good Friday but Easter.

When Christians ignore Good Friday and just want to celebrate Easter, they miss the reality of a fragmented world and the cost of our redemption. But while we must face the horror of Good Friday and the broken character of our world, that is not where we camp. Our worship, Sunday after Sunday, locates our hearts in a different reality, a different sphere of existence. We confess faith in a risen Lord. And this is what, in the end, matters to us most and what captures our hearts.

DISCERNMENT

The rule of discernment that says we should not choose in desolation is complemented by a second: consolation must be tested. We are called to consider what we are experiencing. We are naive if we think that the peace and joy we experience necessarily means that we are walking in faith and aligned with the Spirit.

While we can only choose in consolation, we must test the consolation and ascertain if it is indeed genuine and truly a reflection of the Spirit's presence in our lives. Evil can masquerade as a spirit of light. And sometimes we need to frankly acknowledge that it is not so much an angel of darkness as our own misguided longings that have produced a sense of peace. Our feeling of satisfaction or well-being may not be rooted in the good, the noble, the true and the excellent (Phil 4:8).

Thus we must not be naive. This is not merely a matter of discerning whether one should buy a luxury car or a second house overlooking the sea. As Ignatius reminded those who read the *Exercises*, it is most critical that we become discerning when religious motives and aspirations are present. We can easily proclaim our desire to feed the poor or solve an organization's problems or provide care. We can truly want to do something that is good. But is this the good to which we are being called? Just because people say they have great peace and feel called to serve in some sacrificial way does not necessarily mean that God is in it.

All of this is but a reminder that logic is never in itself a trustworthy method of choosing well. We always need to test the movements of our hearts for what is happening to us emotionally. We must, then, ask straightforward and honest questions that probe our emotional responses to the issues that are before us. In part, this is a recognition that we never choose just because we feel like it. The great danger is that we would be guided by anger or resentment or jealousy (acting in desolation) or that we would choose out of some romantic or sentimental idealism, such as those who choose to respond to the call for religious or missionary service after the singing of a rousing hymn of faith.

We must be discerning. It has been my experience that one of the most beneficial ways of testing the peace we feel is by asking some honest questions that enable us to clarify our motives. The reason we test the peace is that we cannot assume that our motives are truly aligned with the life of God. It follows that we need to cultivate the spiritual practice of intentional self-appraisal in which we face the following questions openly and seriously, not as an irritating or discouraging block to our aspirations but as something that enables us to be honest with ourselves and foster our capacity to live in truth and freedom.[6]

The question of wealth and pleasure. We can ask ourselves, does this peace and joy I am experiencing arise out of a desire for wealth and pleasure? In order to answer this truly, we need to understand the character of the temptation to pursue wealth and pleasure.

When the human community was created, God established the earth as a kind of garden of delight and enjoyment. We were created to enjoy God, and most certainly we were also designed to enjoy the natural world in all its beauty and wonder. However, this perfectly good arrangement has been twisted by evil. The temptation we consistently face suggests that we will be happier and have more pleasure, joy and peace if we have more wealth. In other words, we are tempted to think that we will be happier if more of the

---

[6]The questions are one way of framing the three temptations that Jesus encountered in the desert immediately following his baptism (see Mt 4:1-11).

created world is in our possession, whether in the form of property, a bank account, a quantity of goods or more leisure time. But the Christian community has always recognized that this is a lie.

There is not more joy, or pleasure even, in more wealth. Wealthier people are not happier people. In this regard I particularly enjoy the unique biography of St. Francis of Assisi by G. K. Chesterton. What is striking about this book is that it shows us an individual of deep joy and contentment, with a childlike delight in life, writing about another such person. As I read it, I have the impression that the second happiest person I have ever encountered (Chesterton) was writing about the happiest man who ever lived (St. Francis)! Chesterton stressed that if you were to ask St. Francis why he was so happy, he would answer that he owned nothing and so could enjoy everything![7]

St. Francis stands over every culture and generation and urges us to see the lie that we so easily believe—the lie that if we have more money we will be content and have more joy. He calls us to appreciate the power and grace of simplicity, that is, the freedom that comes in contentment and thanksgiving. Joy comes in simple pleasures and routines and the satisfaction we find in enjoying that which we do not necessarily own.

We are reminded that we must be alert to our rationalizations and that so easily the peace and joy we might experience in a time of choice is really rooted in the longing for wealth and a desire for more money.

The question of honor and recognition. Second, it is important that we ask whether the peace or joy we experience arises from the desire for honor and recognition. As with the first question, here too it would seem that we cannot appreciate the force of the question and the temptation that emerges from it unless we do so in the light of the creation.

When the human community was created, we were each created in the image of God. And as created beings, we naturally—as something built into

---

[7]G. K. Chesterton, *St. Francis of Assisi* (1924; reprint, New York: Doubleday, 1957). One expression of this spiritual posture is captured in Chesterton's line (reflecting on St. Francis) in which he said, "Blessed is he that expecteth nothing, for he shall enjoy everything" (p. 75).

our psyches—have a longing to be recognized and affirmed by the One who created us. We long to know God and for God to know us. We have a legitimate desire for a sense that God sees us and appreciates who we are and what we contribute to creation and to Christ's reign in the world. However, this legitimate longing is also twisted by evil, and so we need to be vigilant and alert to what is happening in our own hearts.

That which in its original form was good and true, a holy and needful aspiration, has gone awry. We are allured into thinking that if we have more honor and more recognition, we will have more significance. We long that many people (the more, the better) would affirm us and -what is even better—praise us. And we can easily get caught up in doing things to be noticed, choosing a course of action because we think it has the potential for securing us more recognition, honor and fame.

The "glory" of this recognition is misleading, for often God calls us to a work that is done in obscurity. In truth, every line of work has within it something that grants to that work its integrity but that is likely known only to the one who does it. Quality work is done ultimately not for others but for God and for oneself. We learn to take joy in a job well done quite apart from any level of recognition we might or might not receive.

So when choices and decisions are before us, we must ask, is this peace driven by the longing to have others praise and affirm us?

The question of power and influence. Then, of course, there is the third question: is this consolation rooted in the desire for power and influence? And here too it is helpful to appeal to the act of our creation.

One of the wonders of our human identity is captured in the opening chapters of Genesis where we read that the first couple were given work to do. They were assigned the task of tilling the garden and naming the animals (Gen 2). At first reading this might seem straightforward and simple, but we must realize that in these activities God invited the human community to act in a way that has extraordinary significance.

The act of tilling the earth speaks of altering the landscape, of shaping the contours of God's creation, of domesticating the earth and enabling it to bring forth fruit, resulting in culture and beauty. And the act of naming the animals is the parallel task that demonstrates authority in stewardship of the wonder of God's creation (a stewardship, of course, that is authentic only if it is responsible and does not selfishly exploit the earth). God has granted real power to the human being—the capacity to make things and to change the way things are. It is an ability that can be used for good or for ill. It is a capacity to make a difference.

Deep within the human psyche is this longing to make a difference, altering the contours of our world in such a way that as a result of our efforts there is more peace, more justice, more goodness than when we first arrived on the scene. We hope that the church can be a better place, and the world can be a better place, because we have contributed in some way to the reign of Christ. And the lie of evil is that if we are going to make a difference, then we need power, and the more power we have, the more we can potentially make a difference. The more power, the more significance to our lives. The more power, the more capacity to influence what happens in the church, in the world, in the workplace, wherever.

And so we read that two of the disciples came to Jesus and asked to sit on his right hand and his left (Mk 10:37-45). In the ancient world this request represented a desire to assume with Jesus the positions of authority in his kingdom. We might be inclined to be hard on these two disciples and wonder about their aspirations to glory. It is likely, however, that what lay behind their request was nothing more than a simple desire to make a difference with and for Christ. And naturally they asked for the power that they thought would make this possible.

It is interesting that Jesus did not scold them for their request. He just showed them that their pursuits were misguided. Indeed he affirmed their desire for greatness, that is, for making a difference. But he turned the lie of evil on its head and declared that greatness is found through service: "Whoever wishes to become great among you must be your servant" (Mk 10:43).

A contemporary term that captures this principle well is *empowerment.* We recognize that power does enable us to make a difference. Yet the wonder of Jesus' words is that those who make a difference are those who have learned to give power away, to serve in such a way that others are enabled through that service to be all they are called to be. In other words, the genius of making a difference in our world is not through the exercise of power, and even less through the accumulation of power, but through the empowerment of others. We make a difference through service.

And so when we feel peace or consolation, it is imperative that we consider the source of our peace to see if what we feel arises from a desire for power or if the energy that motivates us is the desire for service, the willingness and the longing to empower others.

Each of these questions is essentially just another way to ask about the fundamental orientation of our hearts. The issue came up when Peter met the risen Jesus by the seashore and Jesus asked him, "Do you love me more than these?" (Jn 21:15). And it is surely what lay behind the statement of Jesus in the Sermon on the Mount when he urged his hearers to "strive first for the kingdom of God" with the assurance that follows, that "all these things will be given to you as well" (Mt 6:33). And in Romans 12 we find that familiar progression from clarity of commitment to clarity of perspective when the apostle Paul first urged his readers to present themselves to God as a living sacrifice with the assurance that as their minds would be renewed they would be able to "discern what is the will of God" (Rom 12:1-2).

So we test our peace of mind by an honest consideration of the posture and orientation of our hearts. And if we are genuinely open to the Spirit, we will find that we grow in our capacity to recognize our own propensities and capacity for self-deception.

Do we ever have pure motives? Not likely. Not in this life, anyway. But as we practice the art of discernment, we can grow in our ability to recognize what is driving us, and how our fears and misguided aspirations can so easily derail us. We can learn enough about ourselves that we are able to act in a manner that gives us enough confidence that misguided motives are *not* the sustaining energy of our lives. Even when we are confident that we are to move ahead in a decision, we hold our resolution with modesty, will-

ing to be challenged by others, never presuming that we have a unique insight into the will of God.

Humility is critical. The *Spiritual Exercises* include a word that ex-
presses the hope of humility for which we long: *indifference*. Holy indifference is not apathy; it is rather the inner posture of freedom, where we are
able to say and feel that we are open to whatever God wills. If God gives
wealth, this is good. If God withholds wealth, this too is good. If God grants
us the position for which we have applied, that is good. If God grants it to
another, this is good as well. We are indifferent. It is not that we do not care,
but we have chosen to place our hopes and longings in God, and come
what may, we will be content with how God provides. It also means that we
will trust God to do his work in his time.

Does this sound like too high or unreasonable an ideal? It may sound
as such at first. However, the humility of indifference is so fundamental to
authentic spiritual life that we must come back to it and call one another
to it as often as we can. And what we find, of course, is that this is the way
of freedom.[8]

One of the key signs of humility is our willingness to have others speak
to the decision we are making. We must be alert to the inclination within
us that would bristle when anyone challenges what we think is right or what
we have concluded God is saying to us. True humility presumes that we
cannot discern well unless we allow others to challenge us, differ with us
and ask us to rethink our conclusions. If someone told me that, though everyone else disagreed with him, he was confident that God was calling him
to do something, I would urge him to rethink his position or conviction. We
must be willing to enter into conversation with others and test with them
our impressions, our aspirations, our sense of what God is saying.

We do so precisely because we know we are easily self-deceived. All of
us. And so it is imperative that in humble recognition of this we allow oth-

---

[8]Ignatius Loyola, in the *Spiritual Exercises*, suggested that when we are contemplating a
choice, we should imagine ourselves at the Last Day, standing in the presence of the One
who will judge us and our actions (para. 187).

ers—spouse, friends, colleagues, perhaps our pastor or spiritual guide—to call us to wait, to rethink our inclination to act in a particular way, to check and if necessary recheck our motives. It is perilous for a person to be convinced she knows the will of God while also assuming that anyone who questions her is misguided or not as sensitive as she to the presence of the Spirit. When pastors or religious leaders take this stance, they forfeit their capacity to lead; they have assumed a posture that is antithetical to true spirituality and discernment.

Truly discerning persons have an inner confidence that God loves them and guides them. And this confidence is matched by a humility reflected in a willingness to listen to and learn from others. We can never presume to know the voice of Jesus on our own. We are all on a road together, trying to make sense of the longings and aspirations of our hearts. We have a deep need for one another along the way.

When We Do Not Decide

In this discussion about choices, it is important to recognize that the failure to choose is itself a decision. When people procrastinate, we tend to think they are struggling to *make* a decision, and there is truth in this. Except that by not choosing, they *have* chosen. They have chosen not to act. They have chosen to wait, perhaps, but they have chosen. Therefore, it is helpful to know ourselves well enough to recognize any propensity we might have toward procrastination and, as we are able, to be alert to the cause or reason for this inclination. If we are truly in a waiting mode and are at peace in our waiting, that's good. But we need to recognize when we are actually procrastinating, when for whatever reason (perfectionism, a poor self-image, the fear of responsibility or whatever it might be) we are refraining from choosing and acting in consolation.

Part of knowing ourselves includes appreciating what might lie behind our tendency toward procrastination so that we can acknowledge when it is happening. Sometimes we might procrastinate because we are comfortable with the status quo and cannot contemplate a change even though it would clearly be the best thing if we would, with courage, embrace something new that we ought to be doing. In other words, to procrastinate is to choose, but it is to choose either in desolation or in false consolation.

Carlos G. Valles has suggested that one sign of procrastination is the propensity of many to work with impending deadlines. They get into the habit of doing things at the last moment, and consequently they miss doing things at the right time. In other words, the right time to do something may have little to do with an actual deadline. He said, "Each decision has its own timing, its own dawn, its own place in the stars, and that has to be sensed, respected, obeyed. Never trespass on the rhythm of life."[9] He went on to note that students are always interested in the last possible date on which to submit their assignments, not the first possible date! They think in terms of how late they can submit an assignment rather than how early, and this means that they rarely do something at its appropriate time in their lives.

We need deadlines, certainly, but when these markers are the primary criteria for when we will do something, it necessarily means that we have lost the power to act well and to do something at a good time. And often this means that we procrastinate and do something at the last possible moment or make our choices at the last possible moment, if at all. By procrastinating, we have undermined our capacity to choose well.

The same principle applies when people refuse to act because they insist they cannot, that they are victims of forces or persons they cannot challenge, whether these are political or economic factors or individuals who exercise authority in their lives. One will hear people speak of the power of the administration within an organization or of political and economic forces that they say tie their hands. For others, it will be a deeply held conviction that they cannot act because they are living with the consequences of the choices of others. They see their lives as stifled by what has happened to them.

While we must not be naive about the organizational, political and eco-

---

9Carlos G. Valles, S.J., *The Art of Choosing* (New York: Doubleday, 1986), p. 17.

nomic factors that shape our lives, or about the consequences in our lives of the actions of others, it is essential that we develop the capacity to choose within those limitations. And whether we choose to resign or stay, to leave or seek change from within the organization, hopefully we can see how what we are saying and doing comes in response to the presence of the Spirit in our lives. Discerning people refuse to be victims, refuse to be objects of fate and instead choose, within the circumstances (however difficult) in which they find themselves, to seek to know how God is calling them to act.

Then also, some do not decide, or they discount the significance of their choice, because they feel caught in what they consider are two or more less than desirable alternatives. They refuse to vote in an election because none of the candidates is, in their minds, worthy of their vote. Or they do not accept a job offer because they are still waiting for the perfect job. Or they do not marry because "the right person" never seems to materialize. Or they never enroll in a program of study because they cannot find what they think to be the perfect school or course or professor. And then, even if they do (finally) make a choice, in a sense they have not really chosen it because they have not really embraced their decision. For example, if they finally do accept a job—because they need to pay the rent—they do not really *choose* that job but continue to be conscious of the multiple ways in which it is not the job they had hoped for . . . or the person they had dreamed of marrying . . . or the curriculum they had hoped they could follow in their studies . . . or the candidate they had hoped to be able to vote for.

But life is always filled with imperfections and ambiguities. We are always called to discern "the best" within the limitations and imperfections that characterize our lives and our world. Waiting for a perfect candidate, job, spouse or curriculum is useless and tiresome. And having once acted, we gain nothing if we are constantly complaining that our choice was not what we had really hoped for. This is but a subtle form of not choosing, for we have not embraced that which we have been given.

In the end, though, we are often placed in circumstances in which we need to wait—and wait patiently—for God to act. The process of decision making and discernment never obligates God. God will act in good time; we cannot force the hand of God. Neither do we ever put God in our debt. He can and does at times remain silent—a silence that is no doubt perplexing. But if we are patient, he always comes through. God is there, and his providential care is something upon which we can depend. If there is silence from heaven, we can be confident that it is only for a season. And in time, if we have ears to hear, God will speak and his call on our lives will become clear.

8

THE CHARACTER OF
OUR PRAYERS

I have suggested that there are four dimensions to the Spirit's inner witness:

- the assurance that we are loved
- convicting ministry regarding sin
- the illumination of our minds with truth
- guidance in times of choice

There is a theological logic to the order in which these have been presented, one that assumes it is helpful to consider discernment through a progression from the assurance of love to guidance in times of choice. The conviction of sin is intentionally placed after the assurance of love. While we may very well feel the Spirit's convicting ministry before we know we are loved, we can never really embrace this dimension of the Spirit's work in our lives until and unless we know we are loved. The first dimension, in other words, necessarily establishes the parameters for each of the other dimensions of the Spirit's ministry to our hearts.

It follows that we are more likely to be a people who can recognize the inner witness of the Spirit in times of choice if we know we are loved, are conscious of where we are being called to turn from sin and have intentionally chosen to walk in the light we have received. If we doubt we are loved, we will always be handicapped in our capacity to know the call of God. We will have a proclivity to choose and act in ways that strive to find love rather than to live and work out of the assurance that we are loved.

The Spirit's ministry of guidance also presupposes a tender and sensitive conscience, an awareness of our own failings and an awareness that we cannot trust our motives and are easily capable of self-deception. This, in turn, is also reflected in the reality that God's guidance in our lives is but a personalized expression of how we, in particular, are being called to live in the truth. It follows, then, that if we are seeking God's direction for our lives, our posture is one of love for and receptivity to the truth.

But there is also a deepening iterative character to these four dimensions. While there is a logical progression that begins with assurance and love and leads to guidance in times of choice, our experience will be one in which one dimension of the Spirit's witness suddenly opens up new vistas for us to appreciate another. For some, the experience of guidance demonstrates to them more fully how much God loves them. The encounter with truth, of course, opens up new ways by which the Spirit can call us from sin into the light of the truth we now understand. That is, the progression as outlined is not in any way four steps or stages. While we might reflect on one of these on its own, in the end we understand and experience each dimension of the Spirit's witness only in interplay with the other three. And this is a reminder, of course, that there is but one witness of the Spirit to our hearts and minds. We cannot atomize this witness or suggest that we will know one aspect of this witness in isolation from the others.

When we reject the convicting ministry of the Spirit, we are essentially rejecting God's love, for it is by this love that we are being called from sin to life. The same could be said, for example, if we do not walk in the truth we have come to understand or if we know how God is guiding us but have allowed our fears to keep us from accepting a particular call. In other words, when we feel the convicting ministry of the Spirit (as an example of one dimension of the Spirit's witness), what comes to light may well be one or all of the other dimensions. The Spirit is one; the witness of the Spirit is one;

and the Spirit's agenda is one, namely that we would be formed into the image of Christ.

And the invitation of the Spirit is that we would respond intentionally, allowing the Spirit to enable us to know the voice of Jesus so that this transformation, however incremental, would occur. In our intentional response to the Spirit's witness we increasingly we mature in faith, hope and love through the mercy and grace of God. In the meantime, slowly but surely, the Spirit is at work forming within us a Christian conscience — an inner awareness of God, of our world, of others and of ourselves that is informed by the presence of a God of truth, beauty and holiness.

Sometimes we are comforted and encouraged. Our inner fears are calmed and our heads are lifted up as we are enabled to see further and shake off the propensity toward self-pity and self-absorption. But just as often the formation of conscience is one in which we are challenged, admonished and stretched. The inner witness of the Spirit is not an assurance of love that affirms our positions of power, comfort and ease. We cannot assume that a comfortable lifestyle is necessarily a sign of God's blessing. We must beware of the false consolation that links our position of ease and power with a confidence in God's love and be alert to the ways in which Jesus may want to disturb rather than comfort us.

Also, the convicting ministry of the Spirit to our hearts frees us from judging others, particularly those who are different from us. It is a witness to our hearts that transcends our propensity to equate sin with cultural expectations. While our culture might have certain expectations about family or marriage, for example, the Spirit's witness would hopefully enable us to see beyond cultural ideals and appreciate more fully the multiple ways in which the Spirit enables us to grow in faith, hope and love. Through the illumination of our minds, the Spirit challenges our basic cultural assumptions; the gospel is countercultural. The Spirit will continually want to disrupt any propensity we might have toward a selective reading of Scripture.

All of this means that we must be alert to our own comfortable routines and the familiar parameters of our cultural norms, to any assumptions we might have about how the Spirit works in our lives, to any thought that the Spirit will consistently stay on the rails we have set down through our conscience. The Spirit will disrupt as often as comfort. And if we are genuinely open to the Spirit, we will be open to the different ways in which the Spirit might say something totally new to us, whether it is the awareness of love, the way in which we see and feel our sin or the new perspective we might have on the nature of truth.

One of the best ways to do this is to seek out those who are different from ourselves and to be with them in discussion as well as in work and worship. Whether we are meeting people in our travels or are spending time with neighbors of different backgrounds, these encounters and conversations will consistently grant us new perspectives on ourselves, our world and God. We might choose to read the Bible with those who are at the margins of society or with artists and poets. Or if our usual circle does not normally include scholars, we may choose to be with them in a posture in which we hear how an academic reads the Bible and finds Christ. All of us have people whom we consider to be "other," yet it may well be that in the company of the other the Spirit is able to shape and inform our conscience in a manner that enables us to hear the voice of Jesus afresh, in ways not possible within the normal routines and rhythms of our lives.

Through all of this, we seek the formation of a Christian conscience — formed by the Spirit. This is a conscience that reflects the conscience of Christ. In our intentional response to the Spirit, our hearts and minds are incrementally transformed into the image of Christ. We are becoming integrated persons whose inner lives are an expression of our real selves (we no longer live a lie) and our actions in the world are an expression of God's call on our lives. The key to this process is found in the experience of the spirit in our prayers.

THE FORM OF OUR PRAYING

Prayer, as the anchor and center of our lives, enables us to experience the formation of our conscience by the Spirit.[1] This is certainly not the only venue for the formation of conscience. We are in the world and in community. We are in conversation, study, work and play. However, if there is a formation of conscience through these other aspects of our lives, it will in large measure be because prayer lies at the center of daily routine and practice.

Many people assume that decision making is simply about asking God for wisdom (James 1:5 urges precisely this), after which, they suggest, we can act in faith that this prayer will be answered and that God will guide our choices. God will enable us to choose well or at least will keep us from poor decisions.

There are multiple problems with such a perspective on decision making, but for the moment I will highlight two of them. First, this posture discounts the power and significance of our personal encounter with God. It ignores the remarkable reality that God wants to be deeply and fully present to us, particularly in times of choice. It negates the wonder that we are not alone. It does not account for the remarkable reality that God does not merely *give* us wisdom but through his personal presence in our lives enables us to *grow* in wisdom—a wisdom that is formed through personal encounter.

Second, while God may give us this "situational" wisdom, we may not be in a posture to receive it. Through the discipline of prayer we nurture a receptivity to God. While the whole of our lives is lived in relationship with God and in response to the voice of Jesus, it is in prayer where this takes specific form and it is in prayer that we are enabled to know the voice of Jesus in every aspect of our lives. So, then, prayer is not an escape from people or from responsibility. It is instead the exercise of the spirit by which we learn to see reality more clearly, understand our circumstances and appro-

---

[1]I am speaking here of formal prayer. The Christian is encouraged in Scripture to pray at all times, to in a sense be in continual prayer. But this does not negate the need for times of focused prayer, or what is best called "formal" prayer, when all we do is pray. I would observe that we can be continuously in prayer only if we practice the regular habit of formal prayer.

priate afresh the grace to respond with integrity and freedom to our circumstances and to the people with whom we live and work.

PRAYER AS ENCOUNTER AND COMMUNION

Through prayer we seek the formation of conscience. But it is vital to stress that this formation happens specifically through a personal encounter with Christ. Through prayer we have the opportunity and capacity of being in conscious union with Christ, a union that is itself transforming.

To appreciate this, it is essential that we understand the character of prayer. For many Christians, prayer is intercession—an opportunity to ask God to mercifully intervene in our world with grace and power. Prayer is an exercise by which we verbally request that God manifest his divine glory in our lives and in our work. We ask God to do things for us, to respond in mercy to our predicaments, problems and challenges. And this is certainly a vital act of prayer. It is both commanded in Scripture and modeled for us. We see Jesus himself praying a prayer of intercession for his disciples in John 17. However, when it comes to discernment, we speak of a form of prayer that precedes the prayer of intercession, for to discern is to listen and respond to Christ.

Discernment is a response to an inner witness or prompting. More to the point, it is a response to a *person*. As such, it is imperative that we learn to experience prayer as encounter and communion. And therefore intercessory prayer is, properly speaking, a derivative form of prayer—it is prayer that arises out of our encounter and personal communion with Christ. It is the prayer of encounter that gives intercessory prayer its meaning and focus.

The prayer of encounter and communion assumes that it is possible to meet Christ, to listen through and speak through the spheres of time and space and to know the same risen Lord Jesus Christ who met with and taught twelve disciples in Palestine. And it assumes that this encounter is made possible through the ministry of the Spirit. Yet it remains specifically an encounter with Christ.

Obviously such an encounter is experienced by faith. Jesus has ascended to heaven, and now he is known and experienced only through the ministry of the Spirit. We love Jesus and believe in him even though we do not see him as the first disciples saw, felt and heard him (1 Pet 1:8). But this reality in no way detracts from the power and grace we experience in the encounter, and this is so for a simple reason: the Holy Spirit dwells within us and grants us the spiritual capacity to "see," "hear," and "feel."

And so we can speak of prayer as communion. We abide in Christ even as he abides in us (Jn 15). We know a personal engagement with God that is as meaningful, if not more meaningful, than any relationship we have with a human being.

We have intimacy with the Lord of glory, but it is not a sentimentalized intimacy. Here is where the old gospel song "Sweet Hour of Prayer" may not have it quite right. The experience of the church is actually much more like of that of Abraham, Habakkuk, Jeremiah, Daniel, Jacob and other prayers of the Old Testament. Yes, we have the opportunity for extraordinary intimacy with God, but it may be an intimacy in which we are distinctly uncomfortable and ill at ease. For these Old Testament saints, intimacy in prayer meant that they were often distressed, wrestling with God, perplexed by God and even at some points feeling abandoned by God.

Further, this communion is dialogue, a matter of speaking as well as listening. In other words, prayer is not "speaking to God." Yes, true prayer includes the words, longings, affirmations and thanksgivings of the people of God. But in true prayer God has a "privileged voice," one might say. And the final objective of prayer is not experienced in our speaking so much as in our allowing God to speak, to have the final word, but more, to have *the* word that speaks into our lives. It is this word that empowers, liberates, sustains and guides; it is the word we long to hear.[2] Thus all wise counselors of the spiritual life remind us that when it comes to prayer, we must beware of too much

---

[2]Augustine, bishop of Hippo, put it this way: "The [person] who serves you best is the one who is less intent on hearing from you what he wills to hear than on shaping his will according to what he hears from you" (Augustine, *The Confessions of St. Augustine*, ed. and trans. John K. Ryan [New York: Doubleday, 1960], p. 254).

speaking, for God knows us and knows our hearts and knows what we will say before we say it. We must beware of prayer that sounds as though God is uninformed and needs more information so that he can do the job adequately.

Further, the prayer of encounter and communion is also a prayer of submission. The prayer of Jesus recorded in John 17, arising out of his communion with the Father, led to the prayer of Gethsemane, in which he said, "Not my will but yours be done" (Lk 22:42). Likewise, we pray knowing that as God speaks, we hear and obey. We pray as women and men who know that in submission to Christ as Lord we find freedom. In prayer we acquire the posture of heart that is captured in the words of the Lord's Prayer: "Your will be done, on earth as it is in heaven" (Mt 6:10).

So when Samuel prayed, "Speak, LORD, for your servant is listening" (1 Sam 3:10), it was prayer in which the posture of his heart was one of submission. He awaited that which he was being called to do. And when we read in Acts 13 that the elders of the Antioch church were in prayer, it is clear that they heard the call of the Spirit because they were already disposed to respond to the Spirit, as they eventually did in setting aside Paul and Barnabas for their mission to Asia Minor. And Peter, who initially may have resisted the Spirit, was able to receive a call to meet with Cornelius because he was a man prepared to do whatever he was called to do (Acts 10).

THE PLACE OF SILENCE IN PRAYER

What all this presupposes is that the prayer of encounter and communion includes the discipline of silence. And it is here that the experience of the Old Testament prophet Elijah has often been viewed as particularly significant. His story tells us something about the character of prayer, of the way in which God speaks and of what might be required if we are to listen.

First Kings 19 describes Elijah on the run. Even though he had witnessed a powerful display of God's strength and resolve at Mount Carmel, he was discouraged and beaten down. Moreover, he was frustrated with God, who was seemingly inattentive to the circumstances that Elijah and the people of Israel were facing. And to cap it all off, Elijah protested that his own life was in danger. In response God called to him,

> "Go out and stand on the mountain before the LORD, for the LORD
> is about to pass by." Now there was a great wind, so strong that it was
> splitting mountains and breaking rocks in pieces before the LORD,
> but the LORD was not in the wind; and after the wind an earthquake,
> but the LORD was not in the earthquake; and after the earthquake a
> fire, but the LORD was not in the fire; and after the fire a sound of
> sheer silence. When Elijah heard it, he wrapped his face in his man-
> tle and went out and stood at the entrance of the cave. Then there
> came a voice to him that said, "What are you doing here, Elijah?" (1
> Kings 19:11-13)

From this experience, Elijah received specific guidance and assurance.

There is much that is noteworthy in this encounter, but I would highlight particularly the following point: God was not in the earthquake or the
wind or the fire; God was in the "sound of sheer silence." It is an exceptional characterization of silence, in that one would not normally think of
silence as a sound. And translators are challenged to find a way to capture
the idea that it was the sound of nothing, when it was actually the sound of
God making himself known to one person: Elijah.

This text has been a reminder to the church of a truth that is well known
but for which we need regular reminders: if we are going to hear God, we
need to learn silence. We must be still enough to listen, move slowly
enough so that we do not miss the sound of sheer silence. We may be impressed with earthquake, wind and fire, and indeed there may well be times
in which God thunders from the heavens or shouts at us in the streets, but
we will not recognize even this kind of speaking unless we learn silence.
The problem is not that God cannot speak loudly; the issue at hand is our
capacity to hear. There is too much noise in our lives, too much emotional
clutter and intellectual busyness. And all too frequently we are simply "too
busy" to slow down and listen.

For us to hear God, we must learn patience. If we want to be men and

women of discernment, we need to go to the desert, either literally or figu-
ratively. We must move away from the busyness that consumes us, away
from our own hectic activity and that of others. Furthermore, humanly
speaking at least, God tends to move slowly. God's presence, while that of
the omnipresent deity, is usually subtle, quiet, almost imperceptible. And if
we do not learn silence, we will miss it. Indeed the words of Psalm 62, "For
God alone my soul waits in silence" (Ps 62:1, 5), suggests what has been the
experience of many: in silence we discover that now we are only waiting for
One, and that One is God.

A. B. Simpson, a spiritual writer within my own tradition, spoke of the
"still, small voice" and went on to emphasize that we need silence, solitude
and what he called "stillness" if we are going to be able to attend to this voice.
And so he concluded, "Beloved, let us take His stillness, let us dwell in 'the
secret place of the Most High,' let us enter into God and His eternal rest, let
us silence the other sounds, and then we can hear 'the still, small voice.' "[3]

Our Christian heritage would remind us again and again that prayer and
discernment require silence, that we must slow down and find the space
and time to set aside the noise of the world and of our own hearts. And what
we find, as often as not, is that the biggest problem is not so much the noise
in this world as the noise in our own hearts—our own inner fears and anx-
ieties, our own anger and quarrelsomeness and frustrations, our own misguided desires and aspirations. There is so much that stumbles and tumbles
around our hearts and minds and makes them noisy places indeed.

The discipline of silence is a learned art, one that requires persistence
and patience. We seek an interior slowing down. And this is not something
that comes easily for us. The effort is imperative; we seek silence because
we long to hear God and God alone.

Silence is about attentiveness, but silence is also about waiting. Indeed
Psalm 62:1 speaks of the one who "waits in silence." We can hardly be true
disciples of Christ Jesus unless we learn to wait, whether it is waiting for the

---

[3]A. B. Simpson, *The Holy Spirit*, vol. 1 of *The Old Testament* (Harrisburg, Penn.: Christian
Publications, n.d.), p. 162.

consummation of the kingdom or waiting because we accept that God will act in his time. And silence enables us to cultivate this faith in God, this capacity to wait on God and not futilely seek to force the hand of God. Silence, then, fosters one of the most crucial expressions of Christian discipleship.

But even our silence needs a form that orders our prayers. Our encounter is not some vague, empty silence but the silence of personal encounter with Christ. This, then, is a reminder of a historic conviction and practice of Christian spirituality: there is value to intentionality—routine, order, consistency and purpose, both in our public prayers and as in our private prayers. This is one of the ways we assure ourselves that our experience is not merely an escape from the world into a pocket of self-absorption but a genuine encounter with the living God.

THE ORDER OF OUR PRAYER

Public liturgy is the ordered prayers of the people of God. It is appropriate for us to adopt a "liturgy," or order, for our own personal prayers, whether that order is something we adapt from public worship or something else we choose. Either is fine; the important thing is that we establish a regular practice that fosters the prayer of encounter and communion and that nurtures our capacity to discern the inner witness of the Spirit.

One way in which we might order our prayers is suggested by the outline of this book and the four dimensions of the inner witness of the Spirit. For our daily prayers, for example, we might spend thirty minutes in a prayer of attentiveness according to the following pattern:

Thanksgiving. We could begin by spending five minutes in reflection upon the preceding day, identifying those things for which we are grateful. In this portion of the prayer time, the grace we seek is to live in awareness of the goodness and love of God. Our desire, in the immortal words of the hymn "Come, Thou Fount," is this: "Let Thy goodness, like a fetter, bind my wandering heart to Thee."

Confession. Next, we might spend five minutes reviewing the joys and sorrows of the past day, being particularly attentive to the ways that we, in thought, word or deed, were inconsistent with our own confession. Also, this is a good time to acknowledge the presence of desolation in our hearts, whether anger, fear, mourning or discouragement. At this point the grace we seek is to see ourselves in truth and appropriate the grace of God that enables us to turn from darkness and live in the light.

Meditation. The third movement in the suggested order of prayer is ten minutes spent in reading and reflecting on Scripture. We could continue where we left off the day before, meditating on a paragraph of Scripture as we work our way through an Epistle or a Gospel or any of the other books in the Bible. We can choose an order for ourselves that takes us through all the biblical books in a cycle that enables us to appreciate the whole range of Scripture. Here the grace we seek is to know and relish the truth, such that the word of Christ will dwell richly within us and so that through the Scriptures we will know, love and serve Christ.

Guidance for this day. When we are facing major decisions, we would be wise to take time for an extended season of reflection, prayer and discernment. But in our daily prayers it is appropriate to spend ten minutes or so seeking to see the hours ahead of us as Christ sees them and thus engage the responsibilities and challenges of the day in response to the Spirit's witness to our hearts. It is my practice to take out my plan and schedule for the day and either ask God for clarity about my priorities as I face my to-do list, knowing that I cannot do everything I have listed there, or seek grace for what is scheduled in the day—a meeting, a project, a responsibility, whatever lies before me.

While this thirty-minute, four-step process is certainly not the only way in which we might order our daily prayers, it is nevertheless one that structures our time of prayer along lines that could foster the intentionality we need as we open our hearts and minds to the Spirit's work of conscience formation.

Further, this order can be adapted to a day of prayer.[4] The whole day

---

[4]For an example of a day of prayer based on this approach, see my *Alone with the Lord: A Personal Guide to a Day of Prayer* (Vancouver: Regent College Publishing, 2003).

could be divided into four segments, with an extended season of thanksgiving, a more comprehensive review of conscience, an extended reading and meditation on Scripture, followed by a time of critical discernment about choices and decisions we might be making. The day of prayer would be appropriate, for example, if one were facing a major decision and resolved to include an extended season of prayer as part of the discernment process.

Silence, then, finds expression within an order. After an exercise of thanksgiving, we can choose to be silent in the presence of Christ, confident of his love. After confession, once more we can be silent, here conscious that God knows us and that we live under mercy. And in a similar way, both our meditation and our search for guidance can be punctuated by times of silence in which we choose to be attentive to Christ. When we are distracted, we can gently bring our thoughts back to the focus of our prayers. In time our silence is no longer a burden or a challenge but an opportunity for quiet, something that we experience as a part of our daily routine just like anything else we do.

THE DARK NIGHT

Over time, our experience of prayer changes. Sometimes our prayers change because we are negligent or lacking in spiritual discipline. What we seek in those times is the renewal of our first love and a recovery of the joy that comes in prayer and in contemplation. Sometimes, however, the change in our prayers is not due to inattention or negligence so much as to the fact that our prayer has assumed a different character and we no longer recognize it as prayer or appreciate its significance. In other words, it may be that the change in our prayers is a good and necessary change—a change that God encourages.

Many Christians have found that our prayers can become more arid; the prayer lacks sensory joy and immediate pleasure. It does not *feel* as though God is present to us in our prayer. God seems absent.

At such times we remember that in our early days as Christians we found great joy in thinking about God's love. We would delight in a confidence that God loves us. We would feel this love as something that reached down into the core of our beings. Or we remember that we used to experience deep grief for sin and feel the force of our contrition. In turn, we would know great satisfaction in the experience of God's forgiveness. And then also, we remember when our minds were like sponges. Every Scripture text we read was *alive* to us. Truth seemed to be dripping from the text like juice from grapes, vibrant with flavor. But now we find that the sensory awareness of God's love seems to have faded. And we feel a little guilty, wondering if we fall under the admonition of Revelation that we have lost our first love (Rev. 2:4). We can't get the feeling back, and we wonder what has gone wrong.

Now, however much we want to be sincere in our confession of sin, we wonder if we are genuinely open to confession because now it seems we no longer have deep contrition in the face of God's holiness and God's holy law, as we once had. And now truth seems present to us, but it does not seem to overwhelm us anymore. It doesn't consume our hearts and minds like it did when we were beginners in the faith. And we wonder if something has been lost that we should recover. We wonder how it is that our eager love for truth has been dimmed by something, and if all of this requires or calls for some specific correction.

Christians who are experiencing aridity in prayer react in different ways. Some begin to despair. Other Christians continue to go through the motions, acting like nothing has changed but knowing full well that their initial eagerness in prayer has dissipated; there is a sense in which they live a lie. And yet other Christians know full well that nothing is wrong, but they are nevertheless at a loss to explain why their prayers (and their worship) has changed. They know they do not love Christ any less.

We need to make some sense of this aridity, particular as it relates to our prayers and the place of affect in discernment. In this regard many Christians over the past four hundred years have found helpful the insights of St. John of the Cross (1542–1591), who described spiritual aridity as "the dark night of the soul."

INSIGHTS FROM JOHN OF THE CROSS

St. John of the Cross was a remarkable theologian and perhaps Spain's greatest poet. With St. Teresa of Ávila, he founded the Discalced Carmelites. As a Carmelite monk, he had a ministry not only as a spiritual director but also as an administrator and reformer within the movement.

John was very much a theologian of the Scriptures. He actively opposed those who were called "scholastics," whose loyalty was to the tradition of the previous centuries. He identified himself with those who were called "scripturists," who through a study of the original languages sought a literal or plain meaning to the text of holy Scripture. His mentor in this regard was actually at one point imprisoned by the Inquisition. John cherished the Bible, especially the Gospels. Further, John was clearly of the conviction that the chief source of all spiritual instruction is holy Scripture. Nevertheless, it is not so much his consideration of Scripture that makes him a notable contributor to spiritual theology. It is, rather, his viewpoint on prayer.

As a spiritual theologian, John made observations about prayer that are particularly pertinent to discernment, affect and the change we experience in our prayers.[5] John stood in the tradition acknowledging that the goal of the spiritual life is that we would grow in faith so that we may live in perfect love for God and for our neighbor. Faith enables us to achieve the goal of the Christian life: union with Christ.[6] But John believed that the senses are the antithesis of faith and that, consequently, if we are to live by faith, we must deny the senses gratification.

John, like other mystical writers, made a distinction between those who are beginners in prayer and those who are more advanced.[7] Maturity in prayer comes not merely in building on the methods of prayer used by those

---

[5]The most important sources in this regard are the following: *The Ascent of Mount Carmel*, *The Dark Night* (which is essentially a continuation of the *Ascent*), and *The Living Flame of Love*. All of these are found in *The Collected Works of St. John of the Cross*, trans. Kieran Kavanaugh and Otilio Rodriguez (Washington, D.C.: ICS, 1979). References to these works are to book, chapter and paragraph numbers.

[6]See John of the Cross, *Ascent*, 2.1.

[7]Ibid., 1.Prologue.3-4.

who are beginners; it actually means abandoning those methods or at least no longer depending on them.

For the beginner, prayer is highly sensory. It includes an affective awareness of the presence of Christ. We are emotionally conscious of the presence of God in our lives, sensing that Christ loves us, calls us from sin and enables us to walk in the truth. But then, as our prayers mature, we experience what John called a "dark night"—a dark night of the senses, a dark night of the intellect and a dark night of the affections. In summary, it is a dark night for the soul, intellectually and emotionally. By "night" he meant that our senses are no longer gratified.[8] We are, as he put it, "blind." We no longer can look to or depend on what we understand, taste, feel or imagine, for "faith lies beyond all this understanding, taste, feeling, and imaging."[9]

This is necessary, John said, because our sensual appetites (the affections) are as little children in their incessant demand to be gratified. A key indicator of maturity is the capacity to live with delayed gratification. John suggested that just as a child must be weaned of the mother's breast, so we must be weaned of our desire for sensory gratification.[10] Indeed this is what St. Paul was speaking of when he contrasted "milk" and "solid food" (1 Cor 3:1-2).

When the senses are gratified, this satisfaction is a gift from God. But it is just that. It is a gift; it is not God himself. And if we come to love and enjoy God for himself and not for the gifts he gives us, then, John contended, we must with grace accept that in time God withdraws the gifts. He does this perhaps to test us, but more importantly, so that we might know the Giver and find our deepest satisfaction in him. Further, John suggested that we will not mature in prayer (let alone in the whole of life) unless we come to this point. He expressed his longing for those who do not want to mature in their Christian faith: "Some are content with a certain degree of virtue . . . but never achieve spiritual purity. . . . For they still feed and clothe their natural selves with spiritual feelings and consolations instead of divesting

---

[8]Ibid., 2.2.1, 1.3.1.
[9]Ibid., 2.4.2.
[10]Ibid., 1.6.6, 2.17.7.

and denying themselves of these for God's sake."[11]

As many spiritual writers would note, we love God only when we love him through both joy and sorrow. We truly love God when we love him regardless of whether we receive consolation and emotional satisfaction or suffer loss and trial. And it follows that we can learn to love God as God only if God withdraws his rich consolation and purifies our faith and our love for him.[12]

In other words, this critical transition can happen only if the senses are starved (that is, ignored and no longer gratified). Or to state it in the classic way, it can happen only if the senses are purified. We truly live by faith if our deepest desires, longings, aspirations and motives are purified. But these are not purified by an act of our will; they are purified by the Word (Jn 15:3), specifically through the One who is revealed through the Word: Jesus Christ himself. Our will, our passions, our desires and our motives are purified by the encounter with God by faith. Only by faith—vigorous faith—can we come to live in hope and love. But it must be stressed that our purification, the renewal of our wills, comes not so much by suffering and difficulty as through encounter and communion with Christ.[13]

The encounter with Christ is an encounter that is fueled by love and that seeks to purify and mature that love. And here is where the words of Hans Urs von Balthasar are so pertinent, when in his classic theological study on prayer he observed that prayer by its nature is an act of love. Con-

---

[11]Ibid., 2.7.5.

[12]John suggested it is a form of self-love when we love God only for the gifts that we receive from him (ibid., 2.7.12).

[13]Teresa of Ávila used different images (the dry well, for example), but to a similar end. She made a distinction between discursive prayer and contemplative prayer and also noted that it is often, if not consistently, the case that contemplatives are not able to enter into discursive prayer. And she suggested that this is not something about which they need to be concerned; rather, they should accept this as good. As Kieran Kavanaugh put it in the introduction to *The Interior Castle*, "The purification of the person is realized not merely through the sufferings inherent to the human condition but especially through contact with the person of Christ in his humanity and divinity" (Teresa of Ávila, *The Collected Works of St. Teresa of Ávila*, trans. Kieran Kavanaugh and Otilio Rodriquez [Washington, D.C.: ICS, 1980], 2:276). Further references to the *Interior Castle* will identify book, chapter and paragraph numbers.

sequently we should expect that there will be aridity in our prayers. He concluded, " 'Aridity' . . . should not be thought of in terms of penance or of some tragic visitation. It is the normal, 'everyday' face of all love."[14] Balthasar suggested that this dark night, first, is not something we choose at our own initiative, and second, is chosen for those who have a special mission.[15] But he also stressed that this is a reflection of the "normal, everyday" face of love and that this is the kind of faith that God seeks. Thus we must not conclude that it is the quality of prayer or experience that is reserved for a few.

In other words, aridity in our prayers is not a sign that something is broken and needs to be fixed. Rather, it may well be that our prayers have matured. They may have changed in much the same way that the relationship between lovers changes. The expression of love between two newlyweds on their honeymoon may have a character that is very different from that of a couple who have been married for fifty years. Sitting on the veranda at sunset in their rocking chairs, the older couple are clearly not on their honeymoon. Yet they have something incredibly rich—richer, indeed, than anything the honeymoon couple can imagine. They have moved past the effervescent delight of first romance and into a depth of love and joy that reflects their long-term covenant relationship with one another. Similarly, a Christian who is experiencing the dark night may actually have reached a level of exceptional depth with God.

As a side note, then, I need to stress something at this point. When John of the Cross speaks of the "dark night," he is not referring to experiencing a time of great difficulty, perhaps even depression, such as Jesus' experience in Gethsemane or Job's experience. Rather, he is speaking of the quality and character of our prayers.

---

[14]Hans Urs von Balthasar, *Prayer*, trans. Graham Harrison (San Francisco: Ignatius Press, 1986), p. 138. He continued in this vein, writing, "In his economy of salvation God needs faith which feels nothing, self-surrender which sees nothing, blind hope which seems to stretch out its hand into the void. Where will he find such acts of faith, if not among the contemplatives, whose very state of life, so to speak, calls for this kind of response to the word of God?" (p. 140).
[15]Ibid., p. 140.

A DISTINCTION BETWEEN THE GIFT AND THE GIVER

John was not alone in highlighting the development in prayer known as the dark night of the soul. A. B. Simpson made a similar distinction in a hymn where the lyrics read, "Once it was the blessing and now it is the Lord." And we find a similar refrain in the familiar hymn "Dear Lord and Father of Mankind" in the line "Let sense be dumb." There is within these spiritual writings the awareness that emotion and affect, our senses, are a means to an end, not an end in themselves.

The distinction between the blessing (the joy of encounter with Christ, the peace we know as the fruit of our knowing Christ) and the experience of Christ himself is foreign to most Christians. Yet making the distinction is absolutely essential. C. S. Lewis, in a letter to one of his correspondents, stressed that the "presence of God is not the same as the *sense* of God's presence." He went on to write,

> The act which engenders a child ought to be, and usually is, attended by pleasure. But it is not the pleasure that produces the child. Where there is pleasure there may be sterility: where there is no pleasure the act may be fertile. And in the spiritual marriage of God and the soul it is the same. It is the actual presence, not the sensation of the presence, of the Holy Ghost which begets Christ in us.[16]

Teresa of Ávila captured the theological premise behind all of this when she insisted that spiritual maturity "does not consist in spiritual delights but in greater love and in deeds done with greater justice and truth."[17] Elsewhere she reinforced this by saying, "It is in the effects and deeds following afterward that one discerns the true value of prayer; there is no better crucible for testing prayer."[18]

To appreciate what John of the Cross and the others have said, it is impor-

---

[16]C. S. Lewis, *Letters to an American Lady*, ed. Clyde S. Kilby (Grand Rapids, Mich.: Eerdmans, 1967), pp. 36-37.
[17]Teresa, *Interior Castle*, 3.2.10.
[18]Ibid., 4.2.8.

tant to come to some sense of the place of emotional gratification in Christian spiritual experience. And for this, one way forward in our understanding might be to think not so much in terms of our private prayers as of our participation in public prayers, through the liturgy of our worship with the people of God. All authentic worship will be characterized by both an intellectual and an affective response to the presence of Christ and the wonder of God's salvation. Indeed one could easily argue that all true worship involves not only affect and intellect but the whole person. Yet the continual danger for those who plan and lead worship is that the event would be designed for and later judged on its level of emotional satisfaction. Whether it is revivalism that would seek to recall the "old-time religion" through gospel songs or whether it is the contemporary worship forms with their sophisticated use of music, the whole worship event, and particularly the elements that include music forms, have as their intended outcome a delight in God and in God's acts of salvation.

But there is also a danger here. The downside comes when music is used to stir up emotion such that the liturgy no longer really sustains life but becomes an escape from life. Then what we have in worship is not an encounter with God but the experience of a feeling. An emotional package has come to represent for us the presence of God.

Music is a good and necessary part of the worship of the people of God. We can hardly conceive of our worship without it. As noted in an earlier chapter, it is a vital way by which we respond to God with heart and mind, for music has a unique capacity to foster our heart response to truth, to enable us to open our hearts and express truth more deeply, with more heartfelt passion. But something is amiss when the sole purpose of music is to foster a particular emotional sensation.

In the same way, we cannot truly attend to the voice of Jesus if we think that the purpose of prayer is to cultivate a particular emotional response. Rather, we are seeking to know, love and serve Jesus, and we respond to him with heart and mind. An authentic response requires that we be attentive to what is happening to us emotionally, but it does not require, and most urgently should not include, the *manipulation* of emotion.

In our public worship, our goal is to know God, to celebrate Christ and to appropriate afresh the wonder of the Spirit dwelling within us. We do not design the worship to manipulate an emotional response, and just as surely, we need to learn not to judge the quality of the worship experience by how emotionally gratifying it felt. This does not mean that we will not have emotionally rich experiences in worship; it is, rather, that we will not seek these, long for them or judge the quality of the worship event by whether they happened or not.

Having said this, it is important to emphasize that true worship is a response of heart and mind. Indeed an authentic experience of public worship for God's people needs to legitimize *all* emotional experience, rather than just (as is so often the case) that outward display of emotion that appears to be perpetually happy. True worship gives space for us to acknowledge that we live in a broken and cruel world and that we often come to our worship with heavy hearts, mourning loss, discouraged with setback, bearing sorrow, just as Jesus fully acknowledged the grief his disciples felt (Jn 16). When we legitimize only happiness in worship, the irony is that we do not really foster joy, but when we affirm and recognize the whole range of human emotion (as do the Psalms), we actually cultivate our capacity as the people of God to live in joy as the fundamental posture of our hearts.

The wonder of a hymn of mourning and sorrow is that it enables us to know joy. But a hymn of much joy and happiness that is sung because that is *all* we are allowed to sing does not nurture joy, for it denies what we are actually feeling. All the great hymn writers in the history of the church understood the need to affirm the whole range of human emotional experience, following the Psalter. Much contemporary chorus writing, however, tends to affirm what is nothing but a sentimentalized form of joy and peace.

Ideally, public worship should be a means by which our affections are ordered. We can learn how to mourn the great pain that the world bears, how to grieve the loss of life during tragedies, how to respond in anger when there is injustice, how to express joy when two feuding peoples find peace and how to be grateful when an unemployed neighbor finds a job. But this ordering of our affections comes not through emotional manipulation but through our encounter with Christ. And sometimes that encounter is simple, quiet and still. Indeed, more often than not, this is the case.

Perhaps the longer we walk with Christ, the more our encounter with him tends to be quiet and dark or dry. And as we mature, what we need in the liturgy is a worship that allows us to express what we are feeling, certainly, but that mainly allows us to be with God's people in the presence of Christ. When that is all we need, emotional manipulation strikes us as gimmickry, novelty and a distraction from our worship.

In the same way, John of the Cross and others have suggested that as we mature in our prayers, we become less and less conscious of an emotional response in prayer. Our prayers become more flat emotionally. But that does not mean that we are emotionally flat people; it simply means that our emotional responses were a kind of barrier between ourselves and Christ, and now in his grace Christ is allowing us to experience him more directly. The result is "dryness," as some put it, or "darkness," to use the language of John of the Cross. The outcome is not that our lives are emotionally flat; rather, it is our *prayers* that are dry and dark.

The ultimate goal of our prayer is not that we would enjoy a good feeling but that we would mature in humility, advance in faith, hope and love, and grow in our capacity to love God and love our neighbor as ourselves. This comes not by act of our will but by an encounter with God himself. And somehow, mysteriously, when our prayers are dry, Christ is present to us in a manner that is transforming. The fruit is known and seen over time; that is, the test of our prayers is not the immediate emotional response but whether we truly grow in faith, hope and love. And what we learn, experientially, is that Jesus does not just give us food and drink; he *is* our food and drink. What we experience is not just the voice of Jesus but Jesus himself.

RESPONDING TO THE DARK NIGHT

Balthasar offered wise counsel at this point, saying that when we experience aridity in our prayers, "we should always start by attributing it to our own lukewarmness, and leave it to our spiritual director to show us if it be God's doing."[19] This is part of Balthasar's perspective that even the solitude of the dark night is something we experience as members of the community of faith and that we therefore need the community of faith to help us interpret our own prayers.

We should definitely begin with the assumption that the "problem" is on our end. However, few Christians have access to good spiritual direction. Consequently, it seems to me that many who are experiencing this aridity and darkness in their prayers need to begin to trust that experience and follow some of the classic guidelines for prayer in the dark night.[20]

To begin, of course, we need to graciously accept this development and see it as a gift from God. We might wish that there was more emotional fire in our prayers, but God has chosen otherwise, and so the only response is one of acceptance. As Teresa of Ávila attested, we experience the dryness of our prayers so that we will grow in humility. The devil aims that we be disquieted and disturbed, but the Lord calls us to a gentle quietness. "We are fonder of consolations than we are of the cross," Teresa observed. This does not mean that we do not have peace in prayer. Indeed she called her readers to peace. But it is not the inner peace of being regularly consoled by God. Instead it is the peace we have that though God may (as Teresa put it) give "consolations" to beginners in prayer, God is testing us, and the best response to a test is quiet acceptance.[21] This is not

---

[19]Balthasar, *Prayer*, p. 140.

[20]It may be important to make a distinction at this point. The idea of the dark night is never an excuse for self-pity or discouragement. Many believe they are experiencing the dark night and think of this as a justification for their own disappointment, discouragement and bitterness. They have had setbacks in ministry or work and now think this justifies their living under a dark cloud. But this is a terrible misread of the dark night. Those truly in the dark night experience aridity in their prayers, and this aridity actually cultivates a capacity to live with joy in the midst of the challenges of life.

[21]Teresa, *Interior Castle*, 3.1.9. "Consolations" is a translation of Teresa's word *contentos*, by which she meant the joy and pleasures that come in prayer and work, similar to the joys found in everyday life. "Spiritual delights" is a translation of *gustos*, which Teresa distinguished to speak of the deeper, more inward joy and delight that come from God. See footnote 1, p. 487.

something over which we have control; it is God's work.

We need to accept that our prayers have changed, but then we need to be intentional in our response to the aridity and darkness. First, it is vitally important that we continue our regular routine of prayer and meditation. But we do so without the same set of expectations or longing for emotional (or intellectual) gratification. We choose to be content with the simplicity of the act of prayer, whether in thanksgiving or confession or meditation on Scripture, aware that God is present and that this presence is all we really need.

Some who are more activistic respond to the dryness by neglecting their prayers, because they do not seem as useful or meaningful (or, actually, as gratifying) as they once were. Such people wonder what the value would be in sustaining these prayers. And so they fill up their time with activity that gratifies them in a different way but is a poor substitute for the transforming presence of Christ. Others may keep praying but then occupy their prayer with busy activities or exercises or extended intercession to fill up the time, and so in a sense they live distracted by their own busyness rather than choosing to be lovingly attentive to Christ. Instead of either reaction, the wise response is to accept the dryness and sustain the order of one's life and prayers, though without the expectations one once had.

Second, the aridity in our prayers will likely mean that we are less and less inclined to nourish our hearts on special images, places or thoughts. John of the Cross put it this way: "The truly spiritual person never considers nor becomes attached to the particular comfort of a place of prayer, for this would result from attachment to the senses."[22] Holy spaces, such as a sanctuary or a prayer place in our homes, and images that we use to foster our prayers are no longer as immediately meaningful to us. This may seem to be less an issue for Protestant or evangelical Christians, but John spoke not only of the external places and images but also of the use of our imagination and the thoughts or images in which we have found comfort in the past. God weans us of the special places (our church or sanctuary or prayer

---

[22]John of the Cross Ascent 3.39.3.

room), our structures (which can so easily act as spiritual crutches) and even our special liturgies that we find so comforting.

But third and most important, in our dryness we are best advised to learn to be more and more content to just "be." This may sound empty and useless, or it may sound like idleness. But as John noted, when our minds are tranquil and our attention is lovingly focused on Christ, what is happening is that incrementally we are drawn up into the love of Christ and increasingly transformed into his image.[23] It is not something over which we have control; it is, rather, something to which we graciously submit.

In other words, what is happening in our prayers is that we are less and less active so that the Lord may do his work. Thomas Green compared this work to that of a surgeon on an operating table.[24] The image is an apt one. Frequently, in our activistic mindset, we are inclined to think that if there is a problem, we need to fix it. But the wisdom of John of the Cross suggests that we need to be passive before a divine surgeon. And as Green noted, for the surgery to be effective, we need to be "unconscious." The surgery is effective because we do nothing.

For activists, it is hard to believe that when it comes to maturity in our prayers, we are transformed because we consciously and intentionally choose to be still. Furthermore, activists assume that if we are doing nothing, whether in evangelism or worship or prayer, then neither is God doing anything. But what we are invited to appreciate is that God does some of his most important work when we are doing nothing. And when we are called to do nothing in our prayers, that is what we should do.

Further, we learn that in the dryness it is not that God is absent from us but rather that God is much more present. Many Christians believe that God's presence should always be a pleasant experience, but the Bible says God's presence is more like "a consuming fire" (Heb 12:28-29). And therefore, when our prayers are dry or dark, we discover that this does not necessarily mean that something is wrong; we learn that this may actually be an

---

[23]Ibid., 2.15.5.
[24]Thomas H. Green, *Drinking from a Dry Well* (Notre Dame, Ind.: Ave Maria, 1990), p. 24.

indication that things are as they should be. This experience of darkness is not desolation but rather is the quiet presence of Christ, and we accept his presence in faith and accept his work in our lives with submission. But we will not come to this situation unless we let go of a spirituality that demands that we always feel good in the presence of God and unless we accept that the work of God is not something we can control or manipulate. Then we begin to grow into a mature love for God and begin to experience the transforming work of the Spirit.

9

THE CALL OF GOD

Vocational and Moral Discernment

❧

Spiritual discernment is an intentional way by which we respond with courage and integrity to our world. Discernment enables us both to see the world more clearly and to respond well to what we see. We discern our circumstances; we then, in turn, discern the appropriate response.

This discernment includes the capacity to know one's vocation, or how one is being called, at this time and in this place, to give of one's energies, whether that is in a career or in volunteer service. It also involves moral discernment—the capacity to see how one should respond in love and justice to a moral dilemma. Both have to do with discerning how we act in the world, in response to the call of Christ. And in both cases we are being called to offer not a vague, general response to God but a specific response to whom we are being called to be at this time and place.

DISCERNING VOCATION

In probably no aspect of our lives do we more frequently yearn to hear the voice of Jesus than in our work. There may be other times when we long more urgently (the decision to marry, perhaps, or a decision about a child or a family relocation or a major financial move), but the character of our lives and our work is such that we come up against the need to hear this voice again and again when it comes to our vocation.

This is due, in part, to the changing character of our world. None of us can assume that the role or responsibility we now have is one that we will perform indefinitely. In virtually every line of work, whether in the arts, education, the professions or ministry—regardless of occupation, skills or training—no one can think in terms of a single career, that is, a simple line of employment that carries through from one's early adult years until retirement. Those in business have long known that they can make no assumptions about the future of business. One might start a new business now to respond to an opportunity in the marketplace, but it is an opportunity *for now*.

Pastors who have accepted the challenge of long-term ministries (ten years or more in the same congregation) have come to see that they will be effective over the long term only if they appreciate that the church they have been a part of has changed, and thus its pastoral needs have changed as well. These pastors still need to ask the question, how is God calling me to be a pastor of this congregation at this time? And they can make no assumptions based on their previous years of ministry. Certainly there will be continuities, but as often as not in these transitions, it is the discontinuities that we feel most acutely.

Sometimes the changes we face are due to changes in the workplace. Many, for example, feel the force of what is often called a "downturn" in the economy, and through no fault of their own, they discover that they are no longer employed. They have received a notice that their position is being terminated. And thus they are struck with the deep sense of vulnerability that comes when one is unemployed.

For others, natural cycles of life bring about transitions. A young person might be coming to the end of a program of education with the awareness that he is facing the challenge of making it in the job market. A parent who has had primary responsibility for the raising of children sees that the last member of the small tribe is about to leave home, thus changing the contours of the home and the range of opportunities and potential responsibilities that she might assume. And a person coming up to retirement, whether it is forced or not, inevitably faces the challenge that comes with asking,

"Where do I go from here? How do I invest my energies now?"

What this means for the Christian believer is that vocational discernment intersects our lives at regular intervals. It is not now (if it ever was) a spiritual exercise merely for the young person who is trying to choose a career. The task of discerning vocation is fundamental for anyone who wishes to live with personal integrity, courage and authenticity. We come up against the challenge of vocational discernment again and again and again.

Organizations change. They go through cycles of development as much as an individual does. And so even if God were to call us to stay with the same organization throughout the entire course of our career, the challenge of vocational discernment would be no less necessary or demanding for us. While there are points of continuity, we can take nothing for granted. The school, business, church or organization of which we are a part has changed, and will continue to change, and this demands that we make no assumptions based on the past but rather ask, what is God calling me to be and to do in this place at this time? Some transitions we can foresee; others will surprise us. But nothing is routine other than the reality that at frequent intervals we are challenged with discerning vocation—who am I and to what am I being called?

And when we face these passages, what we long for is to hear the voice of Jesus.

Something else needs to be emphasized. No one else will make these critical decisions for us. They might try to do so, but they cannot. Vocation is necessarily something about which we bear personal responsibility. If we are in pastoral ministry, we cannot expect the church board to make our choices for us. They may make decisions that affect what we can or cannot do, but they cannot choose for us and assume responsibility for our lives. If we are in middle management, we may think that the real decisions are being made elsewhere, a long way from our desk, where we feel like pawns on someone else's chessboard. But in the end, though we are inevitably influenced by decisions made elsewhere, the choices we make are ours. We choose how we will respond to this set of circumstances. And no matter

how limiting a set of circumstances may be, we still can ask, how am I being
called to respond to *this* set of circumstances at *this* time and in *this* place?

Further, there is a sense in which part of Christian discipleship is accepting with grace that we each have a cross to bear. This is not some kind of
martyr complex or masochism. Rather, it is an acknowledgment that in our
calling we identify with the suffering of Christ. The brokenness of the world
inevitably impacts our lives, and so our work will, in either an obvious or
more subtle way, be a mysterious means by which we identify with Christ
and his work (Rom 8:17).

But though we are called to bear the cross, we are certainly not called to
bear each and every cross! Jesus, in the last moments before his Passion,
probably had a keen awareness of the cross he was facing. Nevertheless
there, in the Garden of Gethsemane, he discerned with certainty that he
was to accept the horror and humiliation of crucifixion and the abuse of the
religious and political leaders of his day. And in our identification with him,
while we may not have a Gethsemane counterpart, our discernment will often include an awareness of the cross that we are, or may be, called to bear.

I remember one way in which this was highlighted for me in conversation with a friend who was dean of another theological school. He was seriously considering that perhaps he should resign his post and return to a full-
time teaching assignment. I urged him to stay the course, emphasizing as
strongly as I could how much I felt that he had the right strengths, abilities
and vision for the role and also how much his school needed someone like
him. I thought I had been quite persuasive in my little speech, yet I was immediately quieted by his response. He simply and calmly advised me, "Gordon, that may be your cross; but it is not *my* cross." It was not that he was
unwilling to bear up under difficulty, to do what needed to be done, even
if it meant real stress. But he was wise enough to assert that though we are
called to accept the ways in which our calling includes difficulty, we are
called to carry only our own cross.

So it is that the capacity to discern vocation is a critical skill for the Christian believer. It is not the only thing we need when it comes to knowing the

voice of Jesus, but it is one of the most critical issues that will intersect our lives. At this point and in this place, what is it that I am being called to do? Within the range of current opportunities, as I consider a possibility, is this a cross that I am being called to bear?

TWO FOUNDATIONAL QUESTIONS

Discerning vocation requires that we have as much clarity as possible about ourselves and about our circumstances.[1]

We can hardly overstate the critical need for having as much clarity as possible about who we are—our abilities, personality, temperament, longings and desires. This is no less relevant and may be even more critical the older we become, whether in midlife or as we discern for the retirement years. This is not self-absorption so much as a vital expression of personal responsibility. And so Paul urged the Christian believers in Rome to take a sober look at themselves (Rom 12:3), for only then could they respond confidently to the calling and grace of God and live in true humility.

This is not a matter of filling out a questionnaire or personal inventory sheet, though no doubt these can sometimes be helpful. Self-knowledge is more complex and more mysterious. It comes as much through failure as through success, as much through introspection as through conversation with others, as much through a reflection on our current situation as through reflection on the past. It comes in a consideration of some hard data, including our skills and abilities (neither underrating nor overstating them). And it comes through honest reflection on what might be called soft data, namely our dreams and longings and our awareness of what brings us joy. Further, self-knowledge comes in an appreciation of our temperament and personality, since we are not being called to be someone we are not. Our calling will be consistent with how we have been made. Our identity finds expression in how we see and respond to

---

[1]For a more comprehensive study of vocation, some readers may wish to consult my book *Courage and Calling: Embracing Your God-Given Potential* (Downers Grove, Ill.: InterVarsity Press, 1999).

the world: What matters to us? What makes us angry? What sustains hope and beauty and truth for us? What brings us joy? Where do we feel that we have a firm piece of ground on which to stand, so that we can make a difference?

To find such things out about ourselves requires that we engage others in conversation, but it also means that we find some separation from others. The community, especially parents and church, can be so powerfully present that we cannot see ourselves. Even if well intentioned, the expectations of others can undermine our capacity to know who we are. And for many of us, our inability to discern vocation is largely because the still, small voice of Jesus is drowned out by the cacophony that comes from the actual or perceived expectations and suggestions of others, whether in our immediate circle of acquaintances or through the public media. We need time and distance from this noise if we are going to find ourselves. This is true for a young person, for a person in midlife and for a person coming into the senior years. We need both: conversation with others and time and space to ourselves.

Then what matters most is humility, the willingness to accept who we are and embrace the full significance of that identity. What we seek is the grace to take responsibility for our strengths and abilities, to live with contentment within the skin that God has given us rather than aspire to be someone other than who we are. This is humility, and it is liberating in that by it we are freed from the burden of pretense.

Further, we need to match clarity about ourselves with clarity about our world, particularly our immediate circumstances. We urgently need grace to see our world as it is in truth—not a dream world, not the world that would be if we could write the script, but the world as it actually is.

When people are incapable of coming to terms with their vocational identity, it is usually either because they have failed to accept who they are or because they are holding on to illusions about the world in which they live. If we are to discern well, it is imperative that we see the world as it is, not as we wish it were. It is a matter of facing up to the circumstances and opportunities as they actually are, not the circumstances or opportunities for which we hanker.

One of the great dangers in vocational discernment is a sentimentalized view of reality. People will refuse to accept the truth and will continue to wish their world were otherwise than it is. For example, I have heard scholars complain that they were born too late, saying that they are traditional scholars and that the day of the traditional scholar is gone. However, they are describing the type of scholar who belonged to another age, not this age. If men and women today are called to be scholars, it will be for *this* age, for *their* set of circumstances. Similarly, a businessperson may feel a deep longing to do business in a simple economy, not one shaped by global realities. But such a world no longer exists. We either do business in this world or we do not do business.

Regardless of our training or background, our pursuit of employment necessarily includes an analysis of the job market. What is happening in the economy? What kinds of jobs are available? What skills are being sought, particularly in our area of interest?

Further, knowing our world includes an honest and frank evaluation of problems, obstacles and limitations. We may lament the lack of financial resources or feel that people are unfairly critical of our work. And this may be true. We may have been unjustly fired or overlooked for a promotion. Life is unfair. And it may be true (and unfortunate) that we are living with significant financial limitations. But God's call is always within the particular, and consequently the limitations we experience are always the context in which God will call us and enable us to experience his grace.

Part of accepting our world and seeing our circumstances in truth is accepting the opportunities that are given to us rather than bemoaning what is not there. Indeed it is not so much a matter of accepting as of actually *embracing* what we have the opportunity to do. It is a burden and an obstruction to God's grace to wish otherwise. We are only hurting ourselves when we are continually perplexed because the hoped-for job

opening never materializes. We get nowhere by wishing that the phone
would ring with an offer of our dream position, when all the while we are
looking over the shoulder of someone else and wondering why he or she
got the job we might have had.

This does not mean that we are narrow-minded fatalists who see no possibility of change. Neither does it mean we are resigned to unjust systems
of decision making or counterproductive policies and procedures. To the
contrary, a person who sees the opportunities for change in a situation is
one who is in touch with reality. If we are called to be a means of renewal
and change, it will only be as we are able to see what is actually the case,
not what we wish were the circumstances. For if we are realistic about the
way things are, we can also likely see real possibilities for how things could
become, rather than some dream world that could never happen in this
place or at this time.

Again, this is humility. We accept with grace the reality that God has
given us, rather than deploring our fate or complaining that we deserve better. Behind all this lies one of the most fundamental theological principles
with respect to discernment. The reason that it is so important that we see
ourselves and our circumstances clearly is that God speaks into the particular. God speaks to us at this time and in this place. If we have a sentimentalized or idealized view of our world or of ourselves, it will inevitably skew
our capacity to know God's wisdom and direction.

And so as mentioned, part of knowing ourselves and our world includes good conversation. This does not mean that we only do what others agree we should do, but it does mean that we do not face our world or
the process of vocational discernment alone. We walk in company with
others who challenge our perceptions about ourselves as well as our
world. These are people who are prepared to challenge us when we understate our ability and potential and who will just as graciously tell us to
get in touch with reality when we overstate who we are. In conversation
with others we grow in our capacity to see our social environment and our
work potential with greater clarity. This highlights the reality that, what-

ever we do, courage will be the order of the day for all of us. Thus the company of others becomes an essential means of support and encouragement.

Before I address the actual matter of discernment, though, something else needs to be stressed. We will not hear God's call and discern our vocation unless we are persuaded of the potential sacredness of all vocations. If we are convinced that only religious vocations are sacred, if we think that our legitimacy is tied to how much money we can make or if we think the arts are not significant because we view them as less than useful, it may be that we will miss our calling. Our capacity to discern vocation requires that we open our minds as well as our hearts and allow God to challenge our biases and assumptions. This will likely mean that we are in for some surprises along the way!

THE TASK OF DISCERNMENT

We ask the question, Lord Jesus, what are you calling me to be and do in the next chapter of my life? The issue is always the same: we ask God to guide us one step at a time. And we need God's direction. We might wish discerning vocation meant merely a rational, honest consideration of the facts, that facing up to our identity and to our actual circumstances will suddenly bring clarity and freedom. However, vocational discernment is never so simple; it is never purely a matter of rational analysis of ourselves and our circumstances. It is never a simple exercise of reviewing the job market and lining this up with our skills and training.

Vocational discernment will consistently involve emotional turmoil, a confrontation with the fears that so often hound us and the sometimes complicated exercise of coming to terms with our joys. It is not that we are being called to do something irrational; it is merely that we know that if we are going to act with truth and integrity, we need to hear the voice of Jesus and know the witness of his Spirit for this place and this time. And this requires that we come to terms with what is happening to us emotionally, or as Brian J. Mahan has aptly put it: "Vocation finally is less about discovering our occupation than about uncovering preoccupations."[2]

We will choose well only insofar as our hearts and minds are secure in an awareness of God's love (Eph 3:17). We need to choose and act as those who are loved, not as those scrambling to find love. Further, it is prudent that we recognize our potential to choose with motives that are inconsistent with our confession. At this point, our level of honesty makes all the difference—honesty with ourselves, honesty about what we are feeling, thinking and wanting. As mentioned earlier, we never will come to full purity of motive, not in this life. But we can be diligent about what we are thinking and feeling, and it is never a waste of time to systematically review the hard questions that enable us to know if our peace comes from God. These hard questions get at the same temptations that Jesus faced in the desert at the beginning of his public ministry.

Then also, it is wise to honestly accept and recognize if we are feeling threatened or insecure or if the task of discerning vocation is complicated by the awareness that we have been ignored or wronged. If we are facing a vocational choice at a time when our children are growing up and leaving home, we might feel the pang of that loss and be at some level of mourning. Or if we were released from our last employment, overlooked in a potential promotion, forced into retirement or outvoted when we let our name stand for an elected position, wisdom suggests that we acknowledge what is happening to us emotionally.

And we need to be alert to the presence of anger in our hearts; there is probably nothing that can so easily blind us to our actions and reactions. And of course, the possible causes of anger are myriad. We can be angry at the way someone or some organization has treated us. Or we can be angry at ourselves, perhaps for what we did that resulted in a difficult state of affairs. Or we can be angry at a spouse or other family members if for some reason their actions have complicated things for us.

Then, in peace, knowing—as best we can—ourselves and our circum-

---

[2]Brian J. Mahan, *Forgetting Ourselves on Purpose: Vocation and the Ethics of Ambition* (San Francisco: Jossey-Bass, 2002), p. 183.

stances, we can ask, what am I being called to do with this chapter of my life? We do not need to think in terms of one monumental decision that will determine the rest of our lives. The distant future does not need to be a burden to us. But neither does the distant past need to be a burden. We will be able to embrace this moment only if we are prepared to move on from the ways we have been wronged and from those things that in retrospect we wish we had done differently. We can learn from the past and from our mistakes, and we can mourn the losses and pains that have come from the mistakes of others. But we do not need to be locked in the past, victimized by the behavior of others or by our own actions.

Rather, we can embrace the present moment with faith, hope and love, and as God enables us, we can act in such a manner that we seize this opportunity of the joy that is set before us. Our fundamental assurance and point of departure is that God is on our side. God's love and providential care is our bedrock. Even if we do not yet feel this as deeply as we would like, we can at least begin to act on this assumption. Only then will we be able to accept with grace the cross we are being called to bear. And this grace is essential if our difficulties and challenges are to be for us not a badge of honor but something about which we refuse to complain as we identify with Christ.

Eventually, though, we come to the bottom line: the question of our fundamental loyalty. Surely our identity as Christians and our discernment of vocation is marked by coming to clarity about whom we serve. Discerning vocation is as much about obedience as it is about trying to figure out what we are to do with our lives. It is about recognizing before God that this is what we are being *called* to do.

This may mean something very down to earth and pedantic. It may admit a deep sense that we are being called to resign from a prestigious position so that we can be at home to care for an invalid spouse. It may mean that in the face of tremendous opposition and difficulty we have peace, that at least for the time being we are to persevere, even though we feel like quitting. It may mean that we take a substantial cut in pay or accept an assignment that will take us into a role of apparent obscurity and insignificance. Whatever it means, we know that we do what we do because we have come to the conclusion that this is the thing to which God is calling us.[3]

A writer writes because she must. An artist goes about his work convinced that this, so help him God, is what he is supposed to do. Someone in administration accepts the pettiness and details of his work for the simple reason that in the end this is what God would have him do. And a pastor concludes that for now she will remain in a small rural church despite the invitation to a more prestigious urban church, because she has concluded that for now God wants her to be with this particular parish. It is no different in business, law, religious ministry, the arts or education. For the Christian, the bottom line is one of calling and obedience.

FACING OUR FEARS, ACTING IN JOY

Having discerned, we are then called to act with grace and courage. Sometimes (perhaps most of the time) we are called to persevere with grace, courage and strength. We must be alert to a misguided sense of duty. We must beware of any false idea that we cannot resign because we are invaluable to the organization (when I mentioned this about myself once, a dear friend suggested that this was good evidence that it was time to resign!) or we cannot quit because we do not want anyone thinking we are a quitter. No, if we stay and persevere, it is because we have clarity and peace that this is the call of God.

Even when not facing a change, we may nevertheless be called to some

---

[3]This is captured wonderfully in the words of the late Canadian writer Mordecai Richler, who in a letter to a friend wrote, "Before I had my first bk [sic] accepted and until I began work on my second I wanted to be famous. Have position. Anecdotes told abt [sic] me. And the rest of it. But now I do not want or think abt [sic] these things very much. They are trifling in themselves. And worse still, there is no fame big enough or money bribery enough to compensate for the pain that goes into the making of a novel. (Even the mixed joy of publication is paltry, aspirins for cancer). So why do I write? I really don't know. I can thk [sic] of a lot of reasons but all of them wd [sic] be 'thought up' and only partly true. Nearest I can come to it is 'I have to' " (quoted in William Weintraub, "Richler on Writing," *Time*, July 16, 2001, p. 47).

kind of adjustment in our lives and in the pattern of our relationships and our work. A time of discernment might reveal a need for more regularity in our prayers, more consistency in our observance of sabbath rest and renewal or a need for a different pattern of eating and exercise.

At other times the outcome of our discernment will be a call to more training and education, either on the job or as a new chapter of our lives, when we will resign in order to go back to school. This is not an escape from work but a different kind of work, one that calls us to engage heart and mind differently than we might in the marketplace.

And then, of course, we will sometimes be called to make a major change and face a whole new environment for life and work. Perhaps we come to clarity that it is time to resign and explore a new work opportunity. As mentioned above, at this point it is helpful to discern two steps—coming first to clarity about *whether* we are to resign and then to clarity about *when* we are to act on this call. But in the end we act, knowing that we do so in the Lord.

However, all of this is easier said than done. There is still one critical dynamic that can easily distort our thinking and undermine our capacity to act: fear. When it comes to discerning vocation, it may well be that nothing is so crucial as this. We must come to terms with our fear.

In 2 Timothy we read the following: "God did not give us a spirit of cowardice, but rather a spirit of power and of love and of self-discipline" (2 Tim 1:7). This statement follows the call to "fan into flame the gift of God" (NIV). What lies behind this, at least in part, is the assumption that courage is critical to one's capacity to fulfill a call and that one threat we have to face, as we discern and embrace our vocations, is fear. Indeed fear is an obstacle we all encounter, and we do so on multiple levels.

In his helpful study on the vocation of the teacher, *The Courage to Teach*, Parker Palmer wrote about courage and fear in a way that is relevant to all, regardless of whether we are called to be teachers. Palmer observed that we live immersed in a culture of fear: "Fear is everywhere—in our culture, in our institutions, in our students, in ourselves—and it cuts us off from everything."[4] Henri Nouwen echoed this observation when he wrote that "the negative power of fear . . . has invaded every part of our being to such a degree that we no longer know what a life without fear would feel like."[5] That is, we come up against our fears coming and going. We fear failure. We fear isolation. We fear rejection. We fear obscurity. We fear that we will be found out. When we are young, we fear others' opinions. As we get older, we fear letting go of power and influence.

It is here that it seems most naive to think that discerning vocation is only a matter of knowing ourselves and knowing our circumstances. In part, it is never so simple because the dynamic of fear so readily invades every part of the process of discernment. Our fears are so entrenched in our personal identities that they can hardly be separated from us. They are so much a part of our psychological DNA that one could easily think it is impossible to live and choose without being subject to one's fear. To challenge our fears, we might think, is to challenge our fundamental identity. But though we have been formed by fear, we must begin to see that we are not true to ourselves when we live in fear. In fact, we must begin to seek the grace so eloquently expressed in Newton's great hymn, "Amazing Grace":

> 'Twas grace that taught my heart to fear,
> And grace my fears relieved.

Our only way forward is to begin with a frank acknowledgment of our fears, as far as we are able. In the end we may not be able to overcome them, but with God's grace we may be able to keep them at bay. This will be possible, however, only if we are at least able to name them.

What follows is a helpful exercise, one to which I often return as a way

---

[4]Parker Palmer, *The Courage to Teach: Exploring the Inner Landscape of a Teacher's Life* (San Francisco: Jossey-Bass, 1998), p. 56.
[5]Henri J. M. Nouwen, *Lifesigns: Intimacy, Fecundity and Ecstasy in Christian Perspective* (Garden City, N.Y.: Doubleday, 1986), p. 15.

to bring my fears to the surface.[6] It involves asking four questions in sequence; each question builds on the response we make to the prior question or questions. And so as you read this, you might want to consider taking some time between each question to answer it for yourself; and you might find it helpful to come back to these questions more than once.

1. *What do you tend to complain about?* Think particularly about your work, whether it is paid work or your work as a homemaker or in your volunteer church ministry. What tends to be on your lips when you are frustrated, especially when you are let down by or disappointed with others?

2. *What fundamental commitment lies behind the point of frustration?* Your complaint is usually a reflection of a fundamental commitment. It speaks of something that you value and is one way in which you can highlight your priorities. It tells you something about yourself.

For the time being, you might choose just one thing that is particularly important to you, as something that actually does (or at least you hope will) define your life and work.

3. *Is there anything that you are doing or not doing that undermines your capacity to fulfill this fundamental commitment?* In an honest review of our own behavior or pattern of work, we usually know about what we do, or the things we fail to do, that are inconsistent with our values, priorities and commitments. In other words, rather than complaining about others (and quite apart from whether those complaints are legitimate or not), what is it that we are doing or failing to do that undermines our commitments? Rather than seeing ourselves as victims and blaming others, we move forward as we are able to take personal responsibility for our own behavior. And when we do, what do we see?

4. *What lies behind this pattern of behavior?* Now we have come to the most difficult and probing question. As you look at your pattern of behavior, step back from your life for a moment and ask what this behavior means.

---

[6]This is adapted from a presentation by Robert Kegan at a seminar on the vocation of the theological teacher, sponsored by the Association of Theological Schools and held in Riverside, Calif., January 10, 1997.

This involves a good measure of honesty, of course. What we are doing here is acknowledging our own inner contradictions. We are naming the things we are doing that are inconsistent with our confessed values, priorities and commitments. Yet if we can identify these patterns of behavior and then the kinds of commitments that they reflect, we will learn that they help us see the fears that lie behind our own behavior. We begin to see that certain assumptions lie deep within our psyches—assumptions that propel us to do the very things that undermine our capacity to fulfill our vocations.

An exercise like this helps us to see the extent to which what really drives us are not the fundamental commitments, values and priorities we identified in question one but the underlying fears and assumptions that these represent.

Until we meet Christ personally at the consummation of his reign and we hear from him the words "Fear not," we will always have fears nipping at our heels. They may never be dissipated, only disciplined. But they can be tamed only if we acknowledge them. They will blindside us, and indeed blind us, if we do not discern and acknowledge them. And the danger, of course, may be that what actually direct our lives, day in and day out, are our fears and the false assumptions they represent.

When we acknowledge our fears, we can begin to overcome them. We can recognize when our feelings or inclinations are rationalizations to cover our fears. We can anticipate our fears and strive, particularly in conversation with others and through their encouragement, to live and work out of joy in spite of the presence of these fears.

Surely this awareness is the growing edge of both spiritual and vocational development—facing up to our inner contradictions and our fears. We can continue to challenge (again in conversation with others and with their encouragement) the false assumptions that these fears represent. We can ask what it is that encourages us to maintain our belief in them even when we know they are not true. And it is always helpful to face up to the sources of these false assumptions. For many, it is their family of origin. For others, it is discouragement and setback, perhaps met in the workplace as young people. Regardless, we need to insist again and again that these assumptions are false and then act accordingly. At first we might act in little ways, relatively safe acts that quietly subvert the false assumptions. But sometimes we will do big things that are consistent with our priorities, values and commitments and confirm that the assumptions that fuel our fears are in fact false and matter not a whit.

When we do, we find joy. This is not incidental, for what we long for and seek is that our life and work in the world, the vocation to which we are called, would be sustained by joy. It is sheer joy to give oneself to that to which one is called without regrets or halfheartedness but with passion and energy. This gives us a joy that no one can take away. We are doing what we *want* to do.

Ultimately we find and embrace our vocation at the very point where we experience God's deep joy. The calling of God is not burdensome, even though it necessarily includes both challenge and responsibility. Rather, discerning vocation is substantially a matter of discerning what brings us joy and finding through that discernment who we truly are. We learn to live no longer by pretense but in the freedom of humility. We learn to live no longer by duty alone or the expectations of others but in what truly represents the core of our being, that to which God is calling us. We are no longer looking around to compare ourselves with others or resent others or fear their judgments of us. We embrace our call out of joy.

And so, when we go through the critical and necessary process by which we examine our motives and determine what really drives us, when we face up to our fears and the false assumptions that lie behind them, when we ask the tough questions about our fundamental allegiance and our first love, this is not some burdensome act of humiliation to show us what worms we are. These are the exercises that ultimately enable us to be freed of pretense and of those burdens that weigh us down, rob us of joy and drain all the energy out of us.

THE NEED FOR MORAL DISCERNMENT

What I have addressed thus far in this chapter pertains primarily to matters of work, that is, to the activity in the world to which we are called. Yet we also desire to discern the call of God when it comes to our conscience and especially to the presence of moral evil in the church and in the world. The question here is, how do we know what we are called to say and do in response to ethical dilemmas?

The voice of Jesus calls us to act in response to wrong, in a manner that is congruent with his reign in the world. Surely one of the greatest challenges to our Christian identity is the fact that as our capacity for discernment increases, so does our awareness of the multiple ways in which pain and injustice infect this world in which we live. Even more perplexing is that we realize that our own lives, in subtle and sometimes unconscious ways, participate in this wrong and in some ways may even perpetuate it.

Virtually every time I make a purchase, whether it is my weekly groceries or gasoline for my car or an air ticket to attend a theology conference, I am identifying with an organization or a system or a method of production that violates what I believe to be right. In fact, it likely happens *every* time, to some degree. The presence of wrong is that pervasive. Sometimes it is under the surface, something as subtle as the air we breathe. But sometimes we see it full in the face, either in a blatant expression of racism, war or economic injustice or in the powerful systems of taxation, immigration policies and criminal justice that are maintained by governments.

We are confronted with the reality of ethical violations in both the private and public spheres. And whether we are conscious of the subtle forms in which evil surrounds our lives or the more obvious expressions, it is right for us to conclude that something has to be done. We are right to observe and feel that our identification with Christ calls for—yes, demands—that we respond not with apathy but with the engagement of our energies. We reject any notion that passivity is a justifiable Christian posture. If we accept that we are called to identify with Christ, it follows that we seek in this world to make a difference that is compatible with the reign of Christ.

Our moral responsibility increases as soon as we are in a position of power or influence, where our office or role or visibility within a community or organization enables us to see more than we might otherwise see about the community or the organization. And with this comes the opportunity, or leverage, to respond in a way that might make a positive difference: to speak or act on behalf of others.

The church has always affirmed that individual Christians and communities of faith have an obligation to act with integrity and courage in response to human need. This has led to the formation of hospitals and other institutions of compassion and relief. It has also motivated Christians to act in protest and through political associations to confront institutional evil and strive to alter social structures. We see this in the previous century, for example, in the response of Martin Luther King Jr. and others to the racism of the American South as well as the response of Dietrich Bonhoeffer and others to the horrors of Nazi Germany. These were individuals whose Christian conscience led them to a specific and deliberate response to a particular manifestation of wrong

The Character of Moral Discernment

Moral discernment is about making sense of right and wrong. It is about recognizing that evil is subtle, powerful and deadly. It is also, however, about acting in a way that is appropriate in response to both right and wrong. And for anyone who loves life and identifies with the reign of Christ, it only makes sense that we would long to distinguish more clearly between right and wrong so that we can respond appropriately. As we follow Christ, we grow in our longing and capacity to act on his call to justice and love (Phil 1:3-11).

This means, of course, that we learn to see how the good is good and how evil is evil. We want to be alert to evil and not be taken in by its insidious character. We want to learn how to be appropriately angry at the right things, not merely at those matters that irritate us or get under our skin but at that which makes God angry. We also want to mourn when we should mourn and feel discouraged when that response is appropriate. But then, even more, we want to know how to respond in truth, that is, with integrity, in love and justice, and in a manner that is congruent with who we are and with the call of God on us at this time and this place.

In other words, moral discernment is never just an abstract or intellectual exercise of attempting to figure out right and wrong. That is only the first part of the formation of conscience. The second—just as critical—is discerning the appropriate response. It is about discerning what is right, what is wrong *and* what the right response is for this time and in this place. Discernment is always particular. The apostle Paul did not take on the injustice of slavery, even though that institution is unambiguously wrong. It was surely God's will that slavery would not exist, but it was not God's will that Paul should denounce it at that time.

Liberation theologian Jon Sobrino captured well this dual character of moral discernment when he reminded us, "Since God's will is historical rather than eternal or universal, the whole context of the moral subject becomes very complex, going far beyond any straightforward search for what is obviously good and what is obviously evil." There are, then, as Sobrino observed, two stages to Christian discernment: (1) the general "determination of what is good and what is evil," and (2) "the good that one is obliged to do."[7]

Discernment first means that we recognize the presence of injustice and evil. A discerning person is not naive. But second, moral discernment is never solely about identifying what is right and what is wrong so that, like a good gardener, one can water the desired plants and weed out the unwanted ones. Rather, the presence of evil in our world is much more ambiguous. And to complicate matters, we are never sure about the extent of evil in our own hearts. This does not for a moment mean that we cannot make moral judgments and discern how we are to respond; it is merely to

---

[7]Jon Sobrino, *Christology at the Crossroads: A Latin American Approach*, trans. John Drury (Maryknoll, N.Y.: Orbis, 1978), pp. 129-30.

say that the matter is more complicated than might at first appear.

Discernment is about timing. Are we being called to do anything about an issue at *this* time? But it is also about the "what." What are we to do in response to a particular evil or injustice? We seek to discern the appropriate response, recognizing that a lack of proportion and good judgment in our response is a subtle (and sometimes less than subtle) way of participating in evil. An example of such participation in evil is the way that a few pro-life activists have sought to advance their cause by assassinating abortionists. When the response to evil is out of proportion, as in that example, it can become worse than the evil that occasioned it.

Insisting that discernment has two sides in this way is never to be used as an excuse for inactivity or irresponsible passivism. We must be just as alert to the false consolation that would lead us to keep to our comfortable circles, when it is fear that would keep us from speaking or acting in truth. Silence in the face of glaring injustice is inexcusable.

However, the existence of wrong in itself does not end the task of discernment. Jesus saw much that he chose, for the time being, to ignore or at least not denounce. Yet he had no patience with the abusive religious leaders of his day, and he lived with the consequences of his words and his deeds. In fact, he died because of them. He demonstrated a courage to do what he was called to do. What is noteworthy is that he did not respond to everything or feel responsible to act on everything he saw to be wrong. The outcome, though, is that while doing what he was called to do, he sowed seeds that would bear fruit in multiple expressions of the kingdom. In the same way, St. Paul, while not directly addressing slavery, did what he was called to do and in so doing sowed seeds that helped lead to the eventual demise of slavery.

DISCERNING WITH HEART AND MIND

Moral discernment is a learned art, not an innate capacity. The ability to discern how one should respond to a moral dilemma is not in any way automatic nor something that can be taken for granted. Just because one is a

Christian does not mean that one then has the capacity or the inclination to discern well. This is a learned art that flows from an informed and reformed conscience. Ethicist James M. Gustafson compared the capacity to discern to the ability to appreciate and interpret a work of art when he wrote, "The discerning act of moral judgment is impossible to program and difficult to describe. . . . It is probably more akin to the compilation of elements that go into good literary criticism and good literary creativity than it is to the combination of elements that make a good mathematician or logician; it is both rational and affective."[8]

Just as interpreting art is an acquired skill, so moral discernment requires that we learn to cultivate a particular set of skills and perspectives. And this involves more than just rational analysis. It requires that we attend to the affective and intuitive sides of understanding as well. It means that we seek to appreciate the implications of both the reign of Christ and the character of our environment. But it also means that we attend to what is happening to us internally, to our own responses, particularly our affective response to both good and evil.

Moral discernment will involve at least the following three elements.

First, our conscience is informed by a biblical theology of love and justice. Discernment requires the formation of a Christian mind by truth in a way that permeates deeply the way we think and feel and act. However, as has already been stressed, this formation of the mind with truth is never merely an intellectual engagement with a set of values or principles. It is not about understanding or identifying with a cause. It is not about finding out the truth so that we can use it to make moral judgments. Our conscience is formed and informed by our identification with a person, Christ Jesus.

Therefore, what drives us to act is not that we are right (and the world is wrong); it is, rather, the love of Christ that compels us (2 Cor 5:14). And we should thus be suspicious of any inclination to act if we cannot act with compassion, of any propensity toward crusadism, of a spirit of judgmental-

---

[8]James M. Gustafson, *Theology and Christian Ethics* (Philadelphia: United Church Press, 1974), p. 109.

ism toward our world, our culture, our society or our neighbors. Such a posture is inconsistent with a Christian ethic that is governed by both love and justice. If we lack compassion, if there is any inclination to judge and condemn, we know that something is awry.

Second, discernment is about seeing our environment truthfully. We mature in our capacity to see evil for what it is. But it is equally the case that we need to see good for what it is. And further, it means we increase our capacity to see the ambiguity of life, to see how goodness can be altered, if ever so slightly, by evil, and to see the powerful and subtle ways in which the full force of evil is held at bay by the love and providential care of God.

Discernment is about not overstating the extent of the wrong or the presence of evil. To overstate a wrong is to grant it more power than it is due and thus to fail to acknowledge where there is good. To call good evil is equally a violation of discernment. The Christian should celebrate good wherever it finds expression. We cannot discern evil and the appropriate response to evil unless we have a capacity to discern and appreciate good, in whatever form we encounter it. As we mature in our capacity to discern, we begin to see the interplay of the elements of our environment in a way that enables us to see the presence of good as well as that of evil. Indeed the two go together: if we cannot discern good, we cannot discern evil.[9]

Third, moral discernment is about *our* response. Again, it is never in the abstract; it is always about us. It is a response to the world that arises out of our experience of having been loved and forgiven and continuing to be loved and forgiven. We come to see that the evil around us runs through our own hearts and through the Christian communities of which we are a part. It is not just "out there." And so we engage the world while always re-

---

[9]The great English preacher and poet John Donne wrote, "I have not been so pitifully tired with any vanity as with silly old men's exclaiming against our times and extolling their own. Alas, they betray themselves. For if the times be changed, their manners have changed them." And he went on to stress that "good is as ever it was, most plenteous, and must of necessity be more common than evil" (John Donne, *No Man Is an Island: A Selection from the Prose of John Donne*, ed. Rivers Scott [London: Folio Society, 1997], p. 6).

maining alert to judgmentalism, the inclination to crusade against the speck in our neighbor's eye while we are oblivious to the log in our own eye (Mt 7:3-4).

Further, this personal character of moral discernment is a reminder that while we may all agree on what is right and wrong in our assessment of our environment, we will not all be called to respond in the same way. When Dietrich Bonhoeffer felt compelled to participate in a direct action against Adolf Hitler during the Second World War, he was careful to emphasize that integrity and conscience demanded this response of him. But though he had no patience with any appeasement of Hitler and the Nazi regime, he did not necessarily expect others to act as he chose to act.

St. Paul discussed serious moral dilemmas in Romans 14 and 15 as well as 1 Corinthians 10. To abstain from eating meat offered to idols was for the Jewish Christian community a minimal requirement of faithfulness to God. But for the Gentile Christians living in the Greek cities of the ancient world, this was a limitation that made no practical or theological sense. The apostle urged each community to refuse to judge the other, while also urging each to act from faith in a manner consistent with their own conscience. What is striking is that moral and ethical choices cannot be a matter about which one judges one's neighbor. I may well be called to act and respond in a manner different from another.

Further, the personal character of our response is a reminder that what we say and do is necessarily informed by what we are experiencing emotionally. We must be alert to discouragement and anger, to a response to the world that is rooted in anything but peace. But we must also be alert to any inclination to avoid an appropriate response because of fear, possibly a fear that finds expression in a logical and carefully reasoned outline of why we might not do something. Further, we need to be alert to false guilt, which can motivate us to act when we are not called to act or lay on us a perpetual burden of guilt that we are not required to bear. And these two—first, our propensity to act out of guilt, and second, our propensity to inactivity because of fear—speak to the absolute need for intentional discernment if we are to respond with both courage and integrity to the environment in which we live and work.

It is difficult to know our own hearts. But we can learn. And for this, the most valuable means of formation, of the Christian conscience as well as of the discerning response to the world, is good conversation. As Gustafson put it, "The community is in part the present gathering of Christians, in a congregation or some other group, that engages in the moral discourse that informs the conscientiousness of its members through participation in moral deliberation."[10]

Through good conversation with others, particularly (though not limited to) those of the community of faith, we can grow in our capacity to come to terms with both our world and our response to that world. In partnership with others, we can have our assumptions challenged, our comfort disturbed and our fears brought into the open. This, in turn, humbles us before one another and God, and from this posture we can know the necessary encouragement to act with integrity, courage and peace.

---

[10]Gustafson, *Theology and Christian Ethics*, p. 117.

10

SPIRITUAL DIRECTION, PASTORAL CARE AND FRIENDSHIP

❧

W̶e are all called to the task of discernment. Each of us can hear the voice of Jesus. Yet we are able to listen only if we are women and men who live in dynamic community with others who challenge and encourage us. We do not walk this road alone.

One of the critical means by which we live in genuine accountability within the community of faith is by entering into conversation with others about the character of our experience. This is not an abstract discussion — about the spiritual ideals or principles of the spiritual life. Nor is it the re-telling of experiences we may have had in the past. Rather, the conversation that is most beneficial occurs when we speak of our joys and our sorrows, the challenges, hopes and dreams we have, and the temptations and trials that currently shape our experience.

Indeed one of our deepest needs is to have people in our lives who are in a position to ask us the hard questions when we think we know the voice of Jesus. They are individuals who will not flatter us. They are not afraid of our emotional ups and downs, nor fearful that they will hurt our feelings, and they will tell it like it is when they think we have veered off the rails. A true friend listens. Further, true friends recognize that we have to know for ourselves the voice of Jesus. They cannot listen for us; they cannot be the word of God to us. We have to hear for ourselves, and they are committed to helping us know that word. But they are also more than prepared to challenge us when they think that our inflated ego or our fears or our anger is undermining our capacity to hear God. How sad then it must be for those who are alone, who do not have the joy of this kind of friendship! However, we must acknowledge that some do not have it because they have not sought it. They have preferred to walk their own path without the counsel and admonition of true friends.

True friendship, pastoral care and spiritual community include the joy of freeing and empowering others to know with greater confidence what God is saying to them. It is one thing to tell others that God loves them; it is quite another when they know, through the witness in their own hearts, that God loves them. And to the degree that we can empower others to hear more clearly the voice of Jesus, we have given one of the most extraordinary gifts possible.

However, we do not grant this gift by telling others *what* God is saying; rather, we give this gift only as we are able to free them to hear for themselves. This is surely part of what it means to be a friend to another. And we all long for the genuine friendship that frees us to be who God has called us to be. All of this assumes a particular understanding of the human being in community and of the relationship between the community and individual.

THE INDIVIDUAL IN COMMUNITY

In this regard, there are two errors we need to avoid. The first is the error of the West, which assumes the autonomy of the individual. The other is the error of the East, which subsumes the individual within the collective. Neither is true community. Neither presents a biblical view of the human being.

In contrast to both West and East, the biblical perspective on the human being and community highlights a dynamic interplay between the individual and the collective. Our human identity is never found in isolation from community, in a kind of unrestricted self-determination. Yet neither is it found in community per se, if this means that we become an undistinguishable part of a collective. Individuals have a distinctive and personal identity in their own right. The community too has an identity as a collective. But in true community a corporate identity never denies the individuality of its members, and individual identity is always found in healthy interplay within community.

The community, then, while essential to our individual identity, is also a threat to that identity. We do not find ourselves in isolation from the community and we do not find ourselves if we are subsumed within the community. When it comes to discernment, we realize that we do not know the voice of Jesus and the witness of the Spirit if we are lost within the community. The collective can become so strong that we cannot hear what God is saying to us. We must be alone. We must remain "other" from the community and not be absorbed into its powerful collective identity.

However, the community—the others in our world—are an essential means by which we hear the voice of Jesus, experience the assurance that we are loved and know the call of God to respond with courage to the challenges before us. Discernment requires a healthy measure of self-distrust, and it is the community that helps us to see ourselves truthfully. The community is to us a kind of mirror, not in the sense that we see ourselves reflected in the community, but that we cannot see ourselves except when we are in relationship.

The danger, of course, is that the community would presume to hear God for us. Often religious leaders and pastors fall prey to this error, assuming that they know what is best for others (rather than freeing the others to know and respond to God in a manner congruent with their own conscience). When this happens, we lose the power and grace of the individual, that capacity of each person to hear God for himself or herself. The individual's ability to live deeply conscious of both the love of God and the call of God is undermined, and so is the person's ability to respond with courage to his or her world. When this happens, the greatest loss is to the community itself. Our common life is enriched and sustained not by monotony and uniformity but by our diversity and the collective strength of the community as a combination of individuals. But if the individuals are no longer individuals, the community is no longer genuine community.

If we demand uniformity, if we are uncomfortable with the idea that all persons can and must follow their own conscience (Rom 14), then we unwittingly deny not only the individual but also the community. True pastoral care does not have an agenda for others, but rather, in large measure it has no intent other than to free others to know, in their own hearts, the witness of the Spirit. This form of pastoral care actually fosters genuine community.

It is here that, in many respects, we have an opportunity to learn from the classic ministry of spiritual direction.[1] Of course, while some may have the opportunity to receive the formal ministry of spiritual direction, not all do. Yet all will have the opportunity to respond in friendship to another, and all those who are called into pastoral ministry have opportunity to provide some measure of direction.[2] And all of us, as we seek to live in genuine community with one another, have something to learn from this ancient practice. We are regularly in situations in which we can ask, what do you think God is saying to you in this situation? And how do you know that this is the witness of the Spirit to your heart? Further, as I will emphasize more fully below, this ancient practice can give us insight into the character of true friendship.

The Ministry of Spiritual Direction

Spiritual direction is often compared to both counseling and mentoring. Understandably so, for as often as not all three of these occur in conversation between two individuals, usually in private, confidential settings. But spiritual direction is different from both counseling and mentoring, and the distinction on both fronts is an important one. The difference essentially lies in the agenda for the conversation and how this agenda is set.

In counseling, the agenda is set by the emotional needs of the one being counseled. While mentoring and spiritual direction may well include discussion about these kinds of issues, they are addressed along the way, not as

---

[1] I am conscious of the limitations and potential misunderstandings that may exist with the use of the term *direction*. However, the term is gaining broader use and acceptance, and it may well be that it really is the best term, despite the fact that the whole point of spiritual direction is not to "direct" the other, unless we mean that we direct him or her to the Lord.

[2] Eugene Peterson has contended that spiritual direction is actually one of the key elements of authentic pastoral ministry. See Eugene Peterson, *Working the Angles: The Shape of Pastoral Integrity* (Grand Rapids, Mich.: Eerdmans, 1987).

the main focus of discussion. And both spiritual directors and other mentors know that when it comes to emotional pathologies, they are well advised to refer others to a trained counselor.

In mentoring, the agenda is set by the one who mentors. That's because, in a sense, mentoring is a form of teaching. One has a set of skills and trains the other in those skills. A person may want to be a pastor or an artist, and so he or she spends time with a senior pastor or master artist who mentors the person in those professions. Again, it is not that counseling and spiritual direction will not have a teaching element or component; it is, rather, that in mentoring, the *primary* agenda is one of training and teaching, enabling a person to know a craft or to learn a mode of behavior or being.

Spiritual direction is different yet. The agenda is not so much emotional needs, nor is it a program of teaching. Instead the witness of the Spirit determines the course of the conversation. The fundamental posture taken in spiritual direction is one of being with the other, usually in conversation, in a manner that would enhance the capacity of the other to know how God is speaking. As often as not, the focus of spiritual direction is on enabling Christians to mature in faith, hope and love. But the agenda for this maturation is set by the Spirit, not by a formal program of formation, teaching or discipleship. These other programs may be good in themselves, but they are not to be confused with the ministry of direction.

Eugene Peterson has suggested that three basic assumptions lie behind this ministry.[3] First, we can be certain of God's gracious initiative. God is present and at work in each person's life. Second, we can assume that a wealth of spiritual wisdom exists on which we can draw as we seek to respond to the work of God. And third, every person is different. We cannot work with a predetermined outcome or model in spiritual direction for the simple reason that each situation is unique.

The bottom line remains the same: spiritual direction is the ministry of a fellow traveler (perhaps one who is older and more experienced) that en-

---

[3]Ibid., pp. 103-4.

ables another to respond to the initiative of the Spirit. And the one who provides this ministry cannot, and does not, know what the Spirit is saying for the other. Indeed we can never presume to know what the Spirit is saying to another. All we can do, through conversation with the other, is to foster an openness of heart and mind and suggest ways in which the person might come to clarity about the witness of the Spirit.

Spiritual direction, then, is not a ministry of giving counsel about decisions. Of course, it may be quite appropriate for a person to seek counsel in the midst of making a difficult decision. However, in spiritual direction, one of the most effective ways in which we can serve the other is by probing to see how the other can choose well, in intentional response to God.

JOHN OF THE CROSS ON SPIRITUAL DIRECTION

Here is where we see the relevance of one of the great classic commentaries on the ministry of spiritual direction, that of St. John of the Cross. In his classic of spiritual devotion, *Living Flame of Love*, John included an extended section on spiritual direction.[4] What is noteworthy is that he had relatively little to say about *good* spiritual direction but pages and pages on *poor* direction. Thomas H. Green has suggested that this is good reason to pause and realize our potential for doing harm as much as good when we enter into a conversation with another about his or her spiritual life.[5]

From John of the Cross we learn about the ministry of spiritual direction by looking at the dark side of this role, one might say, and its potential for abuse. John observed that there are two approaches that spiritual directors might take that would be injurious. The first is to presume to determine how others should live their lives. This usually means, of course, that the directors expect those they are directing to live according to the directors' expectations. And second, spiritual direction is flawed when the directors assume that oth-

---

[4]John of the Cross, *Living Flame of Love*, vol. 3 of *The Collected Works of St. John of the Cross*, trans. Kieran Kavanaugh and Otilio Rodriguez (Washington, D.C.: ICS, 1979), pp. 29-67.
[5]Thomas H. Green, *The Friend of the Bridegroom: Spiritual Direction and the Encounter with Christ* (Notre Dame, Ind.: Ave Maria, 2000), pp. 76-77.

ers will experience God in the same way that the directors have.

Often, of course, these two go together: the expectations the directors have for those they are directing correspond to the directors' own experience. Yet sometimes they are not the same. Spiritual directors may try to call forth in others a pattern of life or behavior that they themselves had hoped to have, and now the directors seek to live vicariously through the others. On both accounts, the problem is that directors assume they know best. They have an agenda largely because they overvalue their own experience of God and assume it will be replicated in others.

Obviously, we need to be alert to controlling individuals. Not all of those with agendas for others are ill intentioned; they may be generous individuals who truly believe they know what is best. But their generosity and their good intentions are nevertheless dangerous. They may not appreciate how much their good intentions are rooted in their own desire for control and for personal fulfillment. They long to be needed and to have spiritual power in the lives of others.

Some will grant them this power. Many Christians are happy to relinquish their adult responsibility to hear and know the voice of God. They are content to remain in a posture of spiritual dependence on another rather than cultivating their own capacity for discernment. They probably know that the task of discernment is hard work that calls for baring the soul. So if someone else will tell them how they are loved, where they need to face up to sin and what they need to know, they are content to let the other play this role in their lives. And so the fault can easily go both ways.

Yet we cannot stress enough that there is extraordinary freedom, power and joy in knowing, to the depths of our soul, what God is saying to us. Even though this may come slowly and painfully, and even though we will be frustrated at times (with ourselves and perhaps even with God, especially when God seems to be silent), there is no substitute for learning to discern for ourselves. Yet in many respects, we cannot do this alone. We need others to enable us, to encourage us, to challenge the propensities and biases that undermine our capacity to listen to the voice of Jesus. While alert to the dangers, we need to enter eagerly and openly into conversation with a friend, codiscerner, spiritual director or pastor. We need to be in conversation with others about the witness of the Spirit to our hearts.

THE MINISTRY OF CODISCERNMENT

Spiritual direction is a ministry of codiscernment. Though in the actual experience we might be face to face in conversation, it is helpful to think of this as a ministry in which directors walk alongside others. The directors are not so much telling the others anything as seeking, with them, to listen to the voice of Jesus.

Good spiritual directors may have relatively little to say, but what the directors do say will be oriented toward enabling those they serve to listen to what the Spirit is saying. John English put it well when he wrote, "The guide [his term for the director] is not interested in a confession of what the person has done to incur guilt but, rather, in what is happening *to* the person."[6] In other words, spiritual directors seek to help others make sense of what is happening in their experience, and the primary focus of this is what the others are experiencing in prayer.

The directors may well have counsel to give—suggestions for spiritual exercises, good reading to consider, texts of Scripture for meditation. And directors may suggest the need for a day of prayer and may speak directly to an area of neglect or blindness, where this would be appropriate. However, the objective of spiritual direction remains the same: to enable others to grow in their capacity to hear the voice of Jesus. The goal of direction is a relationship, enabling others to mature in their ability to live in communion with Christ.

Therefore, while the ministry of spiritual direction may include a discussion about many aspects of people's lives, notably work and key relationships, the conversation will regularly come back to prayer. Spiritual directors assume that those whom they serve wish to grow in faith, hope and

---

[6]John J. English, *Spiritual Freedom: From an Experience of the Ignatian Exercises to the Art of Spiritual Guidance*, 2nd ed. (Chicago: Loyola Press, 1995), p. 48.

love, and the primary catalyst for this will be their personal encounter with Christ in prayer. Naturally, then, what is happening in people's prayers will be the main focus of conversation.

It also follows that spiritual direction includes conversation about what is being experienced emotionally. Those served through this ministry can acknowledge their feelings, move toward an understanding of their significance and, as appropriate, find some resolution to emotional turmoil or desolation. Tad Dunne has suggested three questions that a director might ask to this end: (1) Is X really the feeling you are experiencing? (2) Is Y really what X is directed toward? (3) How would you feel after choosing option Z?[7] Or to put it differently, are you really feeling what you say you are feeling? Is that feeling really about what you say it is about? And what would you feel if you acted in a particular way and made the decision that is on the table? These questions would be preliminary to the act of choosing, of course, as a means of enabling those being served to be conscious of the emotional terrain in which they are living and choosing. Feelings have an inherent ambiguity; we need someone outside our immediate experience to help us monitor and understand them. This is a vital element in spiritual direction.

First, then, spiritual directors help us monitor our prayers. Second, directors help us come to terms with what is happening to us emotionally. But there is a third element to spiritual direction: this ministry means asking questions about our response to our world.

Here, too, an important distinction needs to be made. Directors are ill advised to use the word *should* about a decision others are making or to offer a judgment about whether a previous decision was wisely made. It is simply not the directors' call to make. Rather, through well-conceived questions, directors can help develop in others a capacity to act well and choose well. Questions about the range of alternatives others might consider would be appropriate. Questions that highlight aspects of the others' world, options or problems they might have overlooked and potential implications

---

[7]Tad Dunne, *Spiritual Mentoring: Guiding People Through Spiritual Exercises to Life Decisions* (San Francisco: HarperSanFrancisco, 1991), p. 152.

for family, friends and colleagues are reasonable as well.

Again, as noted above, spiritual directors are not counselors or therapists but are those who walk beside us as codiscerners, enabling us to monitor our prayers, the emotional terrain of our lives and our actions and reactions to our world. While we might appreciate keenly the value of spiritual directors when we are making a critical decision, the ministry of directors has relevance at all points in our spiritual pilgrimage.

BEING PRESENT TO ONE ANOTHER

Not all will have the opportunity to have a spiritual director, but all will be in conversation with others—pastors and elders within their church, parents and other family members, colleagues in the workplace and friends. Surely part of what we give each other is not our counsel so much as the gift of listening well, insofar as this may enable others to listen well to what God is telling them through the ministry of the Spirit. We might never actually be a spiritual director, but we can be present to others in a way that fosters their capacity to respond to the voice of Jesus. This takes time and patience, yet it is surely one of the most precious gifts we can give to each other.

Other than in a formal ministry of spiritual direction, nowhere does this gift find greater expression than in friendship. We may find pastors and religious leaders who free us and empower us in this way, but sadly this is rare. And we may find that along the way we have experiences of Christian community in which there is freedom—both the freedom to be an individual and the freedom to contribute to the community as an individual. But again, this will likely be rare. This does not mean that we abandon the church or the community of faith; it merely means that we recognize the inherent limitations in our common life.

But along the way, God will grant us the privilege of genuine friendship with one, two or three individuals who are truly codiscerners. They allow us to be individual; they free us to be other. Yet they also enable us to overcome our radical aloneness. As a friend, we have the opportunity to be the presence and voice of Jesus to others, enabling them to know they are loved, because we demonstrate it and free them to experience the inner assurance of God's love. They know God's forgiveness because we forgive them, but then our forgiveness does not obligate them; it is but a sign of the forgiveness of God. Friendship empowers us, as a mirror by which we can see ourselves, but not in a way that distorts our vision with communal expectations or demands.

A true friend believes in others and trusts others to hear the voice of Jesus. A true friend respects the capacity of others to know what God is saying to them. But conversely, the friend is never overly impressed with the others and refuses to flatter. A friend is prepared to challenge and confront as necessary. But this is never because we think we know what the others should do or what God is saying to them. It is only because we are concerned that they are not being themselves and are not truly opening their hearts to the inner witness of the Spirit.

And so, both in community and in friendship, we have much to learn from the classic and ancient ministry of spiritual direction.

First, the ministry of direction encourages us to accept one another. One of the great obstacles to discernment is pretense and inauthenticity. We often try to present ourselves as other than who we are. We cloak our words and our manner in a guise of spiritual maturity and faith, and so who we truly are and what we are really feeling are hidden deep below the surface. We are not living our own lives but those of others.

By accepting one another, we can enable each other to be more honest with God and with ourselves. Only then can we come to terms with what is happening to us emotionally. In other words, we do not really accept others unless they are free, in our company, to speak what they are feeling. Since we cannot discern well unless we come to terms with what is happening to us emotionally, one of our gifts to each other is to establish an environment in which it is safe to speak of what is happening in our hearts.

One of the most significant times of spiritual growth in my own experience was a period of two or three years in which I met with another man over lunch every three weeks or so. And each time we met, we had the same agenda for our conversation. We would ask each other, "Since we met last, what have been your joys and sorrows?" It was an exercise in which we learned to rejoice and mourn with one another (Rom 12:15). And there is no doubt that its primary benefit was to provide a safe environment within which we could acknowledge to one another what we were feeling and how we were making sense of what was happening to us emotionally. This would not have been possible if we did not know that we accepted one another.

Second, from the ministry of direction we can be honest about what we observe. This does not mean that we are cruel or harsh, but it does mean that we are candid with the others, such that the others will learn to trust our words. We do not overstate or understate. If we see something problematic, we say so. They can trust us to speak the truth in love, knowing that we will not flatter or say nice things because we long to be liked or because we fear we will hurt their feelings.

Truthfulness about what we see, and any concerns we have, does not mean that we block others' capacity to hear God. Our honest reaction may well be that we do not understand how what others feel to be the will of God for them can possibly be the will of God. We may honestly say that from our perspective it is not clear how they came up with this idea. But we must always give our observations in a manner that frees the others to act, out of their personal conviction about what God is saying to them.

Of course, if people are doing something, or are about to do something, that could bring irreparable harm to themselves and to others, we need to express concern and raise a note of caution. But usually our honesty is not a burden but a vehicle that frees the other. We can frankly point out that we think they have failed to be honest with themselves, are running from something or someone, or have failed to check their motives. We can be honest if we sense unresolved fear or anger. We can encourage others to be true to themselves with what they are feeling and thinking, especially if we believe they are not facing up to what is happening to them emotionally.

Finally, we can be forthright, after we have listened, when we tell others that as far as we can tell there are no red flags and that our sense is that they have discerned well. We do not need to tell them whether we agree with what they are doing or with the decision they have made. What they most need is the honesty wherein we tell them that it seems they have discerned properly. They have been honest with themselves, with their motives, with their circumstances and with their options. This kind of honesty is an empowering gift.

However, it must be stressed that this kind of truthfulness presupposes acceptance. We cannot be honest with others who are uncertain of our love and acceptance. Mutual openness, trust and honesty can occur only in a climate of acceptance. Until such a foundation is established, we have no right to speak, and in any case others will hear us only when they have chosen to hear us. We are better to remain silent until we can speak from a posture of love and acceptance.

And third, from the ministry of spiritual direction we can learn what it means to offer encouragement and hope. We live and work in a discouraging world. On any given day, whether at home or in the workplace, we come up against much that could cause us to lose heart. Whether it is a major setback or the subtle emotional drain that has us wondering why we should continue to persevere in a disheartening situation, one of the most powerful gifts we give to others is that of encouragement and hope.

By this I do not mean that we say to another, "Let me encourage you, friend." Usually, those who open with this line do not really know us and do not truly know what it might take to encourage us. This is a pseudo-encouragement, however sincere or well intentioned it might be.

Our acceptance and our honesty will likely be significant sources of encouragement. Whether in dealing with our family members, our friends, our colleagues or those with whom we worship on Sunday, few things are as empowering and life giving as knowing others accept us for who we are—others whom we can look to for comfort that is true, plain and simple, with no flattery, no emotional manipulation, no spiritualizing or sentimentalizing.

Beyond this, our encouragement of one another can take several forms. For one thing, we can remind one another of the multiple expressions of the goodness and presence of God, especially when in times of discouragement others might not see it.

Further, we encourage others when we suggest that God may be more present to them than they at first believe. We see this demonstrated in the wonderful exchange between Samuel and Eli when young Samuel three times heard his name called and each time came looking for the older prophet. Eli eventually told him that what he heard was the voice of God and that he should respond with "Speak, LORD, for your servant is listening" (1 Sam 3:9). Similarly, sometimes we are oblivious to the voice of Jesus, and the gift of others is to suggest that God is present and is more than we had at first realized. But again, it is not the role of the friend to tell us *what* God is saying but merely to help us be alert to the fact that God is indeed speaking.

And finally, of course, we encourage when we affirm that we see what is good, what is going well, what is commendable and worthy of praise. False affirmation is detestable and ultimately disheartening; we must speak the truth. But we can, without hesitation, celebrate with the other the ways in which they have every reason to be more hopeful and positive than they might otherwise be.

In the history of the church there have been some wonderful examples of the grace of spiritual direction and friendship. There is the relationship of Francis Xavier and his mentor and friend, Ignatius Loyola. In the latter years of their lives, their communication was entirely through letters. In a similar fashion, we have the notable correspondence between C. S. Lewis and an anonymous American woman in the 1950s and early 1960s up until his death. What stands out in this correspondence (and we only have Lewis's letters in this publication) are the themes that arose and the tone he adopted in his writing.[8]

Lewis repeatedly called for emotional honesty, urging his correspondent to cry and to accept the fact that she was mourning a loss. On one occasion he called her to acknowledge her anger as well as her fears, while simultaneously highlighting the danger of anger and fear in the spiritual life. Fur-

---

[8]C. S. Lewis, *Letters to an American Lady*, ed. Clyde S. Kilby (Grand Rapids, Mich.: Eerdmans, 1967).

ther, the letters make frequent reference to suffering, particularly to the challenge of responding with grace to difficult people. And also, Lewis spoke regularly of prayer and its place in the spiritual life, his correspondent's life in particular. In many respects, these are the three abiding themes of spiritual friendship and conversation: (1) to speak of what is happening to us emotionally, in a manner that fosters a gracious honesty and a lack of pretense; (2) to encourage each other to respond with grace to difficulty and particularly difficult people; and (3) to attend to our prayers. And through all of these, we are to be conscious of the presence and work of the Holy Spirit in our spiritual growth.

Though there is wisdom in these letters, and help for his "American lady" and for all who read this correspondence, what strikes one most in this reading is that Lewis bothered to write at all. As Clyde S. Kilby has noted, Lewis often took the time to write when he was overwhelmed with his work, when he could hardly write because of rheumatic pain in his arm and when he was personally quite averse to writing letters (wishing that the mail carrier would stay away!). As Kilby noted, the reason was that "Lewis believed that taking time out to advise or encourage another Christian was both a humbling of one's talents before the Lord and also as much the work of the Holy Spirit as producing a book."[9] Providing encouragement to a fellow Christian mattered as much to him as anything else he did. His example is a potential encouragement to all of us, to the value of spiritual conversation, of being present to another, of giving generously to one who may have little, if anything, to give in return.

All of this is another way to highlight the wonder that we do not walk the road of life alone. God grants us the grace of knowing the acceptance, the honest words and the encouragement of others. And this is grace indeed. The life of prayer can be difficult and confusing; we are wise to seek the counsel, encouragement and guidance of others and to find another who can be present to us while we make sense of the Spirit's witness to our heart.

---

[9]Ibid., p. 7.

11

MAKING DECISIONS TOGETHER

The Challenge of
Communal Discernment

❧

Decision making in partnership with others is a source of both joy and wonder—and often great frustration. But it is hardly avoidable. If we are married, we make our key life choices with another. We may be in business with a partner who rightly has as much say in the critical choices for the business as we do. We may be members of organizations and groups and committees, and we find that again and again we are making decisions with others.

Can we choose well together? Certainly. But it is appropriate to ask if the matter of discernment applies not only to our individual choices but also to those decisions we make with others. And if so, what form does it take and how might it find practical expression when we are actually facing a decision together?

Many of us are a part of search committees, boards and other decision-making entities in which the question regularly comes to the table: what is God saying to us at this time and in this place? We long to be part of communities and organizations that are intentionally seeking to be responsive to the leadership of Christ. And it is not only church boards or religious organizations that think along these lines; Christians in business partnerships, for example, long to have a sense that their work is led by the Spirit. William Barry stated it well when he wrote, "A burning question for our day . . . is

how to make those institutions [in which we work and worship] and structures more attuned to God's will. . . . There is, perhaps, no greater challenge
to religion today than to foster the conditions that make communal discernment possible."[1] And I would add that this is equally applicable to marriage;
we long to choose well *together*.

Yet while there is a tradition for individual discernment, the same cannot
be said for how we make decisions together in the Lord. In many respects,
within the Christian community we are still finding our way on this matter.
Having said this, though, we must note that there are invaluable resources
at our disposal to guide us and illumine the process for us, both from our
Christian heritage and from more recent perspectives on the nature of our
social entities. We have every reason to believe that we can learn to make
decisions together, that we can do it well and that we can do it through a
process of intentional communal discernment.

Certainly Scripture provides us with some helpful examples of communal discernment, particularly in the book of Acts. Two stand out. In
Acts 13:1-3 we have the example of the church in Antioch coming to resolution about the mission of Barnabas and Saul. The text reads, "Now in
the church at Antioch there were prophets and teachers. . . . While they
were worshiping the Lord and fasting, the Holy Spirit said, 'Set apart for
me Barnabas and Saul for the work to which I have called them.' Then
after fasting and praying they laid their hands on them and sent them
off."

Another example is found in Acts 15. What is noteworthy here is that the
issue at hand was one that included significant tension for the early church.
And at the end they had joy—not the joy of unanimity but the joy of having
chosen well. The elders and apostles came together in a forum in which
they listened to both sides of the issue, reviewed the facts at hand and
reached a decision under the leadership of a moderator, James. And they
factored theological considerations as well as practical matters into the final

---

[1]William A. Barry, "A Theology of Discernment," *The Way Supplement: The Place of Discernment*, spring 1989, p. 136.

decision. When they reached their decision, they communicated it to those affected by it with the wonderful phrase "for it has seemed good to the Holy Spirit and to us" (Acts 15:28). And the announcement was received with great joy (v. 31).

What is most compelling about both examples in Acts is the immediate and conscious presence of the Spirit in the decision. The early believers did not merely ask for wisdom and then act; they were led in their decision by the Spirit. From this we can ask, what might it look like for a group today to come to a decision that would lead them to say, "It seems good to the Holy Spirit and us" about a matter on which they need to make a choice?

What follows is expressed in terms of formal decisions being made by groups or committees. But the principles involved apply just as surely to a married couple who want to know what God might be saying regarding the issues they are facing. Further, two individuals who are working in a partnership need to know principles of communal discernment that would foster their capacity to choose well together. What would it look like for couples, business partners and groups to make decisions through a process of communal discernment?

THE NATURE OF COMMUNAL DISCERNMENT

It is helpful to consider communal discernment in contrast to three other forms of decision making. Most Christians assume that the organizations of which they are a part are of one of three kinds—hierarchical, egalitarian or consensual—and that those organizations make decisions accordingly.

The egalitarian model is no doubt most prominent in the West, where most people make decisions within churches and other organizations on the basis of a clear-headed, rational review of pros and cons. In debate, the merits of opposing views are presented and then a vote is taken. And in a reasonable and democratic way, this majority vote comes to represent not only the will of the people but also the will of God. Thus in the egalitarian model it is assumed that if the Spirit is active in the decision making, this making, this activity will not be immediate but rather mediated through the reasoned decision-making process of the group. We pray for wisdom and then act on the assumption that God will guide the process.[2] However, one could challenge these assumptions on several levels.

While no one is calling for a demise of sensible organization and rational behavior, there are some inherent weaknesses in egalitarian decision making. First, this approach to making decisions naturally favors those who are articulate and highly rational. Second, this approach assumes that each person has not only an equal say but also an equal amount of wisdom or capacity to discern. While the merits of this approach are obvious when it comes to our need for a government that represents the people, this model discounts the reality that some members of the community might have more experience and wisdom to contribute to the process than others. In addition, the Bible specifically speaks of those with the gift of discernment. How is that gift honored in the egalitarian model?

In contrast, other churches and organizations, especially in the East and some parachurch organizations, assume a hierarchical model in which the voice of Jesus is equated not with the will of the majority but with the will of the senior leader. While some Christians may be content with this model, especially if they have deep trust in their leader, the model takes no account of the limitations, weaknesses and potential blind spots of the leader. This model also disregards the wealth of wisdom and insight that is available through the community.

There are times in which the will of the majority should be a point of reference and discussion. Throughout the course of our days, we can make many decisions efficiently and simply through a majority vote. Further, there are also decisions that are made for the sake of expediency, if nothing else, by those in formal office. Where I work, for example, we have a fairly well-developed understanding of which decisions are made by vote of the faculty or the board of trustees and which decisions are made by the presi-

---

[2]This seems to have been the approach of the pre-Pentecost church (see Acts 1:26).

dent. The latter tend to be decisions of implementation rather than policy-making, but the president has real authority, just as it is possible to speak of the real authority of both the board and the faculty when they act in concert by majority rule. However, there are times in the life of any community when a critical decision is on the table and when it is appropriate to ask, what is the Lord saying to us? In this, we are not merely implementing but establishing direction, marking out the contours of our common life. And we want to be able to appropriate the witness of the Spirit to the community as a whole. I will say more on the kinds of decisions that would merit this type of focused attention below, but for now it is important to observe that these kinds of decisions call for a different approach to decision making.

The process of communal discernment chooses to set aside both the democratic model (one vote per person) and the hierarchical model (only the voice of the leadership matters). Inagrace Dietterich describes this well:

> Discerning communities are not hierarchical in structure, but neither are they egalitarian. Because all receive the gifts to contribute to the common good, everyone enjoys the right and the obligation of participating authoritatively in decisions of faith and practice. Yet because the Spirit distributes different gifts, responsibilities and functions, there is also an element of differentiation. Spiritual gifts are not distributed in monotonous uniformity but in rich diversity. *The focus here is not on the prerogatives of the designated leaders or on the equal privileges of the members, but on corporate responsibility for discerning the wisdom and prompting of the Holy Spirit.* Thus communities of giftedness are neither autocratic (the rule of one) nor democratic (the rule of the people) but pneumocratic (the rule of the Holy Spirit). Authority within missional communities is found neither in particular status nor in majority opinion.[3]

---

[3]Darrell L. Guder et al., *Missional Church: A Vision for the Sending of the Church in North America* (Grand Rapids, Mich.: Eerdmans, 1998), pp. 173-74, emphasis added. This is from a chapter written by Inagrace Dietterich.

In response to the limitations of the autocratic and egalitarian approaches, many propose and work on the assumption that the best way forward is what is commonly called "decision making by consensus." In this third model it is assumed that the best way to make a choice together is by a process of informal discussion in which a course of action gradually emerges as different voices are heard and in which eventually unanimous agreement is achieved. While there are approaches to consensus decision making that do not presume the outcome must be unanimous, for many this unanimity is still the ideal. They believe that to be "of the same mind" (Phil 4:2) is to be unanimous. And this unanimity is often viewed as the key sign both of the effectiveness of the process as well as of the legitimacy of the outcome.

An assumption is commonly made: if we all agree, then it must be God's will. But while there are settings in which decision making by an informal process of establishing a consensus is certainly appropriate, decision making by consensus also has its limitations, and each of these is potentially a hindrance to true communal discernment. It is rarely the case, for example, that a group can make a difficult decision by consensus, that is, a creative or imaginative choice that reflects courageous vision. One finds that the naysayers and the pessimists tend to have too much influence in shaping the conversation. Or the sentimentalists and the idealists might sway the discussion by urging all to have more vision or faith. Few if any feel safe to challenge the pessimists or the idealists. Then, also, it has been well documented that decision making by consensus often leads to a decision to which no one is opposed but that also has no strong supporters (what is called the Abilene effect, because the one who coined this apparently observed it to happen in a personal encounter in Abilene, Texas). In the consensus model we come to choices that everyone can accept on some level, but we easily end up with a decision that no one supports enthusiastically.

Furthermore, those involved in consensual decision making too often assume that unanimity is the ideal outcome, and in religious circles this unanimity is presented as a key evidence of God's guidance. The result is that frequently people feel pressured to go along with a group so that the outcome can be called unanimous. But then their own reservations or concerns or disagreements are usually left under the carpet or not taken seriously. Consensual decision making is all too easily influenced by a misplaced niceness in which we choose the safe alternative out of fear that we will offend others, hurt their feelings or be accused of causing conflict. But as Parker Palmer has aptly noted, what we are seeking is not unanimity but a good decision![4] And this is where the consensual approach to decision making often comes up short.

Finally, there is another problem with consensual decision making—what many have concluded is an inherent flaw in this approach. If there are negative or dissonant voices, these are magnified. Their presence frequently takes on a force out of proportion to the sentiments of the group as a whole. And the consequence is that folks agree—perhaps to keep harmony—with the dissonant, intransigent voice as a way of coming to agreement. The outcome of this capitulation, though, does not reflect the true will of the majority. And the group has not chosen well.

There certainly are times when it is appropriate to take a vote and make a decision by an egalitarian, democratic process. And there are other times when it is appropriate to allow those in leadership to choose and act on behalf of the organization. And there definitely are times when decision making through a process of finding a consensus is what is needed. But if we are going to have genuine communal discernment of the will of God, we need to find a model that enables us to listen together to the leadership of Christ for this group at this time, through a conscious and intentional response to the Holy Spirit.

Some will suggest that this is a risky and ambiguous process and one that easily can be abused. This is a legitimate observation. But while there is no doubt that the process can be abused, that is also the case for the hierarchical and egalitarian approaches. I have seen the abuse of power in both cases, both in leaders who have refused to listen to the group and in groups where those who knew how to manipulate Robert's Rules of Order man-

---

[4]Parker Palmer, *To Know as We Are Known: A Spirituality of Education* (San Francisco: Harper & Row, 1983), pp. 95-96.

aged to do so in a way that bypassed the will of the majority. And doubtless some argue for consensual decision making because they know how to work the model to their own ends. All systems are subject to abuse.

But more to the point, if we do not seek (and find) an approach that allows us to respond intentionally to the Spirit, the danger is that our organizations and systems of decision making will remain fundamentally secular. We might have rational, efficient systems of decision making, but our rationality may not serve us well—it can actually marginalize the Spirit! The solution is not some kind of sentimental posture that says, "Let's just pray and God will show us the way." This kind of sentimentality is less than helpful. Neither should we then merely resolve to discount our identity as an organization and our need for reasonable decision-making processes.

We need an approach that is clear, accessible and reasonable. And we need an approach that accounts for the complexity of our organizational life, for both the rational as well as the intuitive, emotional and of course spiritual dynamics that constitute our common life. At the end of the process we should be able to explain why we think God is leading in a particular way. In other words, we should be leery of any kind of "holy hunch" or a "vision" or intuition that no one can challenge. On the other hand, we need a model of communal discernment and decision making that takes intuition seriously and that with this acknowledges the vital place of affect, so that at the end of the day we are able to say, "We have a deep and abiding peace that this is what we are supposed to do."

Some communities will use an intentional process of communal discernment when choosing key personnel. For example, this approach may be used by a search committee that is assigned the task of finding a senior pastor, by a committee that has been given the responsibility to set the direction of an organization, or by a group that is seeking to establish its mission and vision. These are the kinds of decisions that, it would seem, merit a different way of thinking and acting. They set the contours of our common life in a way that requires us to agree together that "it has seemed good to the Holy Spirit and to us" for us to proceed in this course of action.[5]

Not every decision that an organization makes would be subject to the process that will be outlined below. That is neither reasonable nor necessary. As individuals, we make many decisions without prayer or the need for specific prayer. God entrusts us with wisdom and the common sense we need to live our lives.[6] But we all come up against those decisions and choices where the wiser course is to slow down, view the whole situation and then seek a sense of what the Lord is saying to us.

In the same way, each community or group would need to agree about when the approach to certain kinds of choices and decisions will be qualitatively different. In these cases, the group might conclude that this is not a one-person decision nor a majority-vote decision. For this kind of decision, they would resolve to go through a process of communal discernment.

A married couple might be making a decision about family or work or church involvement—a critical choice in which wife and husband agree that this is a matter that alters the contours of their lives. They may feel keenly that this is something not only on which they will decide together but also on which they will consciously seek to make a choice through intentional response to the witness of the Spirit to their hearts. The principles

---

[5]Tad Dunne made a helpful distinction when he spoke of the difference between basic decisions and instrumental decisions (see footnote three in chapter seven). For communal discernment, basic decisions are those that define the fundamental character, orientation and future of the organization. They are those decisions that relate to mission, strategic choices and the appointment of key personnel. Instrumental decisions are those actions that fulfill this agenda.

Using this classification, I would suggest that it is appropriate for a group to use Robert's Rules of Order (or another system that would govern formal debate and group decision making) for instrumental decisions. This would protect the will of the majority and the voice of the minority. And it would keep the process for these kinds of decisions efficient, clear, rational and focused, so that the group can get on with its work.

[6]This is not to discount the call to be in prayer at all times; it is merely to suggest that we do not engage in a period of formal prayer for each and every decision we make. Rather, every day we make a host of decisions that are informed by our prayers, so that we do everything with thanksgiving (Col 3:17), but we do not have a special prayer for guidance and wisdom about each decision.

of communal discernment with groups might be applicable to their joint task of choosing together in the Lord.

CRITICAL AFFIRMATIONS

While communal decision making affirms the place of both the intuitive and the rational, it also affirms three other contributions to the decision-making process: the role of leadership, the contribution of each member of the group and the place of the gift of discernment within the community.

The role of leadership. Communal discernment does not negate the responsibility of leaders to lead, but it insists that leadership find its place *within* the process, as part of a group coming to a common decision. We see this reflected in one of the key biblical texts on discernment—1 Thessalonians 5:12-24, where Paul calls his readers to "not quench the Spirit" but at the same time to "test everything"—in that the text begins with an appeal that the Thessalonians would respect those who "have charge of you in the Lord."

Every community needs leaders, those who are called to govern and give oversight to our common life. Leadership is one of the gifts given to the community. It is naive to discount the need for leadership. Consequently, when God calls someone into leadership within the community, it only makes sense that the community take seriously the perspective and skills that that leadership represents. But it is authentic leadership only if the leader listens to the community and to the voice of the Spirit *through* the community. And so the first task of leadership is to listen. Personal agendas must be set aside. The work of a leader is to serve the community well, and this means that the leader must first learn to listen well.

The voice of each member of the community. Communal discernment shares with egalitarian decision making the conviction that each member of the group plays a significant role in the discernment process. But while the egalitarian model assumes that everyone has an equal voice, communal discernment seeks to affirm the *appropriate* voice and contribution of each one. Although all can speak and all can contribute, the contribution should correspond to a member's giftedness and role within the community.

The gift of discernment. Paul spoke of discernment as one of the gifts of the Spirit to the Christian community (1 Cor 12:10). It follows that this gift should be taken into account in communal discernment. The hierarchical approach to decision making assumes that only the leader has this gift. The egalitarian model attributes it to the body in its corporate expression only and tends to discount the idea that an individual may have a unique gift of discernment that can enable the whole community to discern more effectively. And while there will no doubt be considerable debate on the meaning or character of this gift for our common life, it might be helpful to view it as any individual contribution that enables the group to discern well. Therefore, the gift of discernment will have a variety of expressions. Different persons who have this gift will help the group discern by contributing in different ways. Each expression of this gift will be exercised in deference to the group and with an eager resolve to hear what God is saying through others.

It is helpful to consider four ways in which this gift might find expression within communal discernment:

- Some bring a gift of discernment through their capacity to see beyond the immediate. Every community, it seems, has those who have vision, who see the big picture—a capacity made possible only if they are not caught up in the mundane details of the organization. Those who have this capacity need to be cautious lest they are impatient with those who do not see things as quickly as they do. They need to consciously value and listen to those whose strength is to focus on the details of the immediate situation.

- Some have a gift of discernment exercised through their capacity for critical analysis—they understand the issues and the facts as well as the implications of the various choices a group is considering. Some with this competency have the capacity to read the facts easily, perhaps the financial data that are presented to the group, while others have the capacity to do the research needed to assess and respond well to a situation. The caution for those with this gift of discernment is to remember that though careful analysis is critical to the process of discernment, the process always includes more than rational analysis.

- Some are intuitives and have been given the capacity to identify the emotional dimension of organizations and communities. They are able to bring to the discussion an awareness of how a community and individuals within the community are responding emotionally to change or the possibility of change. At their best, intuitives can help the process by attending to the emotional contours of a community and the emotional dimensions of a decision-making process. But there is a caution: they need to recognize the potential of emotional blackmail in a discernment and decision-making process, when one person or a group of individuals tie up the process with a threat—explicit or implicit—that they will be "hurt" if they do not get their way.

- Finally, the gift of discernment is also found in the sage, an individual who has perhaps been with the organization for a long time and is able to speak out of years of experience and observation. This is an invaluable contribution to the community. Yet here too there is a danger, for those who are older or have been with an organization longer can easily discount the contributions of those who bring a fresh perspective. After all, sometimes it is the newcomer who sees what those of us who have been around a while cannot see or have come to take for granted.

God gives leaders to the church. And God grants the church the gift of discernment in all its expressions. But when it comes to communal discernment, the danger is that leaders and those with the gift of discernment would become impatient with the process or see no need for it. It is imperative, though, that these leaders be a *gift*, contributing to a process out of their roles or unique capacities. They are not a gift if they co-opt the process of communal discernment rather than facilitate the process, helping the outcome take shape.

For example, as a pastor I have over the years noted a marked contrast between two kinds of church treasurers—those who are convinced that the facts speak for themselves and those who ask, with the group, what God is saying to us in the light of these facts. And I have celebrated those veterans in our midst, wise sages, who will happily speak to a situation out of their years of experience but then also insist that their observations be seen as one contribution to the process, not the final word on what should be done.

Communities and organizations want to cooperate with those who have been appointed to leadership roles in their midst. But many are weary of leaders who presume to know the mind of God, who have a vision for the organization or the community that cannot be put to the test of discernment and who will tolerate no opposition. Leadership is appointed to lead. But real leadership occurs within the process of communal discernment and welcomes a process of shared leadership that affirms both formal roles and the multiple ways in which the group has been gifted and thus enabled to think well and discern well. In the process of discernment, then, leadership may come from different members of the group, at different times, in a way congruent with varied strengths, abilities and contributions to the conversation. If a person in a formal role of leadership has a proposal for a new direction or strategic initiative, that person ought to be happy to see this proposal put on the table so that the community can discern together whether this is truly of God. But the leaders and the whole community need a process of discernment that both gives the proposal a fair hearing and leads to an outcome that can be embraced by all because the group senses that God has been an active participant in the conversation.

Communal discernment assumes that God speaks *through* the communal process—a process that affirms the role of leadership and the gift of discernment. But it is nevertheless a process wherein God speaks to the group as a group. It is also important to recognize that though the gift of discernment *may* be linked with specific people (the visionary, the expert in data analysis, the intuitive and the sage), this is not necessarily the case. Even if we cannot link this gift to specific individuals in the group, we can assume that it is present. As a group, we have the gift of discernment, for the Scriptures speak of this as a gift that is given to the church (1 Cor 12:10). We may not know precisely how it will be exercised, so we need to be open to surprises. God may speak to us not through the strong among us but through the weak, not through the senior but through the child in our midst, not through the veteran but through the newcomer, not through the established and articulate voices but through those who till now have said little. However, we hear only if we have ears to hear.

THE CONDITIONS FOR COMMUNAL DISCERNMENT

The conditions that make communal discernment possible are as important as the process itself. Ideally, of course, those who participate in the process of communal discernment are themselves discerning people, with a personal pattern of prayer and of seeking to be attentive to the Spirit. Still, it has been my experience that if a significant number within the group have this posture of heart, they will as often as not set the tone for the whole group—a tone that is governed by the commitment to discern together the mind of the Spirit. Having said this, though, I hasten to add that communal discernment can easily be derailed by a belligerent, aggressive or cynical person. The process is vulnerable to anyone bent on derailing it.

And of course, the possibility of communal discernment presumes a common commitment that our church or organization wants to be led by Christ, however this is framed or understood. Moreover, the values and principles by which we will be governed and by which we will live are, as much as possible, those that we find within the pages of holy Scripture. Communal discernment, in other words, presupposes that the Spirit is present in our midst. And we can attest to this presence through the three classic signs of the Spirit's presence: Christ is glorified; the Scriptures are honored; and our common life is characterized by unity with diversity. And the abiding test of all three is joy.

With these assumptions regarding our individual and common commitments identified, there are as yet several critical conditions to note. Each makes communal discernment possible.

A common purpose. We will be able to discern well together only if we have a common sense about who we are as a group, organization or movement. If we cannot agree on what business we are in and what we are here for, then we will not be able to discern together a vision for the next chapter of our lives. We can decide together on these matters only if we hold a common understanding about our corporate identity—a common charism.[7]

A resolve to decide together. We will be able to decide well together only if we have a resolve to do so. This means that we are prepared to set aside our personal agendas and prior convictions and come to the process with an open heart and mind. This does not mean that we do not have strong feelings and passionate opinions; the process can handle those. But it does mean that we have determined to seek the mind of God *together*. We consciously choose not to approach the process with a preconceived outcome in mind or the thought that all we need to do is persuade the others of what we already know is right. We resolve to choose together. And of course, this means that we will respect the process and the outcome (more later on what it means to respect the outcome if one cannot agree with it).

The classic description for this disposition in discernment is "holy indifference." Again, as noted in an earlier chapter, indifference here does not suggest apathy but rather that we have taken our hands off the outcome. With open hearts and minds, we enter into a process in which we seek with each other an outcome that is possible only if we think and pray together and that as much as possible respects the call of God to our community.

Here, too, is where we need to be alert to what might be called the "strong" individual whose personal will and ability to exert that will can undermine our capacity to discern together as a group. This may be a person in official leadership—the pastor of a church or the dean of a college or a senior stakeholder with a long-term commitment to the group. Any one of these could

---

[7]While the idea of a "charism" is more prevalent in Roman Catholic circles, many non-Catholics appreciate that the idea captures the simple yet significant reality that our congregations and organizations have been brought into being by the Spirit and that they are a gift (a charism) through which the Spirit graces the church and the world. When we discern our charism, we discern the unique way in which this group or community or organization is a gift of the Spirit.

assume that his or her vision is the right vision and that any dissent lacks either intelligence or faith or both. But sometimes this kind of person exerts a dominating influence without really being aware of it. Often these people insist that they have no power. But this only highlights the need for alertness about the role that individuals actually play in the life of a group or a community. We must ask, do these persons so cherish their personal vision that they are incapable of letting it go and seeking to make a decision together?[8]

Mutual regard and acceptance. Communal discernment requires, as a basic condition, a high degree of mutual respect and the acceptance of the other as one with whom we will choose. This means that we respect each other's voice and the contribution that each one will make to the decision. It means that we cannot come to a good decision except we come to it together. We will find wisdom in each other along the way, and we need each other's input.

Communal discernment asserts the intelligence of the other, the sincerity of the other (we do not assume ill intentions) and the capability of the other to help us come to a good decision. This finds expression in our resolve to listen to one another. In listening we set aside our own agendas and attend to each other. And we do so in the conviction that God is going to speak to us through one another. Communal discernment is not the act of waiting for God to speak from the sky or to write something on the wall; God speaks to us through the conversation we will have as well as the prayer that is part of that conversation. And so we need each other. We are discerning together and thus must listen to each other. If we cannot listen well, we cannot discern well.[9]

---

[8]In my first pastorate it took several months for me to realize that the board meetings were not the place where key decisions were being made; the real authority and influence was held by two widows—sisters who had always been in the church and whom no one dared question. Though they held no official role as elders or deacons in the church, it was clearly the case that for many years they were the source of real power and decision making. Nothing happened to which they did not agree, and no one acted without first consulting them. This explained why all board decisions happened over two meetings (so that, as I later found out, members of the board could consult with the two sisters before a final decision was made).
[9]Just as individual discernment requires that we respect the voice of others while sustaining

A foundation of mutual regard and acceptance means that we can handle conflict graciously. We do not need to fear disagreements or passion about diverse opinions, because we honor one another. And our diverse perspectives become the means by which we will come to a common mind, as we see clearly in the example of communal discernment described in Acts 15. But we cannot handle conflict and disagreement constructively if there is personal tension within the group, that is, if there are individuals who have unresolved anger with one another. Where this discord exists, the disagreement will, almost invariably, be fueled by this anger and thus will not be constructive. Mutual respect and acceptance mean that we have forgiven wrongs. We have spoken with one another, if need be in private, to resolve the wrong so that we can truly seek an outcome where we are of "one mind" or the "same mind" (Phil 2:1-4; 4:2).

We need to accept difference of opinion as part of our common life. If we fear disagreement, we will not discern well, for we will avoid (sometimes at all costs) hearing both sides of an argument or more than one perspective. Further, our diversity within community suggests that communal discernment will always be a tough challenge. And it has been my experience that if we evade differences of opinion early in the process, it will always come out later, only then in unhealthy ways and with much more stress and conflict. I have more than once observed a group trying to get along by skirting disagreement because it would dampen the enthusiasm for something or hurt someone's feelings. But avoiding disagreement usually means that we will have to deal with it eventually.

The reality of diversity of opinion is but another reminder of the need to be suspicious of premature unanimity. It could seem as though all are in agreement, but significant disagreement may exist, not in the open but under the surface. To ignore it now and give it no opportunity for expression only means that it will appear at a later date, likely in regrettable ways. A difference of opinion does not prevent a decision from being made; rather,

---

our individual identity, so communal discernment requires that we respect the contribution of the individual without allowing the individual's agenda to co-opt the community.

points of disagreement and conflict need to come into play as part of the process of discernment.

A clearly framed matter for discernment. When we come together to seek the mind of the Spirit, it is best (if not essential) that we have clarity about the issue we are to discuss and about which we are seeking a resolution. This should be clear for each participant in the process. For example, we have two or more candidates for a position and we are to discern which name we will bring forward in nomination.

While the issue at hand does not always call for a simple yes or no, communal discernment does require clarity about the matter for discernment. Without this clarity and agreement, much energy will be dissipated in peripheral concerns. And while these may be legitimate matters for discussion, they will be just that: matters for discussion. But communal discernment is specifically about reaching a decision.

Good information and good research. Communal discernment is not a matter of "holy hunches" or "acting on faith rather than being bothered with the facts." God speaks into the particularities of our lives and the actual circumstances, challenges, problems, opportunities and resources of the communities of which we are a part. Let us always be alert to the false spirituality that suggests good research is not needed for a good decision because "all we need is prayer."

We cannot discern well unless we understand our environment and accept this environment as the context into which God will speak to us. This includes accepting our limitations. We are not wise to speak of our limitations (such as financial constraints) as merely a bump on the road that faith can overlook. True faith seeks to hear what God is saying within the limitations in which we find ourselves, and effective discernment grants us the capacity to see possibilities in light of those limitations.

One could potentially respond to this outline of the conditions of effective communal discernment with exasperation, wondering when one might ever be part of a group with such a high level of spiritual and psychological maturity.We can all think about the circumstances of our workplace and our church and perhaps our homes and conclude that this ideal is simply not within our grasp. We live in a fallen world; our communities reflect this brokenness. But we can and must affirm that the Spirit is offered to broken, sinful groups as well. We can and must affirm that even where the conditions are not ideal, the Spirit is present. And finally, we can seek within our homes, churches and places of work to be the kinds of individuals who foster effective communal discernment.

In this connection, I am impressed with the words of Paul in Romans 12:18, where he wrote, "If it is possible, so far as it depends on you, live peaceably with all." In other words, we can choose to do all we can do to foster a climate of effective discernment. We can be alert to those who might undermine the communal process while also becoming more alert to the ways in which we ourselves might hinder that process. And we can intentionally partner with others in whom we recognize this same resolve to know what God is saying to this community at this time. We can embrace the words of Paul in Philippians 2, where he called his readers to be "of one mind" and followed this with a call to do nothing out of selfish ambition but rather to respond with humility and grace, looking to the interests of others. When we do, we will be surprised at the multiple ways in which the Spirit is present in our midst. This will not mean that our decision making is infallible. If only! But it will mean that we ourselves will grow in our capacity to hear the voice of Jesus as we seek to make decisions with others.

12

MAKING DECISIONS TOGETHER

The Process of
Communal Discernment

❧

The previous chapter described the unique challenge of communal discernment. This chapter describes the process itself as well as the resources available to those who propose to follow an intentional approach to communal discernment.[1]

This process is best engaged in by a relatively small group of from six to eight individuals. It may be possible to enter into a genuine process of communal discernment with nine persons or perhaps a few more. But the larger the group, the greater the likelihood that group dynamics will unduly complicate the process. Furthermore, communal discernment by its nature requires full participation: no one is on the margins; everyone has a voice that must be heard if we are going to know the mind of God. And it is my observation that as soon as you have a group of more than eight, inevitably it means that someone will no longer be comfortable speaking or expressing

---

[1]Though here I offer an approach to communal discernment, it is important to recognize that the best approach may often be contextual within specific denominational and theological traditions. In other words, while it is appropriate for Roman Catholics, Presbyterians and Pentecostal Christians to learn from one another, it is also vital that they appeal to their respective faith traditions as a source of wisdom and guidance in making a decision together. Furthermore, the approved policies and procedures of a denominational group will also be a setting that could either enhance the process or provide some critical limitations that need to be taken into account.

a difference of opinion. Even for highly confident, articulate and extroverted persons, the larger the group, the more reticent they tend to be with their comments and observations. The group may be so large that it is not a safe place for true discernment.[2]

Larger groups need to assign committees or smaller groups to enter into a process of discernment on their behalf. This does not discount the critical role of the larger group to test and approve what is discerned by the smaller company; it is simply that communal discernment by nature is a small-group activity. The larger group might hold a preliminary meeting to share ideas and express concerns as well as to provide information for the discernment group. Also, the smaller group, during the course of their work, might bring a regular communiqué back to the larger assembly as well as, of course, a final report with their proposal or nomination. But the actual process of communal discernment, while it includes the regular interchange between the smaller group and the assembly, will still be focused on this smaller company of individuals.

One reason a smaller core is needed is that God speaks through the group as a group, and so each participant in the process needs to be present each time the group meets. For other types of decision making, people can come and go and can wait until the end of the process to see if they agree. But in communal discernment, we are deciding *together*. And if the process of discernment involves several meetings (as is often the case for a search committee, for example), then it is more likely that a smaller committee or group can consistently have all its members present.

THE RESOURCES FOR COMMUNAL DISCERNMENT

Several tools, resources and techniques are at our disposal for the critical task of communal discernment.

The classic principles of discernment. While the dynamics for commu-

---

[2]With more than eight people, and definitely more than twelve, the relational dynamics are such that we are wiser to find recourse in a formal method of decision making, such as Robert's Rules of Order.

nal discernment will be different from those for individual discernment, the principles that have already been outlined in this study apply to communal discernment. Here, too, we are seeking to listen with heart and mind, only now as a community, out of a conviction that God is on our side and has a positive regard for us. As with individual discernment, we live and work and discern knowing that God loves us. This conviction does not come with the thought that we are the best church or the best organization or the best school (such pride, in fact, will undermine our capacity to choose well), but rather it comes in humility and awe over the fact that God would look upon us with favor. Furthermore, we are reminded of the necessity to be alert to our own sinful propensities. The process of discernment may well call to mind our need to acknowledge wrong. And in some cases this may involve institutional sin that needs to be addressed before we can discern well. Then also, communal discernment takes truth seriously, both the hard data (the facts as they present themselves) and the need for critical thinking and intelligent analysis. But communal discernment also pays primary attention to what is happening to us emotionally—to our affective response to one another and to possible outcomes of our choices, to our need for courage, to the reality that we so easily function, even as groups, out of fear (fear of one another, fear of others outside our circle, fear of failure) rather than courage and confidence.

The science of strategic planning and appreciative inquiry. For some the term "strategic planning" sounds like an overly rational way of thinking about organizational life, and they bristle at the thought that Christians and churches would engage in something so managerial. But strategic planning is nothing more than the elemental task of asking and responding to the question, what are we being called to do in the next chapter of our common life? We cannot do everything and should not even try to do everything that we might consider doing. So, in the light of our mission, our charism, the resources available to us and the gifts and passions God has granted us, where will we invest our energies? This is a reasonable and also a responsible mode of action. It is an inquiry into our circumstances that enables good stewardship of the mission and resources of the organization where we serve. When strategic planning is no more than rational analysis, it fails to be an effective means of empowering a community. But when it becomes a vehicle for genuine conversation in partnership with the principles of discernment, it is an invaluable aid to our decision making and communal discernment.

Strategic planning has more recently been complemented by the discipline of *appreciative inquiry*. This more contemporary technique may well be one of the most significant means by which we could facilitate communal discernment, because it is precisely the kind of tool we can use to open up a community to the witness of the Spirit.

Appreciative inquiry has two central components, as evident in the two words that form the phrase. By "inquiry" we mean the discipline of listening. Inquiry is the intentional exploration that enables those within an organization to learn about their mission, their common work and their contribution together. It asks others what they see and what they appreciate about what is happening. Appreciative inquiry involves an intentional act of asking questions both within the organization and outside it. A church would query its members about their dreams, their needs, their involvement in the church and what they value about their church community. But we would also ask those on the outside (perhaps companies that do business with the church or members of other churches in the same neighborhood), and here too we would ask in a way that enables us to know how this church at this time is being seen. We learn something, in other words, by listening to others. And this listening is congruent with and essential to the task of communal discernment.

But appreciative inquiry does not involve indiscriminate questioning. A particular interest characterizes the following questions: What are we doing well? What do we value about this place and this organization and these opportunities? Usually when we ask questions, we tend to ask, "What's wrong?" or "What's the problem?" But appreciative inquiry suggests that we might instead ask in terms of what is "right." Thus our point of departure is not so much what is missing as what is present. Our bias may be to look for problems, but appreciative inquiry prompts us instead to identify where there has been success and highlight what has gone well. This is significant for communal discernment because it alerts us to how the Spirit has been at work in this community, and we identify this on the assumption that the Spirit's work in the future will be in continuity with the Spirit's work among us thus far. It enables us to think about our work as arising out of our strengths, out of what we have done well, rather than out of our areas of problem or weakness. The strength of this form of inquiry is its positive character, a posture that has the capacity to foster hope.

As appropriate, therefore, groups and organizations might wish to take advantage of the science of strategic planning and appreciative inquiry, as a tool or resource that would foster communal discernment.

The art of leading small groups toward decisions. The principles of group dynamics are especially helpful when it comes to group discussions around decisions and can serve the process of communal discernment. Some basic elements to a group discussion enable the group to have a conversation that leads to a good decision.[3] They include the resolve that we will seek an agreement without sacrificing our own opinions and commitments. We can enter into the discussion free to share our opinion, but we are not out to win an argument and end the discussion. We offer what we see and what we feel strongly about, not as a means of persuading the others in the group to see things our way but as part of the data that will inform our discussion. And we can assume that if we do not share these convictions with others in the group, something vital is missing to the process. We are not seeking to persuade or press our point. That may come later, but it will come as something that arises out of the discussion rather than something that we bring to the discussion. And this means that we can be both passionate about what we offer and open

---

[3]My comments in this section are based in part on the input from two noteworthy sources on this topic. Parker Palmer, *To Know as We Are Known: A Spirituality of Education* (San Francisco: Harper & Row, 1983) has a good set of guidelines and suggestions, pp. 95-96. See also the helpful presentation on the "skillful discussion" by Rick Ross in Peter Senge et al., *The Fifth Discipline Fieldbook: Strategies and Tools for Building a Learning Organization* (New York: Doubleday, 1994), pp. 385-89.

to a change of mind. We can vigorously put our contribution on the table for review and discussion, but also we can eagerly listen to others so as to appreciate the perspective they offer. Our advocacy for one perspective is more than matched by our inquiry into how others see things.

This means that we approach the discussion without thinking in terms of winners and losers. We are not going to take a vote. In contrast to parliamentarian debate or Robert's Rules of Order, we are not speaking for or against a motion that will ultimately be defeated or carried. Rather, we are contributing to a process. As such, we speak with conviction, but we also explore with others their convictions and opinions, not as a way to persuade them of what we have to offer, but as a way to appreciate what they are bringing to the discussion. And we can actually seek out points of difference. Disagreements are not a threat to the process but a critical ingredient that will enable us to make a good decision together. According to Robert's Rules, one must state if one is for or against a motion before one can speak to it. However, in communal discernment we need the freedom to make observations, speak to something, even with passion, when we are still unsure of all that is implied by what we are saying. We may even bring things into the discussion that we may not agree with but that we feel need to be considered. We can suspend assumptions while we probe potential outcomes.

Then also, this form of discussion should include honesty about what people are feeling, their intuitive hunches and affective responses to what emerges in the discussion. We do not fear affect or press to keep the discussion entirely on a rational plane (as though that were possible). We are conscious that we engage one another with heart and mind. Consequently, what is happening to us emotionally, and our intuitive responses to one another and to the ideas and suggestions placed on the table, is as significant as anything else that informs the conversation and influences the decision we will make together.

Finally, this form of discussion leads to resolution. What we are seeking is not polite small talk. Such conversation may be fine in another setting but does not serve for communal discernment. Similarly, dinner-table conversation and discourse may be great fun and highly profitable when nothing needs to be resolved. And debate, whether it takes place on the bus or in a formal academic setting, may persuade someone of something; as often as not, the encounter itself is a useful exercise quite apart from whether there is any resolution. But when it comes to decision making, the group discussion necessarily moves toward a resolution. In formal parliamentary debate there as such things as filibusters and delaying tactics, when one party seeks to keep a formal decision from coming to implementation. And in polite discussion around a dinner table, we might consciously not press a point because we do not want to offend our guests or our hosts. But this kind of conversation does not foster good decision making. It has its place, but not when it comes to a community that is seeking resolution to something. Further, communal discernment requires that each participant be conscious of the process, particularly that it is a process that will (and must) move toward resolution. We do not rush in this direction, yet we all agree that even if we move slowly, a *decision* is the intended outcome that we seek and we agree together to work to this end.

The role of the moderator. In communal discernment the role of the moderator is critical. A great deal depends on having a moderator who understands the character of this role. The moderator is not a "leader," out ahead of the others and seeking to persuade them of a vision or a direction or a decision they should make. Nor is the moderator a neutral observer, as is intended by the role of the "speaker" in parliamentarian debate or the "chair" in Robert's Rules of Order, who is charged to maintain a neutral position, explicitly intended not to take sides but to moderate the opposing views that come to the table for discussion. Rather, in communal discernment the moderator is an active participant, not one who stands outside of the process but one who discerns along with the others. As a participant, the moderator acts as a midwife for the deliberations.

- The moderator fosters a safe environment for genuine conversation, where opinions are called for and considered without a sense of judgment or premature debate. The group needs openness and trust, along with mutual respect.

- The moderator establishes a posture of openness to the Spirit and to the new perspectives and surprises that may come through the awareness of the Spirit's presence in the process. In this sense, the moderator sets the tone, as often as not through leadership in prayer.

- The moderator sets an agenda for the discussion, but it is an agenda that provides general guidelines while remaining flexible to developments or perspectives that may emerge during the conversation.

- The moderator enables the discussion to move forward at an appropriate pace toward resolution. This includes suggesting when the group may be ready for closure.

Effective moderators, while responsible in these ways, are always open to suggestions from the group about anything that might facilitate the conversation and the decision that is being sought. In other words, this is not a controlling role or even a position of power per se but one that has a single objective: to foster good discussion that builds toward a decision.

An external consultant? Some groups may wonder if their decision-making process would be enhanced and strengthened by the presence of an external consultant. They may feel that the issues they are facing are so complex and the decision itself so weighted with emotional baggage that it would be helpful to have a consultant participate as adviser to the process (not to the outcome).

In some situations an outsider can provide invaluable assistance through bringing in a perspective from outside the organization. As such, a consultant is comparable to a spiritual director for an individual. Just as a good director would not presume to guide the spiritual life of a person and would not presume to know what is best for that individual, so a good consultant would not be called on to propose an outcome for the group. If a consultant is effective, it will be only insofar as this person is able to

- ask questions that enable the discerning group to confirm that they have come to a full understanding of their environment and resources

- suggest ways in which the process might move forward if there is an impasse in the discussion

- make observations about the emotional quotient in the discussion, if it seems that either the moderator or others are not alert to this factor

- advise the moderator on ways in which the process might better be facilitated—both within a session and between sessions of the discerning group

- help the group to debrief after a decision is reached, looking at the experience and interpreting elements of the process that they might not appreciate as fully as someone from the outside

An external consultant might be invited in under unusual situations, but normally a group should have within its own circle the resources and capacities to discern well. Indeed the biggest and most valuable resource is the group itself, with its commitment to work together and decide together, its depth of cordiality and good humor that enables the group to process the stressful points in the discussion, the common wisdom that comes when several thinking people get together in one room and, most of all, the wonder that as they gather, the Spirit of the living God gathers with them. Each of these tools, techniques and resources is, in the end, but a means by which the wonder and witness of the Spirit can be known and experienced in their conversation.

THE MEETING TO DISCERN

A group may follow any of several formats when it meets, with the purpose that together its members will seek a decision that reflects the mind of the Spirit. What follows is merely a suggestion of one way in which the moderator of such a gathering might structure the meeting.[4]

---

[4]Readers may wish to consider the "ten movement" process suggested by Morris and Olsen, which has much to commend it, though it does seem a bit more complicated than is really needed. Danny E. Morris and Charles M. Olsen, *Discerning God's Will Together: A Spiritual Practice for the Church* (Nashville: Upper Room, 1997), pp. 65-93.

It is most helpful to plan for ninety-minute sessions—no longer. In most social and cultural contexts we can only be mentally and emotionally present to one another for this length of time. Anything longer and minds begin to wander, spirits flag and energy diminishes. Unless the moderator senses that with a few more minutes the group might be able to come to closure or some kind of decision, when the ninety minutes have expired, it is better to plan to meet another time.

The ninety-minute session can be divided into three parts of approximately thirty minutes each, as follows:

1. **Open discussion.** It is good to begin with open-ended conversation where the issues, concerns, observations and perspectives of all members of the group are freely put on the table without assumptions and without debate.

2. **Prayer and silent reflection.** After the information needed for a decision (or at least a preliminary decision) has been provided, that is, after the various opinions and observations have been made and the scope of the issue at hand has been laid out, the moderator can suggest that the group enter into a season of extended prayer. The prayer could include the request that God would grant the group the grace to discern well, that God would illumine the members' minds, granting them a true indifference to the outcome of the deliberations as well as enabling them to listen well to one another and give them the courage to do what they feel they are being called to do.

In other words, we do not merely want God's blessing on the process. Neither are we only asking for God's wisdom, so that *we* can choose wisely. Though we surely want God's blessing and wisdom, what we most urgently need is the actual presence of God, by the Spirit, in and through and around the process, in our speaking and listening, in our deliberations and in our times of silence together. Jesus needs to be at the table, an active participant in the discussion.

It is appropriate, then, to ask what focus there might be to our prayers. In Philippians 4:2-6 the apostle spoke of the call to be of one mind and then urged his readers to rejoice, to refuse to be worried about anything and to pray with supplication and thanksgiving. James, in turn, beckoned us to call out for wisdom in faith believing that God will grant wisdom (Jas 1:5). And any number of texts highlight the need for a posture of confession and humility in our praying. These texts would suggest, then, at least three foci to our prayers:

- *Thanksgiving*, particularly the prayer of gratitude that opens our hearts to the multiple expressions of God's goodness. We turn from a posture of complaint to one of thanks, and the focus of our prayers could be the actual elements highlighted through the process of appreciative inquiry (Col 3:15-17).

- *Confession* and the prayer of humility that acknowledges where we have strayed from our confession and common convictions. We do not need to browbeat one another or forage for what is not there, but we do need to acknowledge sin and as appropriate confess our sin to one another.

- *Supplication* and the prayer that acknowledges our fears. On the one hand, we ask for wisdom in acknowledgment of our need for insight, understanding and courage. But it is appropriate that our prayers of intercession be focused specifically on our points of fear and anxiety. We seek the peace of God in our deliberations; it follows, then, that our prayers would acknowledge our fears as we cast our anxiety on God (1 Pet 5:6-7) and embrace the peace of God that would guard our hearts and minds in Christ Jesus (Phil 4:7).

Ideally, the members of the group would each vocalize their own intercessions and requests, articulating their own longings for the process, in the company of the others. The time set for prayer can and probably should include segments of silence for reflection on what has been said thus far in the meeting and for attentiveness to the Spirit. Here is where it is so important for the participants to be alert to what is happening in their own hearts and to how the Spirit may be impressing upon them something that they could offer the group as a whole.

3. *Discussion toward resolution.* After the time of prayer and silence, the moderator can call the group back into discussion and begin by soliciting comments and observations that arise out of the prayer. In some cases, it is possible to move toward a decision. In other cases, what is being sought is a preliminary decision, perhaps a tentative choice about what the group will do next as part of their assignment. A search committee, for example, might at this point choose to shorten their list from a large number of candidates to a list of three, or they may decide, as a tentative measure, that they will invite a candidate in for formal interviews (without actually, as yet, confirming a decision).

This third segment of the gathering is in many respects the most crucial. Here is where it is so important that each participant be fully present—committed to the full ninety minutes. The whole group sifts what is being heard and felt, and together they begin to identify what is significant and meaningful and to note in particular if there are diverse opinions or perspectives on the issue at hand. Agreement (if the group is ready for it) will usually be tentative at first and will probably come slowly. A sense will emerge for the group that there is more agreement among them than they had originally realized or thought possible. On the other hand, it is important to allow differences of opinion to arise and to discourage anyone from changing their minds just because they see that others are coming to agreement and they want to avoid conflict.

The group may come to a decision. Or it may be clear that the group is at an impasse, seemingly not only far from agreement but so far apart in their views that concurrence seems beyond their reach. Or there may be an agreement, but with a significant minority voice in which one or two hold perspectives or opinions that differ from the majority. Each of these calls for a different response.

If there is a significant measure of agreement, perhaps a growing concurrence in the group on a way forward, then it is appropriate to ask questions that would probe and confirm what the group is sensing. If there is unanimity, it is important to probe what lies behind this broad agreement, what gives the group such confidence that they have together. If there is a strong majority, there will be opportunity to explore the meaning of the minority voice, but at this point, it is helpful to consider three critical questions.[5]

- *The question of consequences.* What are the likely consequences of this course of action, and is this outcome one that fosters the reign of Christ in the world and in our community? Does this potential outcome enable the proclamation of the gospel and our capacity to live in truth, justice and freedom, in response to the gospel? And I would add that the consequences should call us to live with courage rather than timidity and fear. The potential outcome should be one that challenges us.

- *The question of continuity.* Is this potential choice and its outcomes consistent with *our* story? What God is leading us to do will be consistent with how God has led this group or organization thus far. Can we see how the next chapter in our life together will have continuity with previous chapters? While all new initiatives and directions represent potentially significant discontinuities, these changes will always resonate with the mission or charism of the community or organization. This new direction should be consistent with who we are and it should fit who we are in this time and place. It should, thus, also be contextual: it "fits" us.

- *The question of community.* Is this potential outcome one that can be embraced by the larger community of which we are a part, if we are discerning together for this community? And is this outcome one that we can celebrate and explain with integrity to the broader Christian community, that is, to the whole church? As a local church, can we describe what we are doing, to another church in the same city or to our judicatory authorities (or both), in a way that these external entities can embrace and endorse it? In other words, if we have to be secretive about our decision, we may have good reason to question the choice we have made.

---

[5]These three questions are adapted from Thomas H. Groome, *Christian Religious Education: Sharing Our Story and Vision* (San Francisco: Harper & Row, 1980), pp. 198-201.

These questions are designed to probe our joy and sense of peace in the direction we have chosen, to help us confirm that we have indeed discerned well.

However, it is also quite possible that the group will come to an impasse. This does not have to mean an even split of opinion among the group or even a breakdown in the discussion. Rather, there is an impasse because we cannot detect that a significant level of concurrence is emerging for the group. Even though we are not seeking unanimity, it is clear that there is not a strong enough majority in favor of a particular outcome to indicate that we may be approaching a decision. Sometimes it is simply a matter of agreeing together that we need another meeting in order to find resolution. But it could be that the moderator and the group will recognize that a genuine impasse has been reached.

It is helpful at this point to clarify the terms and the level of disagreement. Without recrimination or any judgments made one way or the other, the group can seek to identify actual differences. As Rick Ross has noted, it is helpful to identify or clarify in which areas the group is in agreement and in which they differ.[6] Do they differ on the facts or on what the facts mean? Do they differ on method—on how they should do what they need to do? Or do they differ on their goals and objectives? Do they differ on values—on what they believe to be important? If they are able to identify where they differ, they may find a way forward, if the group can devote sufficient time to clarify their differences and, if they are able, to work from those differences toward resolution.[7] If the reason for the impasse is not one of difference of opinion on matters such as these, then it might be helpful to probe the emotional content of the discussion and examine openly together how people are feeling and if there is a sense of discontent, anger, frustration or fear that is shaping the conversation.

---

[6]Rick Ross in Senge et al., *Fifth Discipline Fieldbook*, p. 389.

[7]However, if the group differs on three or all four of these areas, then likely the only way forward is either to work entirely within a regulated system of democratic procedures, such as Robert's Rules of Order (there is not enough consensus in the group for genuine communal discernment), or to conclude that they cannot come to a decision and act accordingly.

THE MINORITY VOICE

Then, of course, there may be a strong concurrence in the group, but also a minority voice of one or two who either cannot go along with the group's decision or have agreed to go along with it but with significant reservation. And it is important to speak to this from both sides of the equation. Not only do we, as a group, need to know how the minority voice informs our process of discernment, but we also, as individuals, need to know how to express our opinion and then respond to the possibility that we might differ with the group's decision.

On the one hand, it is vital that the group seek to interpret the significance of the minority voice in their midst. Unanimity is not needed, but the minority voice may be part of the Spirit's guidance of the group, and so it is important to assess its significance.[8] Indeed the presence of a minority voice is a kind of reminder that few choices we make as individuals or as communities are unambiguous. In our individual decisions we often have our own internal dissenting voices, and in group decisions there will often be those who have sought the mind of God with us but who at the end of the process do not see as we do. And thus it is vital that we respect this minority voice and seek to interpret its significance by asking, what is the Spirit telling us through this voice? The dissenting voice could be a note of caution that would slow us down and call us to rethink our decision. Perhaps this person is a prophet in our midst who is calling us to reexamine the direction in which we have chosen to go. Or it could be that this minority voice in our group is a signal that something needs to be adjusted in the decision we are about to make. Perhaps we should alter the resolution to incorporate the perspective that comes through the minority voice. This does not mean that we dampen the enthusiasm and eagerness with which we embrace the decision to which we are being called, but it does mean that we ask what we can learn

---

[8]Unfortunately, it needs to be acknowledged that the lone minority voice may exist solely because of his or her refusal to listen to others and to relinquish a personal agenda. Such an attitude cannot be permitted to sabotage the entire process. But this situation would, hopefully, be the exception rather than the norm.

from the minority voice. We consciously accept that sometimes we may not understand why there is a minority voice, but then this is a reminder that the joy of unanimity is a gift that the Spirit may not always grant.

Sometimes *we* are that minority voice, and it is important to the discernment process that we decide with grace and courage how we will proceed in our response to such a development. All of us will be outvoted in our lifetime, likely more than once. In fact, if you find that you are always in the majority on all the group decisions of which you are a part, it may mean that you have uncanny political skills, or it could mean that you lack courage and the energy to think for yourself. People who honor their conscience will find that at times they are in group situations where they have voted or spoken in the minority. And now they need to decide what to do about this development. At this point it becomes a matter of *personal* discernment.

Sometimes, of course, we will merely move on with the realization that good people differ on such matters. But sometimes we will find that a decision has been made that we simply cannot accept. In other words, it is *not* a matter of an honest disagreement. The issue on the table is one about which we believe something is clearly wrong and that a decision has been made or is being made that is a violation of good judgment and good discernment. We believe that this is not a matter on which there is an honest difference of opinion; this is a matter on which we feel something is not right. A faculty member may feel that the appointment of a new president at the college was simply wrong—the process was wrong and the outcome was wrong. A member of a church may feel that the appointment of a new pastor for the church is a decision that he or she cannot accept in good conscience. Or perhaps a church body has made a decision on a moral question about which one feels the Scriptures speak clearly, and the outcome seems to violate matters of truth and justice. Such decisions will be made in the workplace and in our church settings, and some may face this kind of situation in their homes.

How we respond is a complex matter intellectually, emotionally and spiritually. These kinds of situations highlight for us the need for critical and careful discernment, partly because we can assume nothing. We cannot assume that if something is wrong, we are supposed to do something about it. One legitimate response is to quietly accept this development as something about which one will choose to be forgo action, at least for the time being. Jesus clearly discerned that the cross was unjust, yet he chose to accept it as something about which he would not raise his fist or protest or even block. In other words, the fact that something is wrong does not mean that no discernment is needed.[9]

God may call us to silence, to a gracious acceptance of what has occurred. On the other hand, God may call us to walk away from this place or this organization, to resign or leave. Or we may discern that the situation demands a response of either confrontation or the way of civil or ecclesiastical disobedience.

We need to accept, in this discernment process, that God may lead some in one direction and some in a different way. Some may be called to stay, while others may be called to leave. And, of course, we cannot assume that if it is wrong, then there is no further need for discernment. We cannot trust our feelings. We need to be alert to any chance that we might act in desolation, out of anger or discouragement rather than peace. Whatever we do, we must respond and act in peace.

EXTERNAL CONFIRMATION

Confirmation and accountability are essential parts of individual discernment. In the same way, when it comes to communal discernment, external confirmation is normally an integral part of the process. A search committee only has authority to nominate a candidate, and so the body that actually appoints will need to confirm the committee's decision. And when a report is brought, regardless of the character of the decision, it is good to summa-

---

[9]This, of course, takes us back to the discussion on moral discernment as found in chapter nine. We need to discern not only whether there is something wrong but also what we need to do in response to the wrong. The fact that we think something is wrong is not the end of the matter.

rize the outcome, that is, the recommendation that is being made, as well as the process by which the group came to this resolution. This can be presented simply, without in any way suggesting that if someone or the whole external group disagrees with the recommendation, then they are not respecting either the committee or the process. External confirmation is meaningful only if the group in question has true freedom to accept or reject the resolution that is being brought forward. If the committee has discerned well, then usually they can assume that this external reckoning will affirm their decision. But this may not happen. It may be, of course, that the group has not discerned well; they need to accept that they did not receive external confirmation because they had either rushed to a premature decision or had not really weighed all the alternatives. It may also be that the community refuses to accept the recommendation, even though the discernment was done well. In this case the discerning committee needs to be content that they have done what they were responsible to do—bring a recommendation to the larger group—and they then need to accept the outcome of the larger group's decisions.

In the end, more often than not, we will know the deep joy that comes in having chosen well together, with a confidence that the Spirit of Christ has enabled us to do this. However, just because we have sought to do this well, and just because we have appealed to the Spirit and prayed for the grace to choose well, we cannot for a moment think that the process will be easy or a solution forthcoming without any doubts or uncertainties. Despite our good intentions and the genuineness of our prayers, we can be led astray; our decision making can go awry due to any number of factors. The ambiguity of life and the complexity of our common experience will always leave us making the best of our circumstances and rarely completely satisfied with the outcomes we embrace. And thus we must be wise about the character of how groups and organizations work, how conflict informs and as often as not is a part of good decisions. We must beware of an idealism that leaves us constantly complaining that the organizations of which we are a part are so far from perfect. We live and work with imperfect people, and they have to accept us with our imperfections into their company. We can do all we can to choose well, yet our best efforts might well be sabotaged. But we must not despair or become cynical; we must persist in our efforts to learn how to discern well, and we must strive to develop the capacity to discern well together. And in the goodness of God we will know the grace that enables us to make good decisions together.

The wonder of both individual and communal discernment is always the extraordinary reality that the Spirit is present. We are not alone. The Spirit walks with us, and in the remarkable words of St. Paul in Romans 8, the Spirit helps us in our weakness and intercedes for us with "sighs too deep for words" (Rom 8:26). While along the way we will no doubt heave sighs deeper than words, it is a great comfort to know that the Spirit dwells with us and that the triune God providentially cares for us as individuals, as couples, as families and as organizations. We do not walk alone. In our discernment we will no doubt experience frustration, uncertainty and setbacks. But in the end, our confidence rests not on our capacity to choose well but on the loving and providential care of the God who guides and whom we long to hear.

Author Index

Subject Index

Scripture Index